War and World History
Part I

Professor Jonathan P. Roth

THE TEACHING COMPANY ®

PUBLISHED BY:

THE TEACHING COMPANY
4840 Westfields Boulevard, Suite 500
Chantilly, Virginia 20151-2299
1-800-TEACH-12
Fax—703-378-3819
www.teach12.com

ISBN 1-59803-572-X

Jonathan P. Roth, Ph.D.

Professor of History, San José State University

Jonathan P. Roth was born and raised in the San Francisco Bay area and received his B.A. in Ancient Near Eastern History and Archaeology from the University of California, Berkeley. After studying at the Georg-August University in Göttingen, Germany, as a Fulbright Scholar, he received his M.A. and Ph.D. from Columbia University.

Professor Roth has taught at Tulane University in New Orleans, New York University, and the University of California, Berkeley. He came to the History Department at San José State University, a part of the California State University system, in 1994 and served for three years as its chair. In 2005, he was honored as San José State University's Outstanding Professor.

Professor Roth has researched, written, and lectured extensively on ancient warfare and warfare in world history. He founded and serves as the director of San José State's Burdick Military History Project. His book *Logistics of the Roman Army at War, 264 B.C. to A.D. 235* was published in 1999, and his *Roman Warfare*, a survey textbook, will be published in 2009. He has contributed chapters to *The Cambridge History of Greek and Roman Warfare. Volume I: Greece, the Hellenistic World and the Rise of Rome* (2007); *Representations of War in Ancient Rome* (2006); and *The Roman Army and the Economy* (2002).

From 1983 to 1989, Professor Roth served in the 69th Infantry Regiment of the New York Army National Guard. He enlisted as a private, was promoted to corporal, and, after graduating from the Empire State Military Academy, was commissioned a second lieutenant. He then served as a platoon leader in Company A, as well as chemical officer and mobilization officer. To paraphrase Edward Gibbon, the officer in the National Guard has not been useless to the military historian.

Table of Contents
War and World History
Part I

War and World History

Scope:

War and World History is not a lecture series on military history as traditionally understood. We will discuss few wars, even fewer battles, and almost no strategy. Even great campaigns of conquest, such as those of Alexander or Genghis Khan, will be studied only to measure their historical impact. Some lectures feature weapons, unit organization, tactics, and logistics, but only to explore the complex interaction between warfare and human society and culture.

War is, and always has been, hell. By its very nature, war involves mass killing and maiming, severe psychological damage, and social dislocation. The long tradition of glorifying war continues into the present, though modern scholars generally view war as a completely negative factor in history, draining resources and attention from civilized activities. In truth, despite its horrific effects, war has always been a remarkable driving force behind invention and innovation. The Greek philosopher Heraclitus said, "War is the father of all things," and although this is an exaggeration, many aspects of civilization arise directly or indirectly due to the needs of warfare. Some of the most beautiful and moving pieces of literature and art have been inspired by war. The relationship between religion and war is often commented on, but it is far more complex and subtle than is generally recognized. Warfare is an integral part of virtually every human culture and society.

The history of world warfare is usually told as a series of regional chapters, such as Western war, Islamic war, and Chinese war. This course has another perspective. While it is important to look at developments around the world in their own contexts, warfare develops both chronologically and geographically. The technology of war spreads much earlier and more globally than is generally recognized. Some of the astonishing similarities in war in very distant regions, such as the use of the chariot in western Europe and China, are due to diffusion and not independent invention. We trace some of these surprising stories of how far and how quickly such weapons and weapons systems traveled. We also look at those cases in which similar weapons were indeed developed separately by different cultures. And we trace the changing ideas of war in a world context.

Our main focus will be on what world historians are increasingly seeing as a single great cultural zone, a broad swath of Europe, northern Africa, and Asia, from Atlantic to Pacific. We will also look at warfare in sub-Saharan Africa, the Americas, and Oceania, especially as their importance grows with increased globalization, starting in the 16th century and continuing to today.

At the beginning of the course, we discuss some of the major themes of world warfare: How do we define "war"? Why do we study war? What are our sources and methods for reconstructing past warfare? This course divides roughly into three periods: the ancient period, up to around A.D. 600; the medieval and early modern period, from 600 to 1700, including looking at the Americas and Oceania before "contact"; and the modern period, ending with a look at 21st-century war.

In each period, we look at how weapons and civilian technology, and military and social organization, changed—with the worlds of war and peace constantly influencing each other. A major theme is the ubiquitous alternation of periods of political centralization and decentralization, generally linked with changes in military practice. We also see how the needs of war, especially changes in its cost, affected the economies and finances of states and societies, including coinage and the stock market. Certain lectures focus specifically on revolutionary military changes—such as the introduction of the horse, the chariot, gunpowder, and the regiment—that transformed not only war but also society and culture, in every place that they were introduced. Conversely, we will see how some purely civilian developments, such as writing and steam power, have had dramatic impacts on the way wars were fought.

Several lectures focus on naval warfare, and we will discuss the relatively recent development of air war. At regular intervals, we will compare the military forces of great states. In each period, a lecture will cover how warfare has influenced arts and letters around the world. We will see how painting, sculpture, books, and even fashion have interacted with war. Certain lectures explore specific themes, such as war and religion; how the concepts of race and rank developed; and the interaction of war and such ideologies and practices as democracy, communism, fascism, and terrorism. The last lecture discusses modern pacifist and disarmament movements and humanity's attempts, so far unsuccessful, to end war.

Lecture One
What Is War?

Scope:

Cultures often have opposing and evolving views of warfare. Modern military thinkers and scholars have defined war in different, often contradictory, ways. New studies in neuroscience offer important insights into understanding war. "Nature versus nurture" turned out to be "nature *and* nurture." The theory of war is important, but we also need to understand its practice.

Outline

I. "What is war?" seems to be a very simple question, but the more deeply we examine it, the more complex it becomes.

    A. Individuals and groups often hold different, ambiguous, and sometimes contradictory, views about war.

        1. The ancient Sumerians saw war as descending from heaven and making humans civilized. On the other hand, Nergal was an uncontrollable Sumerian god of war and plague.

        2. The Greeks and Romans saw war both as a part of nature, as in the Platonic idea of earthly war reflecting an ideal reality of war, but also as a plague on humankind brought by war gods such as Ares and Mars.

        3. In both Chinese and Indian writings, we also see similar conflicting ideas. Warfare is seen as one of the elements of the degeneration of humankind from the golden age, but war is also a noble activity, especially when defending civilization against the intrusions of barbarians.

    B. There is a tendency in academia to assign particular attitudes about war to particular ancient cultures, sometimes labeling them as naturally peaceful or naturally warlike.

        1. This idea is associated with a multicultural view of history. In the case of war, however, multicultural theories generally do not reflect the historical record.

        2. We shall see cases of very warlike societies becoming relatively peaceful and vice versa.

3. Over time, theories and attitudes about war became more sophisticated in most cultures.

C. With the rise of the nation-state, a more legalistic view of war arose.

    1. Hugo Grotius developed the basis for the modern laws of war. In *On the Law of War and Peace* (1625), he defined war as a condition in which fighting and killing were legally permitted.

    2. By the 18th century, most Western states had accepted the necessity of a formal declaration of war.

    3. The legalistic view of war was not shared by everyone in 18th-century Europe. Denis Diderot defined war as a plague that attacked the body politic.

II. A passage in Carl von Clausewitz's *On War* (1832) is usually translated "War is merely the continuation of politics by other means," though German *Politik* can mean both "politics" and "policy."

A. Most modern historians take this definition to represent a rational, or political, theory of war. As is often the case with great thinkers, what they mean is often less influential than what they are thought to mean.

    1. Von Clausewitz's meaning of war is a conflict between two states. Tribal warfare or gang warfare is thus not war at all but simply a sort of mass violence.

    2. John Keegan, in *A History of Warfare* (1993), argues that warfare is an expression of culture; what war is differs from culture to culture.

B. Professor Christopher Bassford of the National War College points out that von Clausewitz saw the political element of war as only one part of the "paradoxical trinity" of war.

    1. The political part of the trinity von Clausewitz associated with government, which ideally made rational choices for the benefit of the state.

    2. The second part of the trinity, associated with the people, is its opposite: a "blind natural force" of hatred and other deep human drives.

3. The third part of von Clausewitz's trinity is "the play of chance and probability within which the creative spirit is free to roam." This he associated with the army, and here he seems to mean that war is a sort of art or science (or perhaps both).
4. None of these three aspects of war defines it. Rather v on Clausewitz writes: "Our task therefore is to develop a theory that maintains a balance between these three tendencies, like an object suspended between three magnets."

III. Other academic disciplines have also looked at war and tried to understand its essentials.

A. The various definitions and perspectives are not contradictory but rather provide different perspectives on an elusive phenomenon.

B. In philosophy, there has long been a debate between nature and nurture in defining war.

C. Psychologists have long been concerned with the issue of violence, though not much psychological study has been done from a military perspective.

D. Let me sum up with a few of my own ideas about the theory of war.
1. We need to bring von Clausewitz back into the forefront of our theoretical studies.
2. Although the psychology of aggression is important to understand, war is not a matter of individuals but of organized groups.
3. It is not the number of deaths that defines war.
4. While violence or potential violence is a necessary part of war, unrestrained or uncontrolled violence is by definition not war. War involves the restraint and organization of violence.
5. Primitive war is different from modern war, but one did not replace the other. Rather, modern war absorbed primitive war.
6. The psychological idea of an emergent property is very useful in discussing all aspects of war. War and peace both exist as emergent properties of human relations.

7. While it is important to understand cultural and philosophical elements of war, we must not forget to look at the way war was actually fought.

Suggested Reading:

Bassford and Villacres, "Reclaiming the Clausewitzian Trinity."

Keegan, *A History of Warfare*.

Questions to Consider:

1. How does von Clausewitz's theory of war differ from Keegan's?
2. What is the relationship between human violence and war?

Lecture One—Transcript
What Is War?

In this lecture, we will talk about what might seem to be a very simply question, "What is War?" I could give a simple answer: "War is what military historians study." But as with any inquiry, the more we look into what seems to be a very simple question, the more complex this question becomes. The definition of war is no exception.

Ancient thinkers and philosophers faced this question too. We tend to think in terms of a "Greek" idea or a "Chinese" idea, but the fact is that individuals and groups in ancient and medieval cultures, like modern ones, often held different, ambiguous, and sometimes contradictory, views about war. In addition, some of these ideas were remarkably similar across cultures. In subsequent lectures, we will look more deeply at these sorts of attitudes, but now let's take a quick survey of how some ancient peoples viewed war, before we talk about modern theories of warfare.

In some of their myths, for example, ancient Sumerians saw war as descending from heaven. Warfare was like other elements of society such as kingship. War came from the gods, and it's part of what made humans civilized. This idea of war as a mark of civilization has a long history, and underlies some definitions of war even in modern times, as we shall see. On the other hand, we find the god Nergal, represented in Sumerian myth as an uncontrollable god who brought warfare, and plague, to humanity.

There was among the Egyptians an idea that the universe and the human world had a natural state of harmony and balance, which they called *ma'at*. Peace, both within Egypt and between Egypt and its neighbors, was normal and good. Wars, rebellions, and other violence, seen in the same way as drought or plagues, meant that *ma'at* was out of balance, something that the Egyptian king had to address, if necessary by himself, going to war. While internal uprisings, civil war, and invasion were viewed like a plague, the war waged by the pharaoh was just. It was like a medicine. But there was another tradition in Egypt: that the goddess Sekhmet, like the Sumerian god Nergal, were responsible for both warfare and disease. War in this Egyptian view was uncontrolled, and even after a "just" war, Egyptians had to hold a festival to stop Sekhmet from inducing more killing.

Among the Greeks and Romans we also see different views: War is a part of nature. Indeed the Sumerian notion of war descending from heaven is in some ways similar to the Platonic idea of earthly war reflecting an ideal reality of war. We shall discuss this more in a later lecture. For now, it is enough to point out that there were other Greek ideas about war. For example, that war was a plague on mankind brought by war gods such as Ares and Mars, a notion we find in Homer's writings, for example. We also find the idea that war kept a people from becoming decadent and soft, which was a motif in the writings of the Roman historian Tacitus, for example.

In both Chinese and Indian writings we also see conflicting ideas: On one hand, warfare is seen as one of the elements of the degeneration of mankind from the Golden Age. It was an evil but a necessary evil. On the other, war is a noble activity, especially when defending civilization against the intrusion of barbarians.

I have only given a sample of ancient attitudes. The point is that groups within a culture can hold different views on war, indeed the attitude of a group or individual can change, as can the cultural mores of a society as a whole. Some in academia assign so-called authentic or indigenous views to particular cultures. Thus, some cultures are seen as naturally peaceful and others as naturally warlike. This idea is associated with a multicultural view of history. In the case of war, however, multicultural theories generally do not reflect the historical record. We shall see cases of very warlike societies becoming relatively peaceful, and vice versa.

Over time, theories and attitudes toward war become more sophisticated in most cultures. For the present, we will focus on the development of European ideas on war, as they are particularly influential on modern military theory. With the rise of the nation-state, and that system of international law that accompanied it, a more legalistic definition of war arose. The Dutch scholar Hugo Grotius, for example, was one of Europe's leading legal minds in the 17th century, and developed the basis for the modern laws of war. In his book *On the Law of War and Peace*, first published in 1625, Grotius defined war not as the fighting and killing itself, but as the condition in which the fighting and killing were legally permitted.

Grotius is very much in the western tradition of logic, in which something either is, or is not, like pregnancy, and thus war does not exist on a continuum, it is a condition different from and incompatible with peace. In order to engage the laws of war, therefore, a state needed to publicly declare when the condition of war existed between it and another state. By the 18th century, most European states had accepted the necessity of a formal declaration of war, and this idea was adopted elsewhere, for example in the Constitution of the United States, in which Congress is given the power to declare war.

This legalistic view of war was not, however, shared by everyone in 18th century Europe. Denis Diderot, for example. Diderot was a French philosopher who edited the classic work on which all modern encyclopedias are based. He defined war as a plague or disease that attacked the body politic. For him it was the very soul of irrationality, and when the Enlightenment was successful, and all people were rational, there would be no war. This view was very widely held. On the other hand, it was also commonly thought in the 18th century, that war was a noble activity, and military force was necessary not only to protect and spread civilization, but also to protect societies from the threat of internal uprisings.

The 19th century Prussian general, and writer, Carl von Clausewitz is generally considered to be one of the greatest military theorists of all time. In his most famous work, called *On War*, Von Clausewitz wrote that "War is only a continuation of state policy by other means." Well, not exactly. Von Clausewitz wrote in German, and the German word *politik* can mean both "politics" and "policy." The translation of this passage, or indeed anything, reflects how the translator understands the meaning of the original, which is often ambiguous. What von Clausewitz was saying was either that war was like the normal political interaction between states, that is diplomacy, but carried out by other means, that is force; or he meant that war is a way of carrying out national policy, by other means, that is by force instead of diplomacy; or perhaps he meant both, and the ambiguity is deliberate.

In any case, most modern historians take von Clausewitz's definition to represent what we might call a rational or political theory of war. As I will explain a little later in this lecture, Clausewitz's ideas about war are considerably more sophisticated. For the time being, however, let us stay with this idea of war as politics, as that is the way most people have taken von Clausewitz. So as is often the case with great thinkers, what they meant is often less influential than what they are thought to have meant.

According to this rational, political view, a war is a conflict between two political entities, most often defined as states, and that the conflict must have a goal or purpose, that is part of that state's policy. Thus, according to this view, tribal warfare or gang warfare is by this definition not warfare at all but simply a sort of mass violence.

This view has been criticized by John Keegan, also considered the premier living military historian. In 1993, Keegan published an important, though controversial work, *A History of Warfare*. Keegan's theories on the nature of war are, like von Clausewitz's, more sophisticated and nuanced than they are often characterized. Basically, however, Keegan argues that war is an expression of culture, and that von Clausewitz's definition is not a theory of war in general, but only of war in his own time and place, that is Europe of the 18th century. Like other aspects of culture, war expresses, or perhaps more accurately, limits, human impulses, as marriage rites are meant to control sexual impulses. In most places and times, Keegan says, warfare is a ritual, fought for symbolic and not political reasons. This applies as much to a British regiment, a sort of tribe, in his view, as to the Aztecs in Mexico or the Yanomamo tribe in the Amazon. Since war is an expression of culture, what war is differs from culture to culture.

Keegan's dichotomy between War as Culture and War as Politics is a very important idea, but it does not reflect accurately von Clausewitz's idea on war, which is considerably more complex, and useful. Christopher Bassford, a Professor of Strategy at the National War College, has argued, very persuasively as far as I am concerned, that von Clausewitz's ideas about war go far beyond the usual quotations. As Bassford points out, von Clausewitz saw the rational and political element of war, of war "as the continuation of politics" or policy, as only one part of what he considered the "paradoxical trinity" of war.

The political leg of the trinity he associated with government, which, ideally, made rational choices for the benefit of the state. The second part of the trinity, associated with the people, is its opposite: a blind natural force that is violent emotion, hatred, and other deep human drives. Another often-quoted passage from *On War*, states that "War is an act of violence intended to compel our opponent to fulfil our will." Nothing diplomatic about that.

The third part of von Clausewitz's trinity is the most enigmatic, and perhaps the most revealing. It is "the play of chance and probability within which the creative spirit is free to roam." What does this mean? Von Clausewitz associated this leg with the army, and here he seems to be saying that war is a sort of art or science (or again perhaps both). In this sense of war are the weapons, the tactics, and strategies, as well as the context in which an army fights: the unpredictability of weather, of morale, of enemy action, and so forth. In addition, it's the creativity of the general, of the officer, of the sergeant, and of the individual soldier. None of these three aspects of war defines it, according to von Clausewitz. Rather he writes: "Our task therefore is to develop a theory that maintains a balance between these three tendencies, like an object suspended between three magnets."

Far from excluding violent emotion and strategic creativity from the definition of war, von Clausewitz includes them with calculated policy as creating a holistic view of warfare. In this sense, von Clausewitz is far from an out of date relict of the 19th century or a militaristic Prussian advocate of total war, but continues to be one of the premier theorist of war. He saw war as defined by the constantly shifting interaction of various elements, like a metal ball floating between three magnets, a remarkably modern view.

The study of war has not been carried out only by military historians and theorists. Other academic disciplines have also looked at war and tried to understand its essentials. Let us take von Clausewitz's lead and not see the various definitions and perspectives as necessarily contradictory, but as providing different perspectives on an elusive phenomenon.

Political scientists have been writing about war since the time of Machiavelli. The American political scientist Quincy Wright, like many of his generation, was horrified by the carnage of World War I. Wright felt that understanding war would be a tool in ending it, so he decided to undertake a critical and quantitative study of war, using social scientific tools. Ironically, the first edition of his great work, called *A Study of War*, was published in 1942, in the midst of the carnage of the Second World War. A revised and abridged version came out in 1964. Wright defined war as a relationship with distinct characteristics. For example, it occurs between organized groups and is recognized by both groups as a specific type of legal or conventional condition, with distinctive standards of behavior, that are acceptable in time of war, though not necessarily in time of peace. Thus, killing the enemy in war is not murder. For Wright, violent conflicts can be defined either as a war or not and therefore can be counted and categorized. He counted, for example, 284 distinct wars between 1480 and 1964.

Sociologists have also been concerned with war. Stanislav Andreski, for example, was one of the century's most important sociologists of military force. In 1954 he published his classic *Military Organization and Society*. Andreski assumed that war was a constant in human relations, driven by motives such as profit, prestige, and power. His focus was not on how warfare affects the relations of groups, whether states or tribes, but how warfare influences societies internally, fostering hierarchies and altering social relations between classes.

It would seem natural that war would be a major avenue of study for anthropologists. But Harry Turney-High, one of the most important anthropologists of war, as well as one of the first, complained in his book *Primitive War* published in 1949, that anthropologists of his day paid little attention to the wars of the tribes they studied. Turney-High's own area of research was the Plains Indians, including the Sioux. And in interviewing members of the tribe in the 1930s, he found many who took part in the wars of the 19th century. Turney-High distinguished Primitive from Modern War, but did it functionally rather than racially or ethnically, as was common at the time. According to him, primitive warriors follow leaders and their orders voluntarily, inspired by a war chiefs bravery and charisma. Modern soldiers, on the other hand, follow the orders of their commanders by compulsion, either real or potential. Thus, according to Turney-High, the Plains Indians practiced primitive war, whereas not only European states, but the 19th-century traditional kingdoms of West Africa practiced modern war.

Although there are many problems with Turney-High's analysis, he was right to point out that much of the anthropological view of war, especially war among tribal societies, was based more on philosophy, one might say wishful thinking, than on observations. Philosophers have argued about war since there have been philosophers, and the discussion continues. In modern philosophy there has long been a debate between "nature" versus "nurture" with most anthropologists taking the position that group violence is learned, with the strong implication, or even the explicit assertion, that primitive cultures were peaceful, somewhat like Jean-Jacques Rousseau's noble savage. This idea has had a great deal of influence on anthropologists, and there is a school of thought that sees war as introduced by what is cruelly called "civilization." Of course, the opposite philosophical and anthropological view has existed for a long time. Thomas Hobbes famously referred to life in the state of nature as "solitary, poor, nasty, brutish and short" and he thought that this was mainly due to incessant violence. This school of thought sees civilization as a moderating force and is thought of, if not always termed, "primitive" society.

The cultural anthropologist Lawrence Keeley has stepped into this debate with the most important work on the anthropology of war since Turney-High. His *War Before Civilization*, published in 1996, presents very convincing evidence, based on historical sources as well as field studies that "primitive" societies, his term as well as mine, were quite the opposite of peaceful. Casualty rates, relative to the population as a whole were much higher, as high as 60 percent as compared to about one percent in modern war. Primitive war was frequent, if not incessant: In a survey of North American Indians, Keeley found that at least 87 percent engaged in wars at least once a year. And scalping, by the way, was practiced long before the Europeans arrived. Although ritual was part of primitive war, as it is of modern war, tribal peoples were very efficient at fighting and killing and they fought to win. Sociologists and anthropologists study groups, but of course groups are made up of individuals. Psychologists have long been concerned with the issue of violence, although like anthropologists, there has not been much study of psychology from a military perspective, at least on a theoretical basis.

Sigmund Freud developed the idea of the unconscious, but his theories about human motivation fell rather flat in explaining war, attributing it merely to unconscious aggression and suggesting, almost literally, that we make love, not war. Carl Jung agreed that war was the expression of inner aggression, although in his writings before the outbreak of the Second World War, he almost seemed to welcome it as being more honest, if not nicer, than peace. The psychological theories of both Freud and Jung have been discredited by new discoveries, especially with the extraordinary recent discoveries in neuroscience. Psychologists today very rarely use Freudian or Jungian theory, although both are still cited by social scientists, including, I am sad to say, many historians.

Much of the discussion of psychologists in the early part of the 20th century revolved around the fundamental argument that had engaged the anthropologists, that is whether violence is innate or learned. There were some important insights in this period that related to war. One is the idea that war is not simply a condition or phenomenon, but is a state of mind. Human beings have a different sense of perception in war, and this applies both to the battlefield and to the civilians who stay at home. This is a fact that we need to keep in mind.

Another important psychological idea that retains its relevance is the theory of cognitive dissonance. Developed by Leon Festinger, cognitive dissonance describes the feeling of holding two contradictory ideas simultaneously. Such cognitive dissonance not only occurs in war, but is a necessary part of it. A modern military officer is responsible for the well-being of his or her soldiers, and minimizing casualties. He or she may also carry out a combat mission, which necessarily places soldiers in harm's way. Success on the battlefield necessitates the resulting cognitive dissonance.

The modern advances in brain science, which have made Freud and Jung's theories obsolete, have shown us that the innate and the learned are not separate. Our genetic structure affects our environment and behavior, but remarkably, our environment and behavior also affect our genetic structure. "Nature" versus "nurture" turns out to be "nature and nurture." Psychologists now see consciousness not as something separate from the physical brain, but as an emergent property. An emergent property is one that arises from an interaction of some sort. I'll return to this idea in a moment.

A very important discovery is the key importance of inhibition in the functioning of the brain. Thus, there are parts of the brain that create violent aggressive impulses, and other parts of the brain that inhibit these impulses, shutting them down, weakening them or redirecting them. This idea of inhibition is very important and quite relevant to the study of war. Not only aggression, but uncontrollable panic is also an impulse closely linked to war. In some respects, all training, culture, and method of war can be seen as ways of trying to induce panic in the enemy, and inhibit it in one's own men.

Let me sum up with a few ideas of my own about the theory of war. In the first place, I agree with Bassford that we need to bring von Clausewitz back into the forefront of our theoretical studies. He is the Charles Darwin of military historians, and although many of his ideas, like Darwin's are rooted in the 19th century, the fundamentals remain relevant. We also need to remember, that although the psychology of aggression is important to understand, war is not a matter of condition of individuals in conflict. One person attacking or killing another in isolation, regardless of the motives, can be many things: a crime or a justified action, but it certainly is not an act or war. Even if we accept with Keegan, that tribes or even gangs can fight wars, in war, there is always an "our side" and a "their side" and all wars have rules and conventions based at least on this simple division.

War also has temporal limits, that is, it has a beginning and it has an end. Of course, in a sense, everything has a beginning and an end: our lives, our country, even our world, started at some point and will eventually end at another point. "War," however, is a condition that is understandable only as a counter-point to something called "peace." There is an almost universal distinction: "time of war" and "time of peace." Just as there is always "in" group and "out" group, there is also in war an "on" and "off" time. Thus, in a time of war, one takes an enemy's life with impunity or even praise, but in time of peace the same act becomes something different.

War is generally characterized by killing, some times on an almost unimaginably vast scale. The wars of the 20th century resulted literally in tens of millions of deaths. From a relative point of view, earlier wars were even more destructive. Entire tribes or a people could be entirely destroyed. It is clear, however, that it is not the number of deaths, or even the relative number of deaths, that defines war. It is possible for a serial killer to be responsible for dozens or even hundreds of deaths, but these murders are clearly not a war.

There are cases of targeted and organized mass killing which are generally not viewed as wars, but in many respects can be seen as such. In these cases, the victims are almost exclusively innocent civilians, and the killers are government officials, at times military or paramilitary personnel. The Nazi genocide against European Jewry that we call the Holocaust can be seen as a war against the Jews, as Lucy Davidowicz argued in her book of the same title. The massacres of Armenians under the Ottoman government, the man-made famine in the Ukraine organized by the Soviets, Mao Tse-tung's Cultural Revolution, Pol Pot's purges, and many more, can be put in this category. The discussion of these tragic events, and whether or not they should be seen as wars, could take up an entire lecture series, and indeed has.

In any case, although not all violence is war, all wars are characterized by violence and the threat of violence. A virulent debate in print between to schools of thought, even one carried on for years and with great vehemence, can be considered a war only metaphorically. While violence or potential violence is a necessary part of war, unrestrained or uncontrolled violence is by definition not war.

A very important point to remember is that war is not unrestrained violence. The constraint of violence by custom or command is a key element defining a war. In order to be war, there must be limits: who one can kill, when one can kill, the circumstances under which one can kill. Paradoxically, war is best understood not as a condition in which one can freely kill, but rather one in which ones killing is strictly limited. War involves the restraint of violence, but it is more than that. War involves the organization of violence, and it is exactly in this organizational element that it has the most impact on the development of societies. I agree with Keeley that primitive war is different from modern war, or civilized war, but it is important to keep in mind that one did not replace the other, rather modern war absorbs primitive war and, in a sense, represses it. But primitive war is also implicit in modern war.

This insight is understood by those psychiatrists and psychologists working with soldiers dealing with the trauma of war. The psychiatrist Jonathan Shay wrote *Achilles in Vietnam* as a book of therapy, and it has helped, and continues to help, thousands of veterans. He points out some soldiers can go berserk or feel that way, on the death of a comrade, killing enemies in a blind rage. This is an example of how primitive war still exists within the context of modern war. I recommend Shay's book to anyone interested in the theory of war. The psychological idea of an emergent property, which I mentioned earlier in this lecture, is very useful in discussing all elements of war. I've said that war has a beginning and an end, an "on" and an "off" time and an "in" and an "out" group. But human relations, both in individuals and groups, exist on a continuum from emotional to rational, with not so much as a dividing line, as a point of interaction. War or peace can also be seen as an emergent property of certain of these interactions.

Another point often forgotten by theorists, is that war is about winning, and whatever the impulses or goals that lead to war, individuals and societies will try their best to win. This applies as much to the most primitive tribe as to the most civilized society. In addition, every fighting force needs to arm itself and eat and motivate its warriors or soldiers. Whether a tribal war party or an organized army, technologies and methods need to be adopted—and adapted—to meet these needs. War is about changing conditions: both changes in the physical world, such as weather, and changes introduced by interaction with the opposing force. Thus, while it is important to understand the cultural and philosophical and psychological elements of war, we should not forget to look at the way war was actually fought.

In this series, we shall see that these methods are more often similar than different across cultures, and that cultures and individuals of any culture can adapt readily to the changing conditions of war. The theory of war is important, but theory must be based on the reality of war. In the next lecture, we shall explore how we can reconstruct and understand the wars of both the distant and the recent past.

Lecture Two
The Historiography of War

Scope:

Written traditions help us reconstruct war. Ancient writing is most valuable when a historical narrative is established, such as among the Greeks and the Chinese. When perishable material, such as papyrus, is used, the narrative's survival relies on manuscript transmission. Some original documents survive due to being written on durable material, such as stone or metal, or because of special conditions. We can also learn much from archaeology. Graphic art is a source of information, both about the reality and the perception of war. Our focus depends on the historical method and philosophy being used. Therefore, an understanding of historiography is vital.

Outline

I. To understand war and its effects, historians must go beyond theory and try to understand as much as possible about the reality of war. In this lecture, we will discuss ways in which historians try to reconstruct warfare in the past.

   A. Storytelling about war was originally the only way of preserving its memory. Today, war stories remain an important part of culture and continue to influence our ideas.
   1. When we try to reconstruct war in nonliterate societies, oral histories can take on an important role.
   2. Oral histories must, however, be viewed critically.
   3. World War I veterans incorporated scenes from the movie *Gallipoli* into their memories of the war.
   4. Studies have shown that within three generations, oral histories tend to resemble more fiction than fact.

   B. Virtually all of our information about the history of war comes from written sources.
   1. Remarkably, there are original ancient and medieval military documents that have survived sometimes thousands of years.
   2. Most of our information about the premodern world, however, does not come from original documents but from texts that have been recopied.

3. To be useful, texts must not only survive but also be readable by scholars. Scholars are constantly working to decipher and translate scripts.
4. Much writing about war is derived from an author's personal experience.
5. After the introduction of printing, written sources multiplied exponentially. There was a surprising number of works printed simply to record the experiences of common soldiers.

C. As important as writing is, nonwritten sources are sometimes even more valuable.
1. Even when we have access to the writing of a culture, archaeology can give us insight and sometimes even correct misconceptions derived from written material.
2. Traditional archaeology, based on the study of fortifications, only occasionally yields evidence of battle. This has changed in recent years with the development of battlefield archaeology.
3. Many physical objects of soldiers and armies remain. Armor and weapons are common survivors, even from ancient cultures.
4. Reconstruction and reenactment are tools often underutilized.
5. Art in its various forms is a very important source of information, both about the reality and the perception of war. Audio recordings, photographs, and film are particularly valuable, but must still be viewed critically.

D. In the study of war, each fact is made up of a combination of evidence and analysis using a process called the historical method.
1. History is always changing. Sometimes our view of the past changes because of new evidence.
2. Sometimes history changes through the reinterpretation of existing evidence.
3. We cannot expect our sources to record everything. What our sources do not say is often as important as what they do.

II. Historiography—the method and philosophy of understanding the past—is as critical to the study of war as to any other historical study.

A. In modern terms, history means not just a chronicle or narrative of the past but rather an active inquiry into why the past occurred the way it did.

B. The changing methods and theory of the Western historical tradition have had a particular influence on our view of world warfare.

C. The 19th century also saw the beginning of professional history. Despite the often racist or nationalist views of academic historians during this period, these scholars were committed to instituting more scientific and critical methods of understanding the past.

III. Another important direction in 19th-century historical thinking was the idea of historical dialectics, proposed by Hegel and adopted by Marx and Engels.

A. Dialectical thinking had a great deal of influence on von Clausewitz's ideas.

B. The 20th century saw the development of a number of historical schools, though these had much less impact on military history than on intellectual and social history.

C. Most military history published today remains focused on the West in general, and Europe in particular.

Suggested Reading:

Ferguson, "A Paradigm for the Study of War and Society."

Perlmutter, *Visions of War*.

Whitby, "Reconstructing Ancient Warfare."

Questions to Consider:

1. What factors have led to a tendency to Eurocentrism among military historians?

2. How could we judge if the West has a distinct military tradition?

Lecture Two—Transcript
The Historiography of War

In the last lecture, we talked about war from a theoretical perspective. War, however, is not a theory. It's an event that actually occurred in the past. To understand war, and its effects, historians must try to understand as much as possible about the reality of wars. In this lecture, we will discuss how historians try to reconstruct warfare in the past. Storytelling about war was originally the only way of preserving its memory. Of course, until modern times, this oral history only survived when it was written down. Homer, for example, drew on oral legends and myths to create the *Iliad*, and such epic literature is found in many different cultures. Today, war stories remain an important part of our culture, and continue to influence our ideas. My own view of war, for example, has been shaped by listening to the stories of my father, and my father-in-law, both combat veterans of World War II.

When trying to reconstruct war in nonliterate society, oral histories can take on an important role. They must, however, be viewed critically. Some Australian World War I veterans, for example, were found to have incorporated scenes from movies, such as *Gallipoli* into their memories of the war. Academic studies of oral history indicate that although certain details, such as names, can survive in stories for a very long time, historical events are so changed in the retelling that after three generations or so fact usually cannot be distinguished from fiction. Therefore, for reliable information to survive about most of history, it needs to be written down.

Indeed, virtually all of our information about war comes from written sources. Remarkably, there are original ancient and medieval military documents, and other writings about war, that have survived, sometimes for thousands of year, in various forms, such as clay, papyrus, paper, stone, or metal. Examples include military orders on clay tablets from Mesopotamia, a roster of Roman soldiers on papyrus from Egypt, a supply documents on wood from western China, and lists of captives on a stone stele from Mayan Mesoamerica. Such documents can range from a few words, or even a single name, to descriptions of hundreds of lines.

The tombstones of soldiers, for example, can be a very valuable source. Even if each stone might contain little information individually, when a large number are studied, they can provide valuable data. For example, a single Roman military tombstone describes only a particular soldier's life, but studying hundreds of them, scholars have reconstructed enlistment patterns, conventions of promotion, and the movement of units. Whether a tombstone is inscribed, however, and whether it contains any military information, varies from culture to culture and from time to time. In Rome, for example, once Christianity became the imperial religion, such detailed military tombstones become very rare.

Most of our information about the premodern world, however, does not come from documents that have survived, but from texts that have been recopied, often multiple times, in what is known as manuscript transmission. In this category we find historical descriptions of wars, such as those of the Greek historian Thucydides, Chinese historian Ssu-ma Chien. There are also military handbooks and technical writing about war, including the famous *Art of War* by Sun-tzu, but also the less famous ancient manuals on camp building, catapults and cavalry. Of course, we can get information about war, both how it was fought and how it was viewed, from all sorts of texts. A great deal has been learned about late Roman warfare, for example, from the writings of the Christian theologians called the church fathers.

Of course, to be useful, such writing must not only survive, but scholars must be able to read it. Some ancient scripts, such as the Indus Valley script, cannot be deciphered. Some scripts can be read but the underlying language is unknown. Scholars are constantly working to decipher and translate ancient scripts. The ability to translate Mayan script, which occurred only in the last few decades, dramatically changed our view of their military culture, and allows us to follow the course of Mayan wars fought in the 7th or 8th century A.D.

Much writing about war derives from the author's personal experiences and not just in modern times. The Jewish historian Josephus, who left our best account of the Roman imperial army at war, fought in the war he was describing—indeed, after going over to the Romans side, he fought on both sides, a rare insight. Babur, who conquered India in the 16th century and founded the Mughal Empire, left a remarkable diary of his wars. Writers of all sorts of literature have included stories, others and their own, into all sorts of texts. And the military historian should be careful not to neglect any possible source of information.

In some cultures, like that of the Greeks war was an important source for literature and art. For various reasons, a relatively large amount of this material has survived and has been critically analyzed. On the other hand, there is an enormous number of military books in Arabic, Turkish, and Persian, most of which have never been translated, and much of which remains in manuscript form in archives. Military historians, and I must say myself included, do not make sufficient use of the material that has been published on non-Western military forces, although the situation is improving. There are other archives, not directly military, which also might well give us an important perspective on world warfare, for example the enormous number of Tibetan Buddhist manuscripts that have survived from the Middle Ages or the thousands of Arabic documents from the West African city of Timbuktu.

After the introduction of printing, written sources multiply exponentially. The development of printing led to an explosion of literature about war. Even a relatively minor war might spawn dozens of books. These including histories, as well as personal accounts, often written either to celebrate victory or to justify defeat. There are a surprising number of accounts that are written simply to record the experiences of common soldiers. Printing also brought an increase in the number of forms used by armies, and these were often saved. In fact since the 17th century, military archives have become enormous and modern archives contain literally millions of documents. The invention of typing made the creation of records easier, and further increased their number, a trend that has only been multiplied by the computer.

As important as writing is, what historians call "non-written" sources are sometimes more so. There are many cases in which we have no written sources at all, either because they never existed, as in the case of nonliterate cultures, or because they have all perished for one reason or another. Even when we have access to writing, as in the case of ancient China or medieval Europe, archaeology gives us insights and often corrects misperceptions based on the written record.

Traditional archaeology studied fortifications, such as the walls of cities. In some cases, traditional archaeologists found the evidence of battle, usually the remains of siege ramps and camps. These sort of studies were relatively rare, as archaeologists rarely sought out battlefield sites. This has changed in recent years with the exciting work done in battlefield archaeology around the world. Battlefield archaeologists identify battle sites and reconstruct battles on the basis of physical remains. In addition, underwater archaeology, made possible by the invention of scuba gear, mini-submarines, and remote explorers, has identified and even raised parts or all of dozens of warships, from the bronze ram of an ancient trireme to the U.S.S. Monitor.

There are many physical objects of soldiers and armies that remain. Even from ancient times, many examples of armor and weapons have survived, found in tombs or excavated from ruins. Enemy armor was often taken as prizes, and looting was an important source for military artifacts, even in modern times. Starting in medieval times, we find that such military equipment was often collected, not only in European castles, but by nobles all over the world. Modern armor, weapons, flags, and uniforms are, of course, more common. Both museums, including military museums, and private collectors contain large collections, and both are important sources for historians. An interesting repository is the Covent Garden Opera House in London, which has an enormous collection of genuine arms and armor from around the world, which was collected to be used as props.

An often-underestimated tool is reconstruction and reenactment. Archaeologist and historians have been reconstructing for many years, for example, building models of catapults to better understand ancient texts. Modern re-enactors, generally amateurs who are devoted to various periods of warfare, have made some important discoveries, for example how the Romans carried their packs.

Art in various forms is a very important source of information, both about the reality and the perception of war. It is obvious that paintings and sculptures can be highly stylized and do not necessarily represent reality. This is true even of realistic looking Greek and Roman reliefs or 19th-century paintings and illustrations. On the other hand, an understanding of a culture and its artistic traditions can reveal much about the underlying truth of the photo or of the painting.

Audio recordings, photographs and film about war are an exciting source, but also must be viewed critically. In the same way that fiction about war can be very informative, the Hollywood—or for that matter, the Bollywood—"war movie," while historically inaccurate can tell us a lot about attitudes about war. It is important to remember, however, that seemingly candid photographs and films are often posed. This is not always obvious. Most people know that the famous photograph of Marines raising the flag on Mount Surabachi was posed. What is less known is that many combat photographs and film footage are also staged. The film of the Battle of Dien Bien Phu, for example, often shown in documentaries, were staged after the fact by the Viet Minh using French and Vietnamese Republican prisoners.

In the study of war, as in any other historical study, each "fact" is made up of a combination of evidence and analysis using a process we call the historical method. In some cases, our evidence is so good, and the consensus among historians so great, that we can be virtually certain of its truth, that is, that the statement accurately describes a real event in the past, for example, that Pearl Harbor was bombed by the Japanese on December 7th, 1941. Other events are much less certain: Was there a Trojan War?

History is constantly changing. The past itself doesn't change, but our understanding of it does. Sometimes our view of the past changes because new evidence changes what we know about war. The 1970s were a time of wonderful new discoveries in China many of which have added to our knowledge of warfare there. The thousands of terracotta warriors found in the tomb of Ch'in Shi Huang-ti, the first emperor, are a famous example. Less well known are the ancient military manuals found in a Han-era tomb, including a copy of a lost book by the famous general and military theorist Sun Bin.

There are times when our understanding of the past changes, not based on new evidence, but based on reinterpretation. My own first published article, for example, argued that the Roman siege of Masada in Israel, lasted only for a few weeks (in the spring of 77 A.D.) not for months (from the winter of 72 to 73) as had previously been thought. My conclusion was not based on any new discoveries, but rather on a reexamination of the already existing evidence. While the length of a siege might not seem important, there are other historical conclusions that have been based on it. So as each piece of the puzzle is changed, historians have to constantly rethink the big picture.

We cannot expect, however, that our sources to record everything. Even in the case of modern wars, in which we have literally tons of documents, certain aspects of war will remain unattested. Of course, this is especially true in ancient and medieval history, with so much less material to work with. What our sources don't say is often as important as what they do. We happen to know a lot about Greek warfare, for example, than most other cultures, but the type of warfare that they practiced was not typical of the ancient world. We must be careful of merely following our sources, lest we make the exception into the rule.

Facts are important, but facts are not history, just as paint is not painting. Historiography is what historians call the method and philosophy of understanding the past. This is as important in the study of war as in any other endeavor of history. The word "history" comes from the Greek word meaning "to ask a question." In modern terms, history means not just a chronicle or narrative of the past, but rather an active inquiry into why the past occurred the way it did. In this series, for example, we will try to answer some of these questions: Why did the earliest cities have no walls? Why do western knights and Japanese samurai seem so similar? How did the Europeans succeed in dominating the modern world?

One of the factors that leads to a regional view of military history is that historical sources actually do derive from various traditions, which use not only different languages and scripts, but had different views of what constituted history and was worth recording for posterity. Some historical traditions, such as that of classical Greece and Rome and that of China, think of war and warfare as very important, and they focus on them. Other historical traditions, such as those in Medieval Europe or ancient India concentrate more on religion, and have much less information about warfare.

The changing methods and theory of the Western historical tradition has had a particular influence on our view of world warfare. In the 16th and 17th century, a truly global historical narrative began to develop as non-Western books were translated into European languages. There were a flurry of translations of historical sources from Chinese, Indian, and Arabic texts, and any number of world histories were written. Ironically, just as the world was turning more global, due to a number of factors—imperialism, racism and theories about history—Europeans started to systematically ignore the non-Western world.

Due both to the influence of the Enlightenment and the Industrial Revolution, the idea of historical progress became more and more influential. The ancient empires of China and India were seen as historical dead-ends which, since they were no longer progressing were therefore not worth study. This included their military histories. By the 19th century, most Western historians held this view. Whig History refers to a type of approach that focused on progress, the Great Man and, in military terms, the "Decisive Battle." This approach develops into the Western Civilization. And this has been very influential in education. Edward Creasy's *Fifteen Decisive Battles of the World*, published in 1851 and still in print, is a classic of Whig History. Although "the World" is in the title, only one of Creasy's battles was fought outside of Europe, and that was the Battle of Saratoga in the American Revolution. The absence of Asian and African battles is something Creasy does not even bother to discuss. It seemed so self-evident to him that no non-European battle could possibly change world history.

Ethnocentrism intensified during the 19th and early 20th century, as racial theory became accepted by virtually all academics. We shall discuss the idea of race in greater detail in a later lecture. But racial theory has had, and continues to have, an enormous impact on historical studies, including those of war. Some military cultures that are very similar, for example the Greek and the Roman, or the Chinese and Japanese, are traditionally treated separately in military history due to the fact that these groups were once considered different races, and thus thought to have different collective mentalities, including in military matters.

Needless to say, racism and racial theory has brought a great deal of misery in its wake, but it has also had a very negative effect on military history. An example is the excavation of the remarkable fortified settlement called the "Great Zimbabwe," now located in the country of the same name. The European excavators were convinced that the local Africans were racially incapable of such impressive stone walls, although, in fact, the stone walls had been built by the ancestors of the local Shona people. The excavators dug through all the levels of the site, discarding all the valuable evidence of the true builders, including no doubt remains of weapons, searching for some sign of Phoenicians or Persians or anything but Africans. Remarkably, the physical evidence they had just dug up was not enough to jar their belief in the immutable laws of race, and at the end they declared the identity of the builders of the Great Zimbabwe to be a mystery.

The 19th century also saw the beginning of professional history. And, in fact, this was not seen as incompatible with racism. Racial theory was considered at the time quite scientific. The racial, nationalist and sometimes imperialist views of professors of history in European universities, especially in Germany, did not prevent them from developing and instituting more scientific and critical methods for understanding the past. These historians saw objectivity and accuracy as their goal, not teaching virtue or propagandizing for a particular side. This attitude is expressed by Leopold von Ranke's famous saying, that the historian's "duty was not to judge the past, nor to instruct the present generation how to best conduct itself in the future, but merely to show how it actually happened." Of course, history continued to be affected by the biases of historians, but the historical method these early professors developed was in practice enormously successful in reconstructing the past.

The historical, and the related scientific methods were so successful that many scholars felt that they could discover the scientific rules of society, just as the physicists had discovered the scientific rules of the universe. This was the rise of social science, and in history it resulted in a school called "positivism." Positivist history did very detailed studies, including studies of wars, with the assumption that from these focused studies they would find the elements with which to reconstruct the past. This was very valuable work, on which historians still build, but the confidence that these small details would form themselves into patterns turned out to be misplaced. Positivism tended to lead to more and more intense studies of detail, seemingly for its own sake. This led to a reaction. The ideas of Frederich Nietzsche, for example, were a powerful retort to both positivism and, by the way, the racial theory. It took some time for Nietzsche's ideas to become part of historiography, but they are now very influential in academic circles, a development that is not necessarily to history's advantage in my opinion.

Another important direction in 19th-century historical thinking was the idea of historical dialectics proposed by Hegel and adopted by Marx and Engels. Whether Hegelian or Marxist, according to historical dialectics, history developed according to a set pattern. There was a historical thesis, a war of conquest, setting forth an antithesis, such as the militarization of a state to defend itself, which resulted in a synthesis, as invaders and conquered form a new type of society. Dialectical thinking, by the way, had a great deal of influence on von Clausewitz's ideas. Since the dialectical process was supposed to move in a particular direction, and so in some respects the dialectic historians resembled the positivists. They both thought of themselves as uncovering the scientific laws of history. The focus of dialectics, however, was on theory and not on detail. The dialectic operated on a much higher level than the individual, even the so-called Great Men, whose impact was thought to be minimal. For example, dialectic historians thought that if Caesar had drowned in the Nile during the Battle of Alexandria, another Caesar would have ultimately created the Roman Empire. Warfare, however, was an important factor in the working out and unfolding of history. Positivism and Marxism, and their various subsets were the two rival schools of historiography up to the Second World War.

The 20th century saw the development of a number of historical schools, although these have had much less impact on military history than on intellectual and social history. Marxism was very influential in both the communist world and in the West, and indeed many of the periods best-known historians were Marxists. Their focus on economic factors and class relations, however, tended to deemphasize war, although it was by no means ignored. The French Annales School argued that we should look at history in the very long term, to really understand it. War was not significant in this historical model, as even the longest war did not compare to other long-term historical trends in terms of duration.

Finally, the modern theories, that we might call collectively postmodernism have challenged the basis of the historical method, that it is possible to separate truth from fiction. This view argues that it is impossible to put aside our class and ethnic biases, to put it simply, that when we think we are looking through a window to the past, we are actually looking at a mirror, at ourselves. History is seen as a way for privileged groups to impose their ideology on the powerless, and of course military history is seen as one of the worst culprits. Overall, however, the postmodernists have failed to convince most historians that one cannot be more or less objective. Simply to "problematize," to use a favorite postmodernist expression, is not to disprove. The reality of war and genocide are particularly difficult subjects for the postmodernists, and some of their writing on the subject is frankly ridiculous.

Just as these approaches had little interest in warfare, seeing it as either irrelevant or reactionary, military historians have generally had little use for them. As a result, writing on warfare did not benefit fully from what was positive in these new theoretical approaches, and generally clung on to the Whig or positivist approaches of the 19th century and was stubbornly Eurocentric. There were exceptions. In 1982 William McNeil, probably the greatest of the first generation of world historians, wrote his *The Pursuit of Power*, a broad-ranging discussion of warfare in the early modern period. Significantly, however, McNeil was not a military historian.

This has changed with the introduction of the so-called New Military History pioneered by Geoffrey Parker, whose groundbreaking book, *The Military Revolution*, came out in 1996. New Military History puts armies, battles, and wars in the context of the societies in which they occurred. The last 20 years have seen an explosion of new and exciting historiography on war and military history, and of course it is on this work that this lecture series is primarily based.

Despite these exciting advances, most of the military history published today remains focused on the West in general, and on Europe in particular. The phrase "ancient military history" for example, still usually means "Greek and Roman military history" and "medieval military history" means "western knights and castles." Even the New Military History, however, remains rather Eurocentric, at a time when world and global history is developing rapidly. This Eurocentrism continues due to a number of factors. There is the fact that the practice of military history has traditionally been, and still is, dominated by Europeans and Americans. Another factor is the continuing influence of the regional approach to history, which tends to put Chinese military history, for example, in the discipline of Chinese studies, for example, instead of general military history. This situation is changing, but the lack of sources, and especially the lack of translation, hinders progress.

There are some military historians, such as Victor Davis Hanson, who argue that Western War is a totally different from war as practiced elsewhere in the world. In both *The Western Way of War* and *Carnage and Culture*, Hanson maintains that since Greek times, Western war has favored the decisive battle in contrast to other traditions. Well, there were certainly periods in which Western warfare differed from that in other parts of the world, but I think that Hanson is fundamentally incorrect. We will discuss this issue throughout the series. On the other hand—and in history there is always another hand—there is the view that the cultures of the East, such as India and China, are very ancient, and that they had a special way of fighting wars, along with other elements of their culture that are distinct and developed independently. I also disagree with this view as the subsequent lectures will show.

Even those who deal with the world history of warfare tend to do so in a series of regional chapters, such as Western War, Islamic War, Indian War, Chinese War, and so forth. To some extent this is unavoidable, and this series will sometimes take this tack. But these regions are all too often treated as if they developed in isolation. In addition, military historians tend to neglect the modern wars of Asia and Africa, except insofar as they involve Europeans or Americans. There are, for example, numerous books on such minor wars as the British-Argentine conflict over the Falkland Islands and the American invasion of Grenada. Yet the modern War in the Congo, in which literally millions have died, is largely ignored. Even Western military history can become quite parochial: You could read a history of World War II from an American, French, and Russian historian and think that you were reading about three different wars.

In recent years, there's been a new generation of military historians, such as Jeremy Black, Christon Archer, Stephen Morillo, and Azar Gat, who have explored and championed the global approach. Although they, and I, recognize the key importance of the West in the development of modern warfare, as well as the continuing importance of Greek and Roman warfare, one of the themes of this series is how similar warfare, and its influence, is around the globe.

I do not take a global approach out of fairness, or political correctness, but because it gives us a better understanding of war. Although it obviously covers more time and geographical space, a world history approach makes history clearer in many respects.

Advances such as the zero or gunpowder no longer just "enter stage right" but we see how they came about and how they spread. As you listen to this series, I hope that you will come to agree that military history has much to offer a world historical perspective.

In the next lecture, we will start our chronological journey of war and world history. We will begin at the beginning, at least as far as humans are concerned: the Paleolithic or Old Stone Age.

Lecture Three
The Stone Age War

Scope:

Evidence is very limited for the Paleolithic era (2.5 million years ago to 10,000 B.C.), and much is subject to multiple interpretations. A stone ax could be used for hunting or fighting, and traumatic injury could result from war, but also from murder or ritual sacrifice. The bow and arrow was a key invention of the late Paleolithic, occurring in Europe around 40,000 B.C. The first evidence of war in cave paintings features the bow. The spread of the bow illustrates the question of diffusion versus independent invention. Evidence of war increases in the Neolithic era, such as mass graves of slaughtered persons and early fortifications. A 5,300-year-old body found frozen in the Alps (Ötzi) gives us a remarkable view of early group conflict.

Outline

I. In this lecture, we address a very basic question: How far back in history does warfare go?

  A. Dating events in prehistory is complex, even with modern tools such as radiocarbon dating.

   1. Thus the dates in this lecture and the next few ones are approximate, at times very approximate.

   2. This is not to say that accurate dating is not important—indeed it is the basis of history—only that in the case of prehistory or early history, accuracy is very difficult and sometimes impossible.

  B. Direct evidence of war or even violence in general during the early and middle Paleolithic eras is very limited, and what little has been discovered can be interpreted in many ways.

   1. The Paleolithic era is defined by the use of stones as tools. But there is some evidence of the development of weapons during this period as well.

   2. The spear is the first identifiable weapon. The earliest direct evidence of it dates from about 400,000 years ago.

3. If early humans were scavengers rather than hunters, it changes our view of the Paleolithic considerably. According to the scavenger theory, the spear was used not to kill prey but to drive off other scavengers like hyenas and vultures.
4. The next innovations in weaponry, the stone spear point on a wooden shaft and the dart, appear to go back to around 80,000 B.C. Their development may have been part of what some paleontologists call the great leap forward.
5. Around 30,000 B.C., the first cave paintings appear. These show the hunting of animals such as bison with spears. Some scholars have interpreted some human figures as showing signs of being wounded by spears, but this is far from clear.
6. Around the same time, about 30,000 B.C., one finds the first evidence of the spear-thrower. This is a notched stick into which the spear was fitted, allowing the spear to be hurled farther.

C. From the point of view of the development of warfare, probably the most important invention of the Paleolithic was the bow and arrow.
1. The earliest evidence dates to about 9000 B.C. The bow was the first machine. It stores kinetic energy when the string is pulled back.
2. The original bow is known as a simple bow: a straight piece of round wood, such as a branch, with a bowstring generally made of sinew, twisted hemp, or even human hair.
3. Our earliest evidence for the use of bow and arrow are stone arrowheads, though these were probably developed sometime after the arrow itself.
4. The bow revolutionized hunting and could, of course, also be used to kill people. The invention of the bow is so important that we can call it the bow revolution.

D. Around 12,000 to 11,000 B.C., we find the first direct evidence of the mass killing of humans, perhaps the first direct evidence of war.

    1. The so-called Cemetery 117 in Egypt dates to this period. It contains 59 bodies, many with evidence of violent and likely lethal wounds.

    2. There is also a cave painting in Spain that depicts two groups of men attacking each other and is often pointed to as the first direct evidence of war. However, this painting probably dates to the Neolithic period.

    3. In any case, there is no reason to doubt that some form of group conflict existed in this period, whether or not we want to call it war.

II. One method of trying to understand prehistoric war is to study the behavior of modern tribal peoples.

    A. This idea was basic to the development of anthropology as a study.

        1. Although tribes can tell us something about the origins of war, we must remember that tribes do not necessarily represent a survival into the present of a previous way of life.

        2. For instance, modern tribal warfare is often motivated by economic factors that would probably not have existed in prehistoric times.

        3. The move from hunting and gathering tribes to agricultural villages was not straightforward one.

    B. The Neolithic, or agricultural revolution, occurred in different regions at different times—as early as 8000 B.C. in the Middle East and Southeast Asia, but much later elsewhere.

        1. Groups probably turned to agriculture due to population pressures and the fact that wild animal populations were no longer large enough to support human ones.

        2. There are scholars who contend that war really came to exist only in the Neolithic. There is certainly no question that the evidence of war increases during this period.

        3. With agriculture, one's food source is tied directly to a piece of land, and thus the stakes of fighting with other groups become higher.

4. One could argue that armies were in fact necessary for agriculture to develop and that organized military was the driving force behind agriculture, not merely the result of it.

5. In his studies of why the West eventually dominated the world, Jared Diamond has argued that the success of early Neolithic societies in the Near East was closely tied to the availability of plants and animals genetically predisposed to domestication.

C. It is in the Neolithic that we find the first defenses being built around settlements.

1. Surprisingly, the earliest such defenses, such as those at Jericho, are the most sophisticated. A stone wall about 5 feet thick and 12 to 17 feet high with a stone tower about 30 feet high dates to around 8000 B.C.

2. Some scholars have suggested the Jericho wall was for flood control, but its height and the presence of the tower strongly suggest a defensive purpose.

3. At Catal Hüyük in modern Turkey, the mud walls of the outermost houses formed a defensive perimeter around the village. This site also contains the first examples of stone daggers, maces, and pictures of slings.

4. Despite their sophistication, neither of these sites seems to have led to any further development in defenses.

5. It is true that some Neolithic villages did have walls and ditches around their perimeters, but these defenses are more primitive than those of Jericho and Catal Hüyük, and from a much later date.

D. There is no question that war, or at least group violence, did exist across the Neolithic world.

1. The 5,300-year-old body of a man (called Ötzi by archaeologists) was found frozen in the Swiss Alps. He was carrying a flint knife, a copper ax, and a longbow. His quiver held 14 bone-tipped arrows with flint heads.

2. It was originally thought that Ötzi died of an arrow wound, but recent investigation concludes he received a fatal blow to the head. Careful analysis has shown he died as part of a group struggle, perhaps a battle.

Suggested Reading:

Ferill, *The Origins of War*.

Keeley, *War before Civilization*.

Otterbein, *How War Began*.

Questions to Consider:

1. What are some of the problems with using modern tribal societies to understand prehistoric ones?

2. At what point could war truly be said to have begun?

Lecture Three—Transcript
The Stone Age War

Welcome back. In our last lecture we looked at the tools, methods, and theory that historians use to try and reconstruct past wars. Today we will address a very basic question. How far back in history does warfare go? In other words, how old is war? Before we begin, let me point out something about dating that's especially relevant here. Dating events in prehistory is complex, even with modern tools such as radiocarbon dating. Thus, the dates that I give in this lecture and the next few ones are approximate, at times very approximate. This is not to say that accurate dating isn't important—indeed it is the basis of history—only that in the case of prehistory and early history, accuracy is very difficult, sometimes, frankly, impossible.

In this lecture series we are concerned with human war, but, of course, human beings evolved out of pre-human primates, so we might theorize, as some have, that war is even older than humanity. Studies of chimpanzees, our closest primate relatives, have shown that they not only practice deliberate murder but carry on group fights which involve killing members of other chimp groups. At least some of these wars, if we might call them that, are fought over territory. Indeed, recent logging activities in the African nation of Gabon set off a series of chimpanzee wars in which some 20,000 chimps were killed. These findings are relevant certainly to the issue of warfare among very early humans, but direct evidence for war, or indeed violence of any kind, during the Early and Middle Paleolithic Eras, from about two and half million years ago down to around 40,000–30,000 years ago, is very limited. Very few remains of any kind survive from this very early period, and other than "stones and bones," evidence for aspects of life in the Paleolithic, including war, if it existed, is very, very thin. To make matters worse, what we do discover is usually subject to multiple interpretations. A stone ax, for example, can be used as a weapon of war, but also for hunting, or a tool.

The same problem exists, in human remains, especially if found individually or in small numbers, as is almost always the case. A traumatic injury, such as evidence of a crushed skull, might result from war, but could just as easily be the result of murder or even human sacrifice.

The Paleolithic, or Old Stone Age, is defined, of course, by the use of stones as tools. A stone can easily be used as a weapon, either held in the hand and used for blunt force, or hurled. Unfortunately, there is no way to tell if a particular stone found at a Stone Age site was used as a weapon or not.

The spear is the first identifiable weapon. The first direct evidence for the use of wooden spears dates to around 400,000 years ago, though the use of spear-like weapons by some chimpanzees suggests that humans might have at least used spears much earlier, perhaps millions of years ago.

Spears were long a major weapon of war but also a weapon long used for hunting. War and hunting have always been closely related. Not only are the tools and the methods of war and hunting often quite similar, they both tap into some of the same psychological responses, for example in the production of adrenalin. How Paleolithic people used the spear in obtaining food is quite relevant to our understanding of the development of war. We might think of hunting as being the oldest human activity but, in fact, one of the main debates now being carried out about the Paleolithic is how early humans became hunters. There is increasing evidence that our earliest ancestors were not hunters at all but scavengers.

If we think of early humans as scavengers rather than hunters, it changes our view of the Paleolithic considerably. Rather than humans boldly killing large and fierce animals, they are skulking in the shadows waiting for the predators, like saber-toothed tigers, to finish their meal. In fact, although there are numerous illustrations in modern works that show Stone Age men facing off a mastodon with a spear, I venture to say this is easier to imagine than it was actually to do. According to the scavenger theory, the spear was used not to kill prey but to drive off other scavengers like hyenas and vultures from the leftovers.

Of course, it is possible that even in the Paleolithic times that spears were indeed used to kill animals, and perhaps even other people. Nevertheless, this changing view of early humans does undermine, to some extent, our idea of aggression being part of a long evolutionary process.

In any case, the next innovations in weaponry, the stone spear point tied to a wooden shaft and the dart, appear to go back to around

80,000 B.C., give or take a few tens of thousands of years. Although the stone spear point does not increase the amount of pressure that can be applied against a target, it significantly increases its penetration ability and also reduces the chance of the shaft breaking. Since it increases the weight of the spear toward the head, adding a stone point also makes it easier to throw, and it is likely that this is one of the main purposes of the point. The fact that spears were often thrown probably led to the development of the dart, a shorter version of the spear, which can be hurled more easily and with more accuracy, although since it is lighter, with less force. Accuracy was made possible by the addition of feathers, called "fletch," at the end. It is possible that poisons were also applied to darts to make them more effective. The dart point or head is virtually identical to the later arrowhead and is frequently mistaken for it. Thus, the existence of the bow is often dated too early by confusion with the dart. Both the throwing spear and the dart allowed for killing at a distance, which is not only safer but also psychologically easier. It also made killing animals much easier, and this period may represent the turning of humans from scavenging to hunting as the main source of meat.

The development of the stone spear point and the dart may be part of what some paleontologists have called the "Great Leap Forward," during which humans also invented clothing and sailing. Clothing allowed humans to migrate to the colder regions, such as northern Europe, Siberia, and ultimately to cross over to Alaska and the Americas. Australia has not been connected to the mainland of Asia for millions of years, and so the human beings that arrive there around 40,000 years ago must have sailed there. Some scholars suggest that these inventions are related to a change in the human brain, but this is highly speculative and controversial. In any case, it is also possible that along with hunting animals becoming more common, killing humans may have as well. It was certainly easier.

Around 30,000 B.C., the first cave paintings appear. These show the hunting of animals such as bison with spears. Some scholars have interpreted some human figures as showing signs of being wounded by spears, but this is far from clear. Around the same time, say, say, 30,000 B.C., one finds the first evidence for the spear thrower. This is a notched stick into which the spear was fitted. In effect, it lengthened the arm, allowing the spear to be hurled further.

From the point of view of evidence for the development of warfare, probably the most important invention of the Paleolithic was the bow and arrow. It is also the most difficult, mainly because of the fact that dart heads and arrow heads are so similar. Indeed, the bow probably developed out of the use of the dart, which can become the arrow with the addition of a bow.

The first direct evidence for the bow and arrow comes from the remains of arrows with the shaft still attached comes from Germany and dates to about 9000 BC. Of course, the discovery was probably earlier, although how much earlier, we cannot say.

The bow is the first machine. What it does is store kinetic energy when the string is pulled back. The archer controls when, and in what direction, this energy is released, propelling an arrow with sufficient force to kill an animal, or a human, farther than a spear or dart can be hurled.

The original bow is known as a simple bow, that is a straight piece of wood, such as a branch, with a bowstring, generally made of sinew, that is, the tendons of an animal. Other material could also be used, such as twisted hemp or even human hair. The basic element of the arrow is the wooden shaft, with a notch at the end to fit it to the bowstring.

Since the arrow developed out of the dart, stone points or heads were a feature from the beginning, fitted to the shaft with sinew or string. The feathers placed at the back of the shaft, near the notch, was also a feature of the dart. These feathers stabilized the arrow in flight and improved range and accuracy. Our earliest evidence for the use of bow and arrow are stone arrowheads, though these were probably developed sometime after the arrow itself. What looks to us to be an arrowhead, or even an arrow shaft, however, might be the point or shaft of a javelin or dart. The bow revolutionized hunting and could, of course, also be used to kill people.

The invention of the bow is so important, that we can actually call it a "Bow Revolution." Indeed, we should call it the "First Bow Revolution" as there is another that occurs in the Americas many tens of thousands of years later. We will discuss the American, or Second Bow Revolution, in a later lecture.

Around 12,000 to 11,000 B.C., we find the first direct evidence of the mass killing of humans, perhaps the first direct evidence of war.

The so-called "Cemetery 117," found in Egypt, dates to around 12,000 to 11,000 B.C. It contained 59 bodies: those that could be identified by age and sex were 24 females, 19 males, and 13 children. About 40 percent died from violent wounds which, since none of them had healed, had almost certainly been administered at the same time. Stone projectile points, either from arrows or spears or darts, were found among the bodies. The most plausible explanation of these findings is of a surprise attack by an enemy that caught these people sleeping. Some may have escaped, but the killing may represent not a part, but virtually all of a tribe. This may or may not be true. All we have here actually is the remains of humans who died violent deaths. The evidence for warfare is only circumstantial, although it must be said that it is strong circumstantial evidence.

There is a cave painting from Spain that is often pointed to as the first direct evidence of war. This painting illustrates two groups, five individuals on the left and three on the right, who are shooting at each other with bows. Whether this is war depends in large part on how we define war, but it is almost certainly evidence for some sort of organized group fighting. We should not assume that the eight figures are necessarily representative of a larger group. Human groups in the Paleolithic were quite small, and a "war" with fewer than a dozen combatants on both sides is certainly conceivable.

The problem with this painting, however, is that it does not date to the Mesolithic. It is true that Spanish cave paintings in this style date to the Paleolithic. True that Spanish cave paintings in this style do date to the late Paleolithic period. But this particular painting probably dates to the Neolithic between 4000 and 3500 B.C. Some scholars have claimed that it reflects the practice of the earlier period, but it should be borne in mind that it might well date to same period as the first direct evidence of war in Mesopotamia.

In any case, there is no reason to doubt that some form of group conflict existed in the Paleolithic, whether or not we want to call it "war." Other Paleolithic paintings do illustrate bowmen in hunting scenes: one shows a file of archers, for example, though it is a bit of a stretch to call this military organization.

One method of trying to understand prehistoric war, however or whenever we imagine that it started, is to try to think our way back into these very remote times in the past to study the behavior of modern tribal peoples. This idea was basic to the development of anthropology as a study. The problem of this approach is that tribes do not necessarily represent a survival into the present or a previous way of life. There is good reason to think that tribal organizations often arise due to groups being pushed into marginal areas.

Nevertheless, there is good reason to think that the study of tribal societies can tell us something about nature and the origins of war. In a recent article in the *New Yorker*, UCLA Geography professor Jared Diamond discussed vengeance and cycles of violence among certain clans in Papua New Guinea, where he had done research. His driver there was a man named Daniel Wemp, who described to him an ongoing war between Wemp's clan, called the "Handa," and a neighboring clan, the Ombal. Wemp became involved in this war, this fight, in 1992, when his beloved uncle was killed by an Ombal, and he took it upon himself to revenge his uncle's death. Before Daniel felt he was sufficiently avenged, 29 more people had been killed. Diamond concludes that the desire for vengeance expressed by Wemp and his hostility to other clans does not differ much from modern times. Indeed, it seems very similar to the desire for vengeance discussed in much of human literature, such as the *Iliad*, and expressed by modern participants in war, for example the Vietnam veterans described by the psychiatrist Jonathan Shay, that I mentioned in the last lecture.

We have to be careful, however, in using such descriptions, which are not of prehistoric people, but of modern people, albeit ones living in what we can call a more primitive society. Daniel Wemp's society in Papua New Guinea, for example, differs in many different ways from that of prehistoric peoples. As Diamond points out, Papuan wars are not only fought about vengeance, but also over pigs, which are one of the bases of the economy. The stealing of pigs is often the cause of fighting. Even those people who truly have a hunting and gathering economy, and there are very few left today, cannot be said to be living in the same way as prehistoric peoples. Modern primitive people have often been pushed into very marginal lands, and their cultures may very well represent a response to relatively recent migration, rather than some age-old tradition. We certainly see this phenomenon occurring among the North American Indians of the 18th and 19th centuries.

An important reality of prehistoric life to keep in mind when thinking about warfare is that populations of prehistoric periods were very small. Individual groups or tribes may well have numbered a few dozen at most. In addition, the territory in which humans wandered was very large, and there was usually little difference in the economic productivity of one area over another, that is in how good hunting and gathering was in one valley over another. These facts made war rather unprofitable from the point of view of the Paleolithic economy. Other human bands would have been much more valuable as sources of mates, of trading goods, and even of information about herds and other food sources, to risk what minor gains could be gained from killing them under normal circumstances. War would seem to be a dangerous luxury under Paleolithic conditions. This assumes, of course, a level of rational cost-benefit analysis that may not have been common during the Stone Age. In any case, it is just speculation. Nevertheless, most of the primitive people of today are generally dealing with a much reduced and marginal territory, to which they have been pushed by more modern societies, and their tendency to go to war may be a result of these stresses.

Let me stop for a moment. We have to distinguish between the psychology of primitive war and the functionality of primitive war. In addition, we have to see that prehistoric conditions could differ. And that the evidence for prehistoric war might reflect conditions in which there were stresses or benefits of fight.

To go on, it is reasonable to imagine that the sort of vengeance war described by Diamond and indeed by other scholars, such as the anthropologist Lawrence Keeley, was indeed a pattern, found in prehistoric hunting and gathering societies. But we should think of this sort of war as not being replaced by, but rather being absorbed into, modern war. It is not difficult to think of civilized counterparts to this sort of behavior. All of this discussion, however, will have to remain in the realm of theory.

Before we turn to the Neolithic era, which is understood by scholars to mean the period of the domestication of plants and animals, we need to understand that the move from hunting and gathering tribes to agricultural villages was not a straightforward one. There were a number of human experiments with more dense populations, with many characteristics found later on, which were often based on food sources, such as shell fish, but not yet on farming. The Natufian culture found in what is today Israel is a good example. Around 12,000 to 11,000 B.C., the Natufians developed settlements made up of groupings of thatch huts. Not only are they not nomadic, but these settlements have the same density of population that we find in the early Neolithic villages thousands of years later. There is no evidence or sign of any kind of defenses, although there are skeletons of domesticated dogs. It is possible that the dog was used as a sort of "early warning system," but they also might have been used for hunting or as companions. Now these experiments in this period, called by some scholars the "Epipaleolithic" or "Mesolithic," generally failed. The Natufian culture, for example, simply disappeared.

The Neolithic or agricultural revolution itself occurs in different regions at different times, as early as 8000 B.C. in the Middle East and Southeast Asia, but much later elsewhere. Agriculture completely changed every society that adopted it. Modern studies have shown that, contrary to an earlier view, collecting food from domesticated animal and plant sources was not easier than hunting and gathering, and did not lead to better lives. Indeed, evidence indicates that Neolithic populations lived shorter, less healthy lives than hunter-gatherers. Populations probably turned to agriculture due to population pressures and the fact that wild animal populations were no longer large enough to support human ones. Thus, agriculture developed out of a situation of demographic stress. The same sort of stress that may lead to war. In fact, there are scholars who really think that war begins only in the Neolithic. There is no question that our evidence for war increases. When we think about war in this period, we should keep in mind the various societal stresses that led to the adoption of agriculture.

Since one's food source is tied to a piece of land, the stakes of fighting with other groups becomes higher. The development of agriculture allowed for denser populations but also necessitated a more vigorous military force. While a hunting and gathering group could survive even a serious defeat by simply migrating, this was usually not an option for farmers. One could actually argue that war was necessary to allow agriculture, and that military force was a driving impulse behind, and not merely the result of, the Neolithic revolution.

Of course, the domestication of plants and animals did allow for a relatively steady and stable production of food. In addition, there is an incentive to raise more children, as instead of being simply an extra mouth that needed to be carried around while following herds, young children could be used to work in the fields. Thus agriculture naturally led to much higher and denser populations. And fairly quickly the population density reached a point that it was too great to be supported by the wild animals or plants in a region. So once a population turned to agriculture, it could not return to a hunting and gathering lifestyle. For better or worse, people became reliant on agriculture for food, as we still are today.

Jared Diamond, whom I mentioned before in the context of his description of vengeance wars in Papua, is best known for his remarkable book, *Guns, Germs and Steel*. Although Diamond is not a historian, his book has become a basic text of world history, and should really be read by everyone with an interest in the subject. Diamond wrote this book to try to answer a basic question: Why did the west come to dominate the world? We shall refer to his ideas throughout this series, but for now we will concentrate on his important insights on the agricultural revolution. Diamond is an evolutionary biologist, and he pointed out that out of the thousands and tens of thousands of animal and plant species, only a handful are capable of being domesticated. A zebra, for example, can be tamed, but it cannot, unlike its very close relative the horse, be domesticated. Thus the success of a particular Neolithic is related to the local plants and animals that were genetically predisposed to be domesticated. Many more such plants and animals were available, for example, in the Near East, than in Mesoamerica, and Diamond argues that this fact affected the development of societies long after the Neolithic.

Diamond makes another point, which is related to the theme of core and margin, which runs through our lecture series. Plants and animal species are more likely to be able to spread in an east-west direction, along the same latitude and climactic zones, than on a north-south axis, which will cross several climates. This is why, he argues, that the western Neolithic and eastern Neolithic eventually combine, trading domestic animals and plants and create what we are referring to as the Eurasian core. From a military perspective, probably the most important animal to be domesticated is not the goat or the sheep or the pig but rather the donkey. As we shall see, the donkey has a long, if not glorious, connection to the history of warfare.

It is in the Neolithic that we find the first defenses being built around settlements. Surprisingly, the earliest such defenses are also the most sophisticated. At Jericho, north of the Dead Sea in what is now the Palestinian Authority, a stone wall about five feet thick and from 12 to 17 feet high dates to around 8000 B.C., early in the Near Eastern Neolithic. A stone tower about 30 feet high and containing a staircase was built next to it. Some scholars have suggested the Jericho wall was for flood control, but its height and the presence of the tower strongly suggest a defensive purpose. Jericho was a large town by Neolithic standards, some six acres, with a population of 2,000 to 3,000 people. The town was already 500 years old when the wall was built, but the wall may well predate the introduction of agriculture. It may have been the safety provided by the wall that led to farming, not the productivity of farming that led to the wall. The first weapon used solely for war, the club, appears in the late Neolithic.

At Catal Hüyük located in Anatolia, modern Turkey, mud brick houses were built tightly packed on top of a plateau around 7000 B.C. The walls of the outermost houses formed a defensive perimeter, much as we see in the adobe buildings of the Pueblo Indians. Found at Catal Hüyük were the first examples of stone daggers, maces, and pictures of slings being used. Sling stones have been found at other Anatolian sites dating to around the same time.

Both Jericho and Catal Hüyük are almost always illustrated in works on the Neolithic with the implication that these are examples of settlements of the period. In fact, they are unique, and neither of them seem to have led to any further development in defensive fortifications. After Jericho and Catal Hüyük were abandoned, it is thousands of years before anything like them, either stone walls or contiguous houses, are found anywhere in the world. It is certainly not a coincidence that these are the two most densely populated settlements in the world when they existed or that both were located in most unusual locations: where fertile soil allowed agriculture and near the source of valuable trade items: obsidian (that is volcanic glass, very useful for stone tools and for blades) in the case of Catal Hüyük and naphta (natural petroleum, probably used for magic) in the case of Jericho.

It is true that some Neolithic villages did have walls and ditches around their perimeter, almost certainly for defense. These defenses, however, while more primitive than those found at Jericho and Catal Hüyük and are all from a much later period. In the Samarra culture of Mesopotamia, around 5500 B.C., we find walls and ditches just when these people were expanding into fertile Tigris-Euphrates. Early European Neolithic villages also had ditches. Neolithic villages in China, dating to around 5000 B.C., have deep ditches around them, almost certainly for defense. Ditches appear in the Yangshao culture in the Yellow Valley about 4000 B.C. and their settlements were built on terraces, perhaps for defense. There is, however, no evidence for defense around most Neolithic villages. Of course, it is possible that they used armed force to defend themselves and did not feel walls or ditches worth the effort. The lack of such defenses, however, should warn us against assuming that war was a major factor in the Neolithic, at least in most cases.

There is no question, however, that war or at least group violence, did exist, and not only at Jericho or Catal Hüyük. A 5,300-year-old body found frozen in the Alps gives us a remarkable view of early group conflict. Swiss scholars gave this body the name of Ötzi, it sounds better in Swiss German than English. In any case, Ötzi was carrying a flint knife with an ash handle, a copper ax with a handle made of yew wood, and a longbow, some 72 inches tall, made of the same wood. He had a quiver of 14 bone-tipped arrows and shafts made of Viburnum, a common source of shafts in early times. It was originally thought that Ötzi died of an arrow wound, but recent investigations conclude that he received a fatal blow to the head. Careful analysis has shown that neither he, nor his enemy, was alone. In fact, DNA analysis of the blood found at the site shows there was at least four individuals. He died at part of a group struggle, perhaps a battle.

In this lecture, we have considered the complex and enigmatic evidence for war in the Stone Age. In the next lecture, we will consider the relationship of war to the first civilizations: those of Mesopotamia and Egypt.

Lecture Four
Peace, War, and Civilization

Scope:

The evidence for war in the rise of the first civilizations is thin and ambiguous. Especially striking is the lack of walls in Mesopotamian cities such as Uruk. Nevertheless, the first evidence for city fortifications occurs at Hamoukar in Syria, around 3500 B.C. There is evidence for war during the so-called Dynasty 0 of Egypt (c. 3300 B.C.), but the earliest written records in both Egypt and Mesopotamia reflect a remarkably unmilitary society. Starting around 2700 B.C., we start to see indications of increasing warfare, with the first written evidence of a war dating to 2550 B.C. By 2000 B.C., the civilizations of the Near East were highly militarized, with sophisticated weapons, logistical administration, and unit organization.

Outline

I. Since force and coercion have been such an important part of political power for the last 4,000 years, many scholars have surmised that war played a central role in the development of civilization.

   A. It is surprising, then, that war and armies do not seem to have been at the center of Sumer's early city-states.

      1. Beginning around 4000 B.C., a sophisticated culture developed in Sumer (now southern Iraq).
      2. A single city, Uruk, played a leading role in the rise of Sumerian civilization.
      3. By 3500 B.C., with at least 50,000 to 60,000 inhabitants, Uruk had become the center of a colonization movement that seems to have spread based on trade, not warfare.

   B. The earliest Sumerian tablets, engraved on stone around 3000 B.C., are contracts and lists, with no mention of war or soldiers.

      1. Other than some cylinder seals depicting bound men being attacked, scholars have found virtually no evidence of war or military force in this society.
      2. Despite the enormous wealth of Sumerian culture, their cities lacked walls and other defenses.

       3. While city temples were walled and may have functioned as citadels, there is no evidence of any of them being attacked in this period.

  C. In contrast, cities in northern Mesopotamia do seem to have had walls during the 4th millennium.

       1. Archeologists have recently excavated the small city of Hamoukar in northeastern Syria, which was surrounded by a 10-foot mud wall built between 4000 and 3500 B.C.

       2. The wall and the city were destroyed in about 3500 B.C. This is the first known siege of a city.

       3. Hamoukar's attackers used thousands of sling bullets and hundreds of larger clay balls. Hamoukar's wall was destroyed by fire.

       4. The destruction level was replaced by a settlement of the Uruk culture, leading excavators to conclude the attackers were from Uruk.

II. Why did the wealthiest and most advanced cities in southern Mesopotamia not need armies or defenses while fierce fighting was taking place to the north during the same time period?

  A. In comparison to hunter-gatherer societies, the population density of Sumerian cities was so high as to provide an effective defense by itself.

       1. In addition, the Sumerian cities were not close to each other, thus making territorial wars unnecessary.

       2. The northern cities were in the middle of major trade routes but were not in control of them. This trade wealth made city walls necessary. Though Uruk was also wealthy, its merchants were the ones controlling the trade routes, making Uruk less liable to attack.

       3. We can also look to the development of pastoralism in the north, specifically the rise of an early form of nomadic pastoralism called donkey nomads. Donkey nomads could be easily mobilized as a military presence, thus creating a threat in the north that did not exist in the more agricultural south.

  B. This may explain what happened at Hamoukar.

       1. The city was probably the victim of an attack by pastoralists, either hill peoples from the Taurus Mountains to the north or donkey nomads from arid regions to the southwest.

2. Driving the defenders from the walls with missiles, they scaled the 10-foot wall with ladders and pillaged and burned the settlement. Such pastoralists were interested not in occupation but in loot.

3. The people of the Uruk culture who resettled Hamoukar were likely not the attackers but were rebuilding to reestablish an important trade center.

C. In my view, these early peoples were making rational decisions about war making and not simply acting out cultural rituals. We can test this idea by looking at the presence or absence of walls in neighboring cultures.

1. The Indus Valley civilization, in what is now Pakistan, is almost as old as that of Mesopotamia. The absence of walls in most Indus Valley cities may have the same explanation as in southern Mesopotamia: no warlike neighbors and an abundance of land between cities.

2. We do find evidence of weapons and defensive structures in China, where agriculture was in close proximity to hill and nomadic pastoralists.

3. In 4th-millennium Egypt, we also find evidence for war, though not structural evidence. Most of the evidence can be found in illustrations on artifacts like the Narmer Palette, which shows warlike scenes.

4. Early Egypt was characterized by several factors that led them to war: the limited fertile land along the Nile, the valuable trade routes passing through the area, and the proximity of many hill pastoralists and donkey nomads.

5. War images become much less common after the unification of Egypt, as the population grew and internal peace became more profitable.

III. Sometime around 2900 to 2800 B.C., substantial walls were built around Uruk. It was not long before all the southern Mesopotamian cities were walled.

A. Walls had become important symbols both of cities and of kings; the size of the walls of Uruk and other cities might be due as much to prestige as to actual defensive needs.

1. At the same time, we know that a mythology was developing that kingship and war were created at the beginning of the world and had been sent by the gods.

2. Around 2700 B.C., we start to see other indications of increasing warfare in a more densely populated Sumer.
3. The priest-king was replaced by the *lugal*, or war-king. In each city, the new king built a palace surrounded by walls.
4. The royal tombs of Ur contain much evidence of war, including weapons and armor.
5. In a Sumerian document of about 2500 B.C., we find the first written record of a battle.
6. We have much more evidence of war from the middle of the 3rd millennium—not only of struggle between Sumerian city-states, but also with pastoral people and neighboring kingdoms.

B. At the same time that Sumerian cities were becoming more warlike, cities in northern Mesopotamia, Syria, and Palestine were becoming more sophisticated.
1. The city of Ebla had a professional army, and the city of Mari grew to be an impressive regional power.
2. These changes are almost certainly connected to the growing value of the trading networks leading to Mesopotamia and especially Egypt.

C. By the end of the 3rd millennium, despite their differences in writing, religion, and architecture, all cultures of the Near East shared a common military system in most respects.
1. The spear with a bronze tip was used universally, with a bronze ax, sickle sword, dagger, or stone mace as a side weapon.
2. A heavy four-wheeled chariot was used in Mesopotamia and Syria, but not in Egypt.
3. These cultures were already developing the basic forms of siege that remain fixed even today: blockade and assault.
4. Soldiers were contributed by temples, villages, and neighborhoods and commanded by the same officials who led them in peace.
5. We also find the first use of military unit organization and ranks.

Suggested Reading:

Gabriel, *The Culture of War*.

Garlan, *War in the Ancient World*.

Gnirs, "Ancient Egypt."

Questions to Consider:

1. Does our evidence for warfare in this period support a geographic explanation or a cultural one?

2. How do trade routes fit into the pattern of warfare in the Near East?

Lecture Four—Transcript
Peace, War, and Civilization

Welcome back. In our last lecture, we discussed war during the period of the Neolithic, when agriculture arose. In this lecture, we will explore the complicated question of warfare at the time of the rise of the first cities and civilizations. Since force and coercion has been such an important part of political power for the last four thousand years, many scholars of antiquity have naturally surmised that war and the use of armed force played an important role in the development of civilization.

It is striking, therefore, that the Sumerian civilization, that arose in southern Mesopotamia, seems remarkably lacking in military institutions or evidence of extensive warfare. This is not to say that war did not exist. It certainly did. Wars and armies, however, do not seem to have been at the center of Sumer's early city-states, either in reality or in ideology.

Beginning around 4000 B.C. a sophisticated culture developed in Sumer, along the banks of the Tigris and Euphrates rivers in what is today southern Iraq. Although the term "civilization" has fallen out of favor, this is the best way of describing what happened. Within a relatively short period of time, we see the development of densely populated cities, sophisticated irrigation systems, monumental architecture, writing, the use of bronze, the wheel, social hierarchy, and many other developments.

As has been pointed out by Mark van de Mieroop, one of the leading scholars of Mesopotamia working today, what is very interesting is the role played in the rise of civilization by a single city, Uruk. By 3500 B.C., Uruk was the largest and most advanced city in the world, with at least 50–60,000 inhabitants, and perhaps as many as 100,000. In addition to Uruk, there were about a dozen other Sumerian cities, with at least 10,000 people in each. There is evidence that Uruk not only affected the other Sumerian cities, establishing what is named the Uruk culture, but was at the center of a colonization movement, which established settlements from the borders of Egypt to northern Mesopotamia and to what is today Iran. In contrast to similar events, there is no evidence that this colonization was accompanied by military means; rather its seems to be associated with trade.

The earliest Sumerian tablets, engraved on stone around 3000 B.C. are contracts and lists, and there is no mention of war or soldiers in them. In fact, from what we can reconstruct about Sumerian society in this early period, the Sumerian cities were ruled by a priest-king, whose power base was the central city temple that rose in the middle of every Sumerian city. There may be an indication of war in early Sumerian society in the form of some cylinder seals, which have been dated to somewhere around 3200 to 3000 B.C. These show men being bound and attacked with what seemed to be maces. This has been taken to refer to war, although it is possible that they have to do with human sacrifice, which was certainly a feature of early Sumerian society.

Other than these cylinder seals, during more than a century of intensive excavation and study, including the study of many clay tablets, there is virtually no evidence in fourth-millennium southern Mesopotamia in the writing, illustrations, artifacts, or architecture of Sumerian warfare or military force.

The cities of Sumer were certainly the wealthiest places in the world at the time. Yet, despite what must have been the tremendous lure of such luxury to neighboring tribes, the Sumerian cities lacked walls, or evidence of armies in the fourth millennium. It is true that the city-temples in the center of every Sumerian city were surrounded by walls, and they might have functioned as citadels or as places of internal control. Yet, although we can trace the development of some of them archaeological, such as the great temple at Eridu for a thousand years, there is no evidence of such temples ever being attacked in this period.

How can we explain that the cities of Sumer not only did not seem to fight each other, but also were not attacked by surrounding peoples? What is most interesting is that while other aspects of the Uruk culture, such as writing, move from southern to northern Mesopotamia, the building of city walls moves in exactly the opposite direction. A number of small cities in northern Mesopotamia appear to have had walls in the fourth millennium. One example is the settlement of Hamoukar located in northeastern Syria, near the Turkish and Iraqi borders. Sometime between 4000 to 3500 B.C., a ten-foot mud wall was built around the town.

Now I mentioned previously how certain discoveries can completely change our view of history and this is one. In 2005, excavators at

Hamoukar, announced the discovery of the first-known battle site, in fact the most extensive evidence of warfare ever discovered for the fourth millennium. Around 3500 B.C., Hamoukar's wall had been bombarded by attackers with slings and clay balls. Some of these clay balls were the size of ping-pong balls, some tennis balls. Around 120 of these [were] apparently used to hurl at the enemy [along with] about 1,200 sling bullets. The wall had been destroyed by fire.

Above this destruction level, there was a resettlement level belonging to the Uruk culture. This has led the excavators to conclude that the attackers of Hamoukar were from Uruk, and that they had conquered the city. And if this is true, this would be the most convincing evidence for warfare in the Uruk period. Yet, there is a fundamental problem with this analysis. If the city of Uruk could, and did, send a large army far to the north and capture and burn a city there, why is there virtually no evidence of warfare or armies in Uruk itself, or any other southern Mesopotamia city, or indeed anywhere else we find the Uruk culture in this period?

There's another problem. Slings or hurling balls were not weapons generally associated with the Sumerians. The sling is absent from our earliest illustrations of Sumerian war. (I'll discuss these later.) We know that the bow was used by at least 3000 [B.C.] yet there is no evidence of bows at Hamoukar. On the other hand, the sling is associated with pastoral people from an early date, and we know that it was used in Anatolia, to the north of Hamoukar, as early as the Neolithic. How can we make sense of this? Why would the most advanced, and presumably the wealthiest cities in southern Mesopotamia, such as Uruk, not need defenses. At the same time we have evidence for fortifications and fierce fighting at Hamoukar in northern Mesopotamia. Why did the technology of walls that existed in the north in 3500 B.C. not spread south for another 500 years or more? The answer might lie in the issue of population density and the development of pastoralism. In comparison to the hunting-gathering people of the Neolithic that probably existed in early times in neighboring areas, the population density of Sumerian cities was so high as to provide an effective defense in and of itself. An attack on a city of tens of thousands by a hunter-gatherer clan of a few dozen would have been suicidal.

It might seem that pastoral societies, that herd sheep, goats, and other small cattle, have a lot in common with hunter-gatherer tribes. But in fact pastoralism was developed not before but after agriculture. Indeed, pastoral societies cannot exist without agricultural settlements with which to trade. In ancient times we find two basic types of pastoralists. There are hill pastoralists, who take advantage up the pastures in highlands to feed their flocks in the summer months, and nomadic pastoralists, who move their herds from place to place to find forage. In the fourth millennium, neither the horse nor the camel had been domesticated in the Near East, so those who practiced an early form of nomadic pastoralism are called "donkey nomads." Pastoralists of all kinds have one significant advantage over agricultural peoples. A larger proportion of their adult male population can be mobilized for war, and for a longer period, than farmers, whose production is both more labor intensive and more tied to the seasonal needs of crops.

The situation in southern Mesopotamia was so: The desert regions to the south were not very suitable for donkey nomadism. The only hill pastoralists nearby were in the Zagros Mountains to the east, but it may well have taken hundreds of years for these pastoral tribes to grow large enough and strong enough to be a threat. In addition, Sumerian cities were not close to each other. They relied basically on irrigation of land. So there were wastelands separating them, thus making territorial wars unnecessary.

Hamoukar, however, is located in the far north of Mesopotamia. Just to the north were the Taurus Mountains, in which hill pastoralism could flourish, and to the south the Jazirah, a semi-desert region known to have been a center of donkey nomads. This far northern area of Mesopotamia was among the first areas to develop both agriculture and pastoralism. The area was quite fertile, but agriculture was based more on rainfall, rather than irrigation, there were not the regions of wasteland separating cities in the north, which would be more likely to fight over fertile territory lying between them. Thus, walls made sense, in a way that they did not further south.

In addition, northern Mesopotamia was right in the middle of valuable trade routes, trade routes that went back to the Neolithic, but were being expanded by the growth of the Uruk culture, which was no doubt the economic powerhouse of the world at the time. To the north, Anatolia was the source of silver and gold. To the east, lapis lazuli and tin were brought in from what is today Afghanistan.

To the west ran the trade routes both to the Mediterranean, from which timber was brought, and down to Egypt, which provided ivory and other goods. The wealth of this trade could be kept inside these cities, which made having walls worthwhile, as they did, you recall, at Jericho and Catal Hüyük. But these small northern cities were not yet large enough or strong enough to take control of these trade routes themselves. In any case, the fact that Uruk was not only the consumer of the trade, but that Uruk merchants were apparently the ones actually running the trade from these colonies. Intermediate cities no doubt profited far more from its smooth operation than they would from trying to seize this trade.

The pastoral people, however, would have had quite a different point of view. This may explain what happened at Hamoukar. The city was probably the victim of an attack by pastoralists, either hill people from the Taurus to the north or donkey nomads from arid regions to the southwest. Driving the defenders from the walls with missiles, they scaled the 10-foot wall with ladders, and pillaged and burned the settlement. Such pastoralists were not interested in occupation, but loot. The people of the Uruk culture who resettled Hamoukar were likely not the attackers but were rebuilding to reestablish an important trade center. As you can tell, in my view, these early people were making rational decisions about war making and not simply acting out cultural rituals. We can test this idea to some extent by looking at the presence or absence of walls in neighboring cultures.

The Indus Valley civilization, located in what is today Pakistan, is almost as old as that in Mesopotamia. There are numerous and sophisticated mud brick remains of houses and large monumental buildings. There was long distance trade to Sumer and elsewhere in the west. Despite many examples of art, there are no illustrations of war. Some small Indus Valley cities were fortified with brick walls, but the larger ones, for example, Mohenjo-daro and Harappa, had no walls, although they do have internal citadels. The absence of walls in most Indus Valley cities, especially the largest and richest, may well have the same explanation as in southern Mesopotamia: the lack of powerful warlike neighbors and an abundance of land between settlements, which were brought into agricultural production through irrigation. The small cities with walls may have been, like northern Mesopotamia, more vulnerable to attack.

In China, as in Europe, the geography of the early Neolithic put agriculture in close proximity to both hill and nomadic pastoralists. In the Neolithic Longshan period, which flourished around the Yellow and Yangtze rivers about the same time as the Sumerians, around 3000–2000 B.C., villages began to be surrounded by walls. In upland regions walls were made of rocks and boulders, but along the rivers, they were already being made of stamped earth. In this method, layers of earth are placed between wooden frames and hammered with wooden mallets until they become hard as concrete. (This is a method that continues to be used by the Chinese.) In this period, however, the Chinese were still using stone weapons, for example short knives and spears. The stone ax is the prototype of the later Chinese weapon called the *ge*. It would seem, therefore, that war was already known, and even common, in the Chinese Neolithic.

In fourth millennium Egypt, we also find evidence for war. Here the evidence is not in the form of walls or fortifications, as these do not survive well near the Nile. The same annual floods that made this land so fertile destroyed them over time. We do have pictorial evidence, however. As early as 3600 B.C., we find an ivory knife handle illustrating a battle both by land and on a boat, presumably in the Nile. There are illustrations of war during the so-called Dynasty 0, centered at Abydos around 3300 B.C. or so. And then around 3100 B.C. we have the so-called Libyan or Fortress palette, which shows walled settlements being attacked by animals with picks. These animals, such as a scorpion or a lion, may represent clans or kings of tribes or something like that. The fact that we have walled cities illustrated shows that such cities existed and presumably existed long before they were destroyed.

The so-called Narmer palette, which probably dates to the period of the unification of Egypt, also shows warlike scenes and has been interpreted to refer to a war that united upper and lower Egypt. Now whether or not that's true, it's evidence of war. There is good evidence that Egypt in the predynastic and early dynastic periods was made up of various states which were fighting over fertile land along the Nile. In addition, there were valuable trade routes, both across the Red Sea to the east and the Sinai desert to the north, both of which led to the Uruk culture. In addition, there were areas bordering the Nile were very suitable for the growth of both hill pastoralists and donkey nomads.

The growth of population along the Nile would have brought the Egyptians into conflict with bordering pastoralists, and made it possible and desirable to subdue them permanently. It also would have made the conquest of the remaining independent states within the Nile Valley desirable. In the Second Dynasty, around 2600 B.C. an inscription refers to the suppression of "northern enemies," which may refer to a war with the Libyan donkey nomads or the capture, or recapture, of some independent region in the Nile Delta. There is also evidence of Egyptian expansion southwards into what is known as Nubia or Kush (modern Sudan). During the Third Dynasty, substantial forts were built in the south to keep the Kushites or Nubians from moving north up the Nile. There were also forts to keep the "sand dwellers," as the Egyptians called them, from raiding lower Egypt from the Sinai desert to the east.

In the predynastic and early dynastic period, there are many images of the Egyptian king trampling enemies underfoot. The king grasps the hair of a group of enemies while he holds a mace over their heads. Other enemies are shown dead or captured under his feet. Once Egypt is firmly united, however, and the pastoral people are presumably subdued, this image becomes much less common. The Egyptian king in the Old Kingdom is increasingly viewed not as a conqueror but as a god, who fosters peace and prosperity in the land. Once a single authority is established over the Nile Valley, its basis seems to have been partly religious and partly due to its success in fostering productivity through control of the Nile flood. As was the case with early Sumer, in this later period of Egyptian history, there is little written evidence for armies or warfare.

This change might be explained by the dramatic growth in the Egyptian population. It is in the first few dynasties that the population in Egypt absolutely explodes. It has been estimated that in the predynastic period there were only some 100,000 to 200,000 Egyptians. By the Third Dynasty, the beginning of the Old Kingdom, there were one to two million. The change also made internal peace more profitable and desirable than war, as agricultural success was based on knowledge of the Nile flood, which could be calculated by the rise of waters in the far south, but this information was useless unless it could be communicated to the north by a central government. Egypt also outgrew Mesopotamia in population and productivity and now became the economic center of the West. They now did not need to fight over trade routes, as the trade routes now led to them. This process had probably been well established by the beginning of the Old Kingdom. The overall change in the economic situation of Egypt, and its effects on trade routes, may partly explain the changes in warfare that we see occurring in Mesopotamia. Of course, other factors were at work: The general population was growing and land was becoming more scarce. In addition, pastoral people, who neighbored Mesopotamia, were growing more numerous and powerful, as they adopted the weapons and techniques of the more advanced city-states.

Sometime around 2900 to 2800 B.C., walls were built around Uruk. These were the earliest known in Sumer. The brick walls of Uruk—actually they were earth faces with brick—were on a completely different scale than those of the older northern Mesopotamian ones. These walls were 40 feet high and had elaborate gates. It was not long before all southern Mesopotamian cities were walled. Walls become very important symbols both of the cities and of kings. And the size of the walls of Uruk and other cities might be due as much to prestige as actual defensive needs. We also find other changes. While we know that the king was a new development, a mythology develops which made kingship, and war, created at the beginning of the world and sent by the gods. Thus we see mythology itself being transformed to account for a warlike period.

Around 2700 B.C., we see other indications of increasing warfare in a more densely populated Sumer. We have to be a bit careful about our conclusions, since this is the very time that we start to find enough cuneiform tablets to start to build a picture of Sumerian society. This is the time that the priest-king was replaced by the *lugal*, literally the "big man," a war-king. In each city, the new king built a palace surrounded by walls. Sometimes this palace was built next to the old central temple but often it was built on the edge of the outer wall. The fact that the king or the lugal did not simply take over the temple complex in the center of the city suggests there was a certain amount of internal tension. In fact, we almost immediately find stories of kings being overthrown and being replaced by others.

The royal tombs of Ur, which date to around 2600 to 2400 B.C., were the burial places of these new war-kings. They contain much evidence of war, including weapons and armor, as well as the so-called Standard of Ur (probably a music instrument), which dates to this period, illustrates the role of the ideal king in peace and war. On the so-called war panel, there are three registers, which appear to be read from bottom to top. In the bottom register, a row of war chariots tramples enemies underfoot. In the middle register an army of infantry lead off enemy captives, who are presented to the king in the upper register.

In a Sumerian document of around 2500 B.C. or so, we find the first written record of a battle fought between Umma and Lagash, two other Sumerian cities. This is a territorial dispute over a stretch of ground between them, but the war is characterized as the king of Lagash defending the rights of the god Ningirsu.

Another sign of Sumerian war is the limestone stele, called the Stele of the Vultures, dating to around 2450 B.C. The king of Lagash is shown twice, once leading a phalanx of infantry soldiers on foot and leading other infantry from a chariot. The king can be identified by his distinctive helmet, which is virtually identical to one found in the Royal Tombs of Ur. On another fragment of the stele, vultures and lions eat the bodies of the enemy dead, above a written description of the war.

We have a lot more evidence of war from the middle of the third millennium in Mesopotamia. We find not only the struggle between the Sumerian city-states but also with various pastoral people and with the neighboring kingdom of Elam in southwestern Iran. At the same time that the Sumerian cities were becoming more warlike, we find cities growing and becoming more sophisticated in northern Mesopotamia, Syria, and Palestine. The city of Ebla, also in Syria, was founded around 3000 B.C., and reached its height around 2400. Ebla had a professional army and was surrounded by a high wall. Another city, Mari, grows to be a regional power. These changes are almost certainly connected to the growing value of the trading networks leading both to Mesopotamia and now especially Egypt.

Northern Mesopotamia was now in the position to control trade routes, but southern Mesopotamia was also in a position to conquer northern Mesopotamia. Around 2400, the Sumerian king Lugalzagesi created the first empire to unite all of Mesopotamia. This was soon replaced by the Akkadian Empire, founded by Sargon of Akkad, who conquered through Syria all the way to the Mediterranean. Sargon raised the first known professional army, which may have been as large as 5,400 men. At this point the king was wealthy enough, from both tribute and trade, to feed this number of soldiers out of his personal income.

By the end of the third millennium, despite their differences in writing, religion, architecture, and so forth, in most respects all the cultures of the Near East, shared a common military system. The spear with a bronze tip was used universally, with a bronze ax, sickle sword, dagger or stone mace as a side or auxiliary weapon. There were metal helmets and leather armor, studded with bronze disks. The sling is an early missile weapon (as seen at Hamoukar) and continues to be used through the period. The simple bow was used by most armies. Around 2400 B.C., the improved composite bow is invented, which was more powerful and accurate.

A heavy four-wheeled chariot was used in Mesopotamia and Syria, but not in Egypt. Ox- and donkey-drawn carts for civilian purpose had appeared in Sumer around 3000 B.C., but the ox was too slow and the domestic donkey not aggressive enough to use these for military purposes, other than carrying supplies. The four-wheeled chariot of this period was drawn by wild donkeys, or onagers.

Stamped earth slopes were added to the outside of Mesopotamian and Syrian walls as early as 25th century B.C. The appearance of these slopes is probably connected to the invention of better means of taking cities, such as battering rams and mining.

Already we see the development of the basic forms of sieges, which remained fixed, with changes due to technology, even today. The first type is the blockade and the second the assault.

Most soldiers in all cultures were raised in the same way as was the labor that built monumental architecture. They were contributed by temples, villages, or neighborhoods and commanded by the same officials who led them in peace. We also find the first use of military unit organization and ranks, as well as the use of foreign troops, especially for specialist purposes, such as the Nubian archers used by the Egyptians.

At the end of the third millennium, we get an intensification of warfare throughout the Near East. In Egypt, we get a collapse of the Old Kingdom into civil war and an invasion.

In Mesopotamia, the Akkadian Dynasty takes over northern Mesopotamia and Syria but then it self-collapses and is replaced by a short-lived Sumerian dynasty. This is both soon overrun by both the Elamites to the East and by the Amorite pastoralists coming in from the north.

In this lecture we have seen the development of highly militarized societies in the Near East by 2000 B.C. In the next lecture, we will talk about a revolution in technology that affected, and indeed created, a new military culture that will stretch from Europe and Africa to East Asia.

Lecture Five
The Chariot Revolution

Scope:

The Kurgan culture in the steppe region north of the Black and Caspian seas domesticated the horse around 4000 B.C. Too small to ride, these horses were used to pull chariots with spoked wheels and a lightweight fighting platform. With the addition of the composite bow around 2000 B.C., the chariot became a world-transforming weapons system. Using chariots, Indo-European peoples spread to the west, east, and south. This expansion led to the rise of the steppe cultures of Central Asia, as well as a series of dramatic invasions into the Near East and Europe, India, and China. The characteristics of this weapons system created chariot nobilities with similar features throughout the Old World, from Shang China and Aryan India to Mycenaean Greece. Only the wealthiest states, such as New Kingdom Egypt, could afford a professional chariot army.

Outline

I. Before discussing the chariot revolution, I need to clarify two things: my use of the terms "core" and "margin" and the whole idea of military revolutions.

   A. World historians usually use "core" and "margin" to describe the relationship between two geographic regions.
   1. I am using the terms in a broader sense, defined by the use of military technologies and the subsequent sociological changes that accompanied these technologies.
   2. The core region ultimately covered a vast expanse of land running across the breadth of the Old World.

   B. In these lectures, I refer to a whole series of military revolutions: the chariot, the sword, the horse, gunpowder, and so on.
   1. Some historians disagree with me, claiming that these changes were the result of slow development, not revolution.
   2. One factor that tends to obscure the dramatic nature of weapons innovation is that they tend to go through a two-stage process.

3. In its original version, the weapon is important enough to be adopted but does not significantly change warfare. Then, with an addition or innovation, the weapon becomes world transforming.
4. We will discuss this process with the chariot and see the same process occur with other military innovations, such as gunpowder.

II. Now, let's get down to brass tacks—or in this case, to wooden spokes.
A. We have already met the original chariots: the heavy Sumerian versions, with four solid wheels and drawn by wild donkeys.
1. The relationship of the original Sumerian chariot to the new two-wheeled, horse-drawn chariot is a controversial topic among military historians.
2. Some say that the new chariot developed in Mesopotamia out of the older Sumerian version and then spread into the steppes.
3. Others contend that the new chariot was developed in the steppe region, where the horse had first been domesticated.
B. The most significant innovation of the new chariot was the use of horses to draw it.
1. Archaeological evidence has established that the horse was first domesticated around 4000 B.C. in what is now southern Ukraine and Kazakhstan.
2. Horses were probably used for food, for milk, and for breeding mules for pack animals.
3. The advantage of the light, horse-drawn chariot to pastoralism is obvious.
4. The addition of the bit made control and maneuvering much more effective.
C. This new chariot had a dramatic effect on the steppe cultures.
1. The vast grasslands between eastern Europe and western China became an area of prime activity for herd animals.
2. The chariot and bow combination was not only useful for guarding herds and hunting—it also made raiding other tribes easier.

3. Stealing cattle and horses must have been a common way of supplementing income, and soon it must have become apparent that one could easily defeat or terrorize agricultural villages into submission.

4. The steppe pastoralists had a major military advantage: A much higher percentage of their population could be used in war.

III. The rapid spread of chariot technology is closely associated with the Indo-European language family.

  A. It has been recently argued that the region in which the horse was first domesticated was also the homeland of the earliest Indo-European language, called Proto-Indo-European.

    1. There is a great deal of historical resistance to the idea of Indo-European warriors sweeping across the core in their chariots, but there is increasing evidence that this is exactly what happened.

    2. Whatever the reason, it is clear that for the next 2,000 years, the steppes were dominated by Indo-European-speaking people.

  B. Chariot-riding peoples moving into Neolithic regions often resulted in a kick-starting of civilization, usually accompanied by intensive warfare. A good example of this is the impact of the chariot on China.

    1. In 2000 B.C., when the Near East was already part of a literate Bronze Age culture, China still lacked writing and was a Neolithic village culture.

    2. Though Chinese tradition maintains that the rise of the Shang dynasty was an indigenous affair, the introduction of the chariot from the West does coincide with the first archaeological evidence of the Shang.

    3. In the Shang period, we find a dramatic increase in the size of settlements, many with stamped-earth walls.

    4. Shang culture was quite warlike and expansionist from the beginning. We see how war not only established the first Chinese dynasty but also served to spread it.

  C. China, of course, was not the only Neolithic region to be affected by chariot technology.

    1. There are many rock carvings depicting horse-drawn chariots throughout the Sahara.

2. The chariot also moved into Europe, but there are many questions about exactly how—and how dramatically—it impacted the region.

IV. The period of 2200 to 1900 B.C. was one of tremendous conflict in the Near East. There are many theories about what caused these upheavals.

    A. Archaeologists often object to models of invasion as the cause of political and social change, as they often cannot find archaeological evidence for it.

        1. But the invasion of pastoralists into urban areas often took the form of gradually increasing raids.

        2. Additionally, even sudden conquests often leave no archaeological trace, a fact that is not always sufficiently appreciated.

        3. The 3rd-millennium empires of Egypt and Mesopotamia may have been victims of their own success. As their populations thrived, the chances of internal uprisings increased.

        4. By 1900 B.C., we know that there were a number of small Amorite kingdoms established in Mesopotamia.

        5. The relationship of the chariot to the spread of the Amorites is unclear. We do know that the Amorite dynasty of Babylon used the chariot extensively.

    B. The Hittites and Hurrians both used chariots to great advantage in establishing their empires.

        1. To the west, we find chariot states rising both in mainland Greece and on the islands of the Mediterranean.

        2. These new Near Eastern states were characterized by powerful monarchs with centralized bureaucracies, working out of large palace complexes.

        3. Another feature of these Near Eastern empires was the so-called chariot nobility. Since chariots were such an expensive weapons system, kings would give land to nobles in exchange for chariots.

        4. One such empire was New Kingdom Egypt. A new motif developed in Egyptian art during this period: the king riding in his chariot and firing his bow, trampling his enemies.

C. I have left the discussion of the most classic example of the invasion of Indo-European chariot warriors until last. This is the movement of the people known as Aryans into India, which is recorded in the sacred Hindu texts, the Vedas.

> **1.** Though most archaeologists and ancient historians have abandoned the chariot invasion as the cause of the decline in the Indus Valley, I have not—for very good reasons.
>
> **2.** The dating of the decline of the Indus Valley civilization is perfectly compatible with an Aryan invasion. A similar invasion occurred simultaneously in a region near India.
>
> **3.** Most significantly, we have the development in all these regions of a warrior caste; this is almost certainly the chariot nobility that we have seen elsewhere.

Suggested Reading:

Anthony, *The Horse, the Wheel, and Language.*

Cotterell, *The Chariot.*

Gnirs, "Ancient Egypt."

Questions to Consider:

1. How did the chariot make possible the steppe cultures?
2. What kind of impact did the chariot have on agricultural societies?

Lecture Five—Transcript
The Chariot Revolution

Welcome back. In the last lecture we followed the process by which the Near East, by around 2000 B.C., had developed sophisticated military cultures. In today's lecture, I want to talk about the chariot revolution. Before I do so, however, I need to discuss two things: one is my use of the terms "core" and "margin" and the second is the whole idea of military revolutions.

World historians usually use the words "core" and "margin" to describe the relationship between two geographic regions which, of course, changes over time. In this lecture, and subsequently in the series, I will be using the terms "core" and "margin" in a broader sense. We will see that with the spread of the chariot, and later other military technologies, a core region developed that used the same weapons, and because of the nature of those weapons, often adopted similar political, social, and economic systems to use them effectively. This core region ultimately covers a vast expanse of land running across the breadth of the Old World, includes both northern and western Africa and much of western Europe, covers the Mediterranean region, east Africa and the Near East, includes both southern Asia and Central Asia, continues along both sides of the great Himalayan Mountains to east Asia, and ends at the Pacific coast of China.

This core region will be the focus of most of our attention in the rest of the series since it is along its 9,000-mile length that most of the world's innovations in warfare have occurred and initially spread. We will not, however, neglect warfare in what we'll call the "margin," that is central and southern Africa, the Americas, and Oceania, which we will discuss later on.

In this series, I am going to be referring to a whole number of military revolutions: that of the chariot is one, the sword, the horse, gunpowder, and so on. There will be others. There are military historians, however, who reject the whole idea of military revolution, arguing that what we have is not really revolutionary changes, but rather a slow steady ongoing development. This is a complicated issue, but to cut a long story short, I don't agree. I will argue in this series, that there certainly were military revolutions, and that they had broad and dramatic impact over relatively short periods of time.

One factor that tends to obscure the dramatic nature of weapons innovation is that they tend to go through a two-stage process. In its original version, it is important enough to be adopted, yet does not significantly change warfare. Then, with an addition or another innovation, the weapon becomes world-transforming. We will discuss this process with the chariot and see the same process occurring with other military innovations, such as gunpowder, for example.

Now, let's get down to brass tacks—or in this case to wooden spokes. We have already met the original chariots: the heavy Sumerian versions, with four solid wheels and drawn by wild donkeys. The relationship of this Sumerian chariot to this new two-wheeled horse-drawn chariot is a controversial topic among military historians. There are two basic theories: that the new style chariot, with spoked wheels and an axle at the rear, developed in Mesopotamia out of the older Sumerian version, first using the donkey and then the horse, and subsequently spread into the steppe, or that new style that was developed in the Steppe region that had first domesticated the horse, and its use spread south into Mesopotamia.

New evidence is beginning to favor the first view, but whichever direction the technology moved, it was only with the development of the lighter version that the chariot's potential as a weapons system could be fully realized. The most significant new element of the new chariots was the use of horses to draw them. Since the horse is so important to the chariot and to the history of warfare, let's discuss the domestication of this remarkable animal. Archaeological evidence has established that the horse was first domesticated in what is now the southern Ukraine and Kazakhstan, north of the Caspian Sea, around 4000 B.C. They were probably first used for food and milk, horses are natural herd animals, like goats and sheep. Another use of horses is for breeding mules. A mule is the sterile offspring of a horse and a donkey. It is larger and can carry more than a donkey, and it becomes not only a beast of burden, but is also used to pull carts. Like the donkey before it, and I must say, often alongside it, the mule becomes vitally important as a military pack animal.

Already in the third millennium B.C., we find both the use of donkeys and mules to carry burdens on their backs and to pull carts and wagons. This no doubt suggested the same use for horses. Unlike donkeys and mules, these early domesticated horses were too small to ride: If one sat on their spine it would have broken. Horses, however, could be used to pull carts. We don't know who invented the spoked wheel or designed the lightweight platform made of wood or wicker, but once it's hitched to a horse, the advantage for pastoralism is very obvious. The addition of a bit, which attached the reins to the horse's mouth made control and maneuvering much more effective.

In the previous lecture, we discussed how the so-called "donkey nomads," which developed pastoralism in the hill regions and marginal desert areas. With the use of the chariot, herds could be moved farther and farther from a home base. With the bow, wild animals, as well as thieves, could be kept away. In this use, the chariot had a dramatic effect on the steppes. The steppes are the vast grasslands that stretched from eastern Europe to eastern China and went from being hunting grounds supporting small populations, to an area of prime productivity for herd animals, such as goats and sheep.

The chariot and bow combination was not only useful for guarding herds and hunting, it also made raiding on other tribes easier. In its military form, the chariot's basket held at least two soldiers: a driver and an archer, although there was sometimes a third, carrying a spear or some other weapon. The archer used a composite bow, which was small enough to fire in the chariot, but powerful enough to be quite effective.

Stealing cattle and horses must have been a common way of supplementing income and soon it must have become apparent that one could easily defeat the foot soldiers of agricultural villages or terrorize them into submission and providing tribute or simply plundering them. Since the pastoral tribes needed the agricultural people, so taxing them (usually in the form of ransom or tribute) was a way of shearing the sheep, but not killing them.

As with the hill pastoralists, these new steppe pastoralists had a major military advantage: A much higher percentage of their population could be used in war. John Keegan has pointed out that the hunting culture of the steppes helped to develop new and effective tactics, such as encirclement and feigned retreat, which are used by steppe peoples up to early modern times. Once the spoked wheel, horse, and bit had been added to the chariot, its use spread rapidly along the grasslands of the steppes, opening this enormous region to pastoralism, and later to trade. Chariot-riding people not only moved into these lightly populated areas, but also into regions that had already entered the Neolithic, although not the Bronze Age. These regions include China, where we see a rapid civilizing trend, in response. Finally the chariot moved into already urbanized areas such as the Near East, were it had a dramatic effect on empires and social hierarchy. Even though this process occurred over several hundred years, I think it is fair to call this a military revolution.

The rapid spread of chariot technology, first in the steppe and then into more settled regions, is closely associated with the Indo-European language family, of which English is a member. It has been recently, and convincingly argued, based both on linguistic and genetic evidence that the region in which the horse was first domesticated, was also the homeland of the earliest Indo-European language, called Proto-Indo-European. It has long been known that sometime before 2000 B.C. (how long before is a matter of great controversy), Indo-European speakers began from their original homeland, and migrated, or conquered, in every direction. As a result of this spread, we find Indo-European languages spoken from western Europe all the way east to India. Indeed, there is evidence in written documents of Indo-European being spoken as far east as western China.

There is a great deal of historical resistance to the idea of Indo-European warriors sweeping across the core on chariots. In large part this is because the idea was a key part of the racial theory and thinking that dominated history in the 19th and early 20th century. In addition, as I've already mentioned, the idea of slow, gradual change is more attractive to some historical theories than dramatic military revolutions. Nevertheless, there is increasing evidence that this is exactly what happened. In order to accept the idea of the chariot revolution, we need not accept racial theory, and indeed we have to keep in mind that Indo-European refers only to a group of languages and not to a race. In addition, we can recognize that Indo-European spread in other times and ways, and that the chariot and the Indo-European language do not always move together.

It is clear, however, that for the next two thousand years, the steppes were dominated by Indo-European speaking peoples. Most of them speak a language belonging to two closely related branches of Indo-

European. We will meet many well-known Iranian speaking steppe peoples: the Medes and the Persians for example, as well as the Scythians, Sarmatians and others. A second group consists of the Aryan speakers, including the people who later invade India. Keep in mind that "Aryan" here is not the same as the term used in the 20th century. The Nazis used this word to mean any German who wasn't Jewish. The original meaning of the word, still used by linguists refers to a language branch of Indo-European, represented, for example, by ancient Sanskrit. The relationship of the chariot riding peoples with Indo-European can actually be seen in the spread of this very word because "arya," which means "warrior," is the origin of the names of both Iran and Ireland.

We have already discussed the impact of the chariot on the steppes. But this is only one part of the chariot revolution. We see that as chariot riding peoples moved into Neolithic regions, it often resulted in a "kick-starting" of civilization, usually accompanied by intensive warfare. A good example of this is the impact of the chariot in China. We have already seen that although China is normally seen as a very ancient culture, that in 2000 B.C., when the Near East was already part of a literate, urban Bronze Age, China still lacked writing and was a Neolithic village culture. The traditional Chinese historical tradition viewed the rise of the Shang dynasty as an entirely indigenous affair, and indeed for various reasons, including national pride, which is probably the most significant reason, historians of China and in China have been reluctant to admit to foreign, especially western, impact on what is considered to be the first historical Chinese dynasty.

Nevertheless, the introduction of the chariot from the west, to the region does coincide with the first archaeological evidence of the Shang. There are certainly chariots found in royal burials in the Shang capital at Anyang, and these chariots are certainly of western origin. Other than national pride, there is little reason to doubt the significant impact of a migration of probably Indo-European speaking chariot pastoralists from the west.

In China's Shang period we find the dramatic increase in the size of settlements, and for the first time we can really call them cities. Many have stamped earth walls, some with bases up to 60 feet thick. We know that there were Indo-European speakers in western China in a later period. They left writings in the Tocharian language, and it is tempting to think that the people who brought the chariot to China were also Indo-Europeans. There is no direct evidence for this however. We also don't know the relationship between the chariot and the rise of civilization in China: Did chariot warriors found the Shang dynasty or was the Shang founded by local people in order to defend themselves from the steppe people? We don't know, but the importance of the chariot to the process is undeniable.

Shang culture was quite warlike and expansionist from the beginning. They fought both against the so-called "horse barbarians" to the west, that is the steppe chariot warriors, and expanded their domain within what was becoming China. Typically, Shang armies would invade enemy territory, burn the trees and undergrowth and plant crops and sacrifice captured animals and humans. These regions were then absorbed into the Shang state. Military colonies were built, surrounding by stamped earth walls. Thus we see how war not only established the first Chinese dynasty but also served to spread it. Shang society was based on aristocratic clans that were hierarchically organized. These are very likely the same as the chariot nobility we will encounter later in other cultures and which I will discuss in a moment. We know that aristocratic chariot forces served in the Shang army but used bronze weapons and the compound bow, as was common in the west.

Of course, not all elements of the Chinese culture were borrowed. Writing, which is first found on the so-called oracle bones of the Shang dynasty, as well on bronze artifacts, is almost certainly an independent development. What's interesting is the sign for chariot in the script, which appears very early on, clearly shows the same western design as is seen in the western burials. In the Shang we find drums used for military purposes for the first time, as well as flags and pennants. Because white was the color of death, waving a white flag was already the sign of surrender. This was passed to western Asia in the Middle Ages, and subsequently to Europe and around the world.

China, of course, was not the only Neolithic region to be affected by the chariot. There are many rock carvings of horse drawn chariots throughout the Sahara. The region had already undergone the dramatic desertification that occurred around 3400 B.C., and while these rock carvings cannot be accurately dated, the horse and chariot were probably introduced at the time of their more general spread throughout the core. Indeed, it may well be the horse and chariot that allowed the desert to be crossed in this period, connecting west Africa to the core. Unfortunately, we know little else of the period. There is about a thousand year blank spot before the first evidence of urbanization in west Africa, but I would not be surprised, however, to see that denser populations and cultural development go back to the period of the introduction of the horse and chariot. We'll have to await further excavation. We know that the chariot also moved into Europe, though it is a testament to how marginal this region was at the time. There are many questions about exactly how, and how dramatically, chariots impacted the region. In any case, having seen the impact of the chariot on the steppes and on Neolithic cultures in China, we now turn to its very dramatic impact on urban cultures in the Near East.

We left the cultures of the Near East around 2000 B.C. The period of around c. 2200 to c. 1900 is one of a great deal of conflict around the region. The Old Kingdom of Egypt fell, and various parts of the country fought each other—and there was a foreign invasion. In Mesopotamia, the Akkadian Empire collapsed, and the subsequent Sumerian dynasty was overrun by invaders. There are many theories about what caused these upheavals, and there does seem to be a general drying trend, that some historians have looked to as the ultimate cause of social and political collapse.

Archaeologists often object to models of invasion as the cause of political and social change, as they often do not see evidence of sudden change in the archaeological record. In the first place, the invasion of pastoralists into urban areas usually takes the form of gradually increasing raids, and often involves interactions much more complex than simply conquest. We can see such a process in the fall of the Roman and Han Chinese empires, which we will explore in a later lecture. In the second place, even sudden conquests often leave no archaeological trace, a fact that is not always sufficiently appreciated.

The downfall of the third millennium empires of Egypt and Mesopotamia need not have been from drought or social unrest or any other negative factors. They may well have been the victims of their own success. The neighboring pastoral peoples, both hill pastoralists, such as the Gutians, who lived in the Zagros mountains to the east of Mesopotamia, and the donkey-nomads, such as the

Amorites, who lived in the arid regions of Northern Mesopotamia, benefited from the growth of agriculture and trade. They grew in population and also obtained the most advanced military technology of the time. In the same period, growing militarization would have led to greater chances for internal uprisings, as it became clearer that military strongmen could take on the ritual trappings of kingship without too much trouble.

By 1900 B.C., we know that there were a number of small- to medium-sized Amorite kingdoms established in Mesopotamia, for example, the well-known Babylon. These existed elsewhere in the Near East. Other Amorite dynasties arise in Syria, for example, at Mari, which now controlled the trade route from Mesopotamia to the Mediterranean and in Assyria. Not all the new dynasties were Amorites, however, we find the Canaanites established in a number of cities in what is today Lebanon, Israel, and Palestine, for example. By the year 2000, Egypt had been reunited under a noble family from Thebes, which established the Middle Kingdom. This period of Egyptian history is much more militaristic, but we know that the chariot was not yet used by the Egyptians. The relationship of the chariot to the spread of the Amorites is unclear. It may well be that the horse-drawn chariot was already in use in the Near East, either because it had developed there or because it had already been introduced. Whether or not the chariot was in use previously, we know that the Amorite dynasty of Babylon uses the chariot to establish its control over Mesopotamia, mainly due to the conquest of its most famous king, Hammurabi, who lived in the middle of the 18th century B.C. In Canaan, a number of powerful city-states also grew up, also using the chariot.

In any case, there is definitely an invasion of chariot using, and Indo-European speaking peoples into the Near East. Sometime after 1900 B.C., we have the spread of the Hittite Empire. The Hittites were certainly Indo-European speakers, although not part of the Iranian or Aryan branches of that language family. They definitely used the chariot, however, and over the next three hundred years establish a powerful kingdom in Anatolia and Syria. A second people who use the chariot to establish an\ empire are the Hurrians. We cannot read the Hurrian language, so there are many questions about their empire, but it is clear that they created a powerful state in Syria, that rivaled the Hittites.

To the west, we find chariot states rising in both mainland Greece, the Mycenaean culture, and on the islands of the Mediterranean, such as Crete. By around 1600 B.C., the Near East and Greece is dominated by a number of powerful kingdoms: Mycenaean's, Hittites, Hurrians, Babylonians, and Egyptians.

These new Near Eastern states are characterized by a powerful monarch with a centralized bureaucracy, working out of a large palace complex. Thus they are often called palace-centered empires. An interesting feature is the growth of inter-empire trade that is often in the form of a "gift exchange" between monarchs. This sort of trade was in bronze, tin, textiles, pottery, precious metal, and horses. The horse is remarkably suited for warfare. Yet it requires special training, special care, special feeding, and constant exercise. The skills for this would have been second nature to steppe peoples, but at a premium in the agricultural regions. Here we see an example, which we will also see in later lectures, of how war drives the need for specialists, in this case, horse trainers.

Another feature of these Near Eastern empires were the so-called chariot nobility. We have already referred to this in the case of Shang China. Chariots were a very expensive weapons system. The chariot itself was a delicate piece of craftsmanship and even a simple one was quite costly. The horses themselves were quite valuable and, and as I've said, needed to be trained, and maintained, given special food, and constant exercise and care. Drivers for the chariot needed to be quite skilled. The composite bow was another expensive feature. Simply being able to ride in a light chariot was quite a feat, not to mention being able to fire a bow from it. So archers needed to be trained. Even wielding a spear from a wildly bucking chariot is not a simple task. So it was not only the initial purchase of the various elements that were costly, but in addition the fighting men, the archer, and a spears man, had to be trained, had to be maintained. One needed a host of other personnel: the driver, the trainer, grooms, craftsmen to fix broken wheels and baskets, and so forth.

The chariot was such an expensive weapons system to purchase and maintain that most empires were not in the position to take on the cost. This led to the use of chariot nobility. Such nobles were given land by the king, as well as peasants to work it. In exchange, the nobles provided chariots for the royal army. In many of our written sources, we find the word *maryannu*, referring to exactly this type of chariot nobility, especially among the Hurrians and Canaanites. The word *arya* may well be related to the Indo-European term *arya* that we have already met.

The Egyptian Middle Kingdom had collapsed in the middle of the 17th century B.C. due to the attacks of a chariot-riding people that the Egyptians called the Hyksos, who were almost certainly the Canaanites. These Canaanites created a number of small kingdoms in northern Egypt. The Egyptians soon adopted the chariot, drove out the Canaanites, and created the New Kingdom. This became the only Near Eastern state wealthy enough for the central government to create a professional chariot army. With this army the Egyptians moved west, and conquered the Canaanite city-states, and south, conquering Nubia (or Kush). Under the New Kingdom, the Egyptians created a powerful empire that soon came into contact with, and conflict with, the Hurrians and the Hittites.

New Kingdom Egypt created a sophisticated military run by an elaborate military bureaucracy. Taxation and tribute, to pay for it, was collected by an equally complex civil administration, both in Egypt itself, and in its provinces in Nubia and Canaan. The professional chariot forces were originally subordinated to the traditional Egyptian military elite, that is, the ship-borne marines who fought on the Nile. But before long the new chariot fighters became the most prestigious force. A new motif developed in Egyptian art: of the king riding his chariot and firing his bow, trampling Egypt's enemies.

I have left the discussion of perhaps the most classic example of the invasion of Indo-European chariot warriors to the last. This is the movement of the people known collectively as the Aryans into India, recorded in the sacred Hindu books known as the Vedas. As with China, there has been a modern reaction against the idea of invasion, although the view that the Aryans were native to India is held mainly by Indian nationalists and by few serious scholars. On the other hand, although 19th- and early 20th-century scholars saw the chariot invasion as the cause of the decline of the Indus Valley civilization, this view has been abandoned by most archaeologists and ancient historians, although not, in my view, for very good reasons.

The dating of the decline of the Indus Valley civilization is, however, perfectly compatible with an Aryan invasion, and other than a general reluctance to attribute cultural change to military invasion, there seems to be no particular reason to reject the idea. A strong support for it comes from the fact that a very similar invasion, linguistically, culturally, and technologically occurs simultaneously next to India, in Iran and, Afghanistan. Very significantly we have the development in all these regions a warrior caste called the *Kshatriyas*, both in Iran and India, that is almost certainly the chariot nobility that we have seen elsewhere. Scholars should not allow the historical use of the Aryan invasion by racial theorists of the past to blind them to the strong evidence for its existence and powerful impact.

Throughout this lecture, we have seen how in this broad region we are calling the core, the spread of a common military technology occurred: the chariot. Very similar institutions develop in very distant places, partly due to diffusion and partly due to similar reactions to economic and social necessities of the new weapons system. Indeed, the chariot revolution is a basic factor in the creation of the core, which will play a pivotal role in world history. In the next lecture, we will explore another military revolution, the sword revolution, and its relationship to the Iron Age.

Lecture Six
The Sword Revolution

Scope:

The role of iron weapons in the collapse of the Near Eastern Bronze Age cultures has long been debated. The traditional view that iron was an important factor has been rejected by historians but needs to be reconsidered. This period, from about 1200 to 800 B.C., is very difficult to reconstruct due to the paucity of written sources and the complexity of those that do survive, such as the Bible and the Homeric poems. The introduction of a new type of sword, the Naue II sword, was probably a major factor. The sword and ironworking generally spread together throughout the core.

Outline

I. In this lecture, we look at another revolution: the sword revolution. The sword has a long history as a bronze weapon, but it is connected to the adoption of a metal that would transform history—iron.

> **A.** The term Iron Age, like Bronze Age, is a relative one. It simply refers to the time after which a particular culture first used iron. It differs, of course, from place to place.
>
> > **1.** Early archaeologists often explained the replacement of bronze by iron in military terms. This theory was discredited by a number of arguments.
> >
> > **2.** The introduction of iron seemed too early: The palace-centered cultures were at their height in 1500 B.C., when the Hittites first used iron.
> >
> > **3.** In addition, the use of iron was very rare for hundreds of years after its discovery.
> >
> > **4.** Finally, it was doubted that iron weapons were really more effective than bronze ones. Most armies continued to use spears and arrows, in which bronze or even stone points are not much less lethal than iron ones.
> >
> > **5.** A consensus has emerged that it was the downfall of the Bronze Age empires that led to the Iron Age, not vice versa.

B. To explain the way in which iron weapons replaced bronze, we need to explain the differences between the metallurgy of bronze and iron.

    1. Bronze, a combination of copper and tin, was an improvement over copper alone, but its ingredients were rare and it was too soft to make truly effective weapons.

    2. Bronze did improve some weapons, such as the dagger. But bronze swords lacked tensile strength in lengths longer than three feet.

    3. Iron is considerably more difficult to produce than bronze. It requires high temperatures and an enormous amount of strength and skill.

C. From the point of view of weapons technology, the real Iron Age occurred in the 1st millennium B.C., not the 2nd. What happened around 1200 B.C. that might explain the change from bronze to iron? Quite a lot, and most of it has to do with war.

    1. So many of the Near East empires disappeared during this time period that one historian calls it simply the Catastrophe.

    2. This period of history, which runs from about 1200 B.C. to about 900 B.C., is notoriously complex and puzzling. The destruction that occurred brought much of our written record to an end.

    3. The few contemporary sources that we do have, mainly Egyptian, speak of an invasion by the so-called Sea Peoples.

II. Let me say a few words about the Bible as a military historical source.

A. In this lecture we will focus on the books from Genesis through 2 Kings.

    1. These books are indeed historical works, which is not to say that they are necessarily historically accurate but that they were intended to be a history of the Jewish people from Creation to the destruction of the kingdom of Judah in the 6th century B.C.

    2. It is very important to understand that the earliest part of this history, the Five Books of Moses, was the last to be written.

3. The books that contain the oldest and most relevant military material are the Books of Judges, 1 and 2 Samuel, and the Books of Kings.

B. The stories of the *Iliad* and the *Odyssey* may also go back to the period of these conflicts.

1. The texts were probably first written down in the 7th century B.C. and were based on some oral tradition that had developed over the previous century or more.

2. It has been established that the texts that we have contain elements from the Mycenaean period, from the Dark Ages, and from Homer's own time.

C. Despite the paucity of our sources, it is clear that there were a number of major invasions, or migrations, in the 13th and 12th centuries B.C.

1. The first was a series of attacks by the Sea Peoples that destroyed the Hittite Empire, probably destroyed the Hurrian Empire, and demolished most of the Canaanite city-states.

2. At the same time that the Hittites were destroyed, the Mycenaean cities in Greece were sacked, probably by fellow Greek speakers, in the Dorian invasion.

3. Another invasion we can identify is that of the Arameans, who established a number of kingdoms in Syria and probably brought about the end of the Middle Assyrian Empire.

4. One of the most interesting and enigmatic features of this period is the people called Habiru or Apiru. Some scholars have seen a connection between the Habiru and the biblical Hebrews, though there are many difficulties with this connection.

5. We shall discuss the Hebrews later, but we should note that the earliest-written portions of the Bible are filled with stories of wars and conquests.

III. While these invasions are very complicated from an ethnic and political perspective, they may be quite simple from a military one.

A. Historian Robert Drews has suggested that the reason for this massive change was the development of a new type of bronze sword in the region of Austria and Hungary around 1450 B.C.

1. Drews calls this the Naue II sword, a name that has caught on among military historians. It is so-called because it was identified by a German archaeologist named Julius Naue.
2. Naue actually called it the *Griffzungenschwert*, which literally translates to "grip-tongue sword." Other military historians have called it the short slashing sword, which does not really describe the revolutionary feature of this weapon.
3. I will call it the "tongue-hilt sword," which is a bit awkward but gets the message across.
4. The improvement in the tongue-hilt sword is relatively simple: The blade and hilt were cast as a single piece, with the hilt sticking out from the rear of the blade like a tongue.
5. For hundreds of years after their invention, tongue-hilt swords were made of bronze, but the all-in-one casting made them a big improvement over previous swords.

B. Drew's theory is that the use of this tongue-hilt sword made possible the defeat of chariot forces. There are some arguments about this, but it is clear that the sword allowed for a new kind of fighting, close and personal.

C. The success of the tongue-hilt sword may have had another effect. This new type of weapon could be considerably improved by replacing bronze with iron.
1. Iron has much higher strength and tensility, making an iron sword more effective and durable than a bronze one.
2. Iron swords could be made longer, leading to the introduction of the long sword.
3. Not only iron weapons but iron implements of all kinds became more common.
4. Iron is one of the first technologies where we see the increase of scale bringing down costs. Iron soon became significantly cheaper than bronze.

D. As complicated as the Iron Age was in the Near East, it was even more so in places like India, Europe, and China. But scholars can use the same model that we have developed here to look at the Iron Age in those civilizations.

1. One factor that might explain why the Iron Age developed in regional fits and starts is one that often appears in military revolutions. The adoption of a new weapon is often done at the expense of the military caste that developed based on previous technology.
2. It is not inconceivable that the spread of the iron sword and its accompanying technologies was consciously blocked by the elites who would be threatened by its adoption.
3. There is one place where we know that ironworking was not adopted in response to the iron sword. The Bantu culture used iron, but only for spearheads.
4. The Bantu culture is the exception, however. In most places, iron and the sword were closely connected.

Suggested Reading:

Drews, *The End of the Bronze Age*.

Sandars, *The Sea Peoples*.

Questions to Consider:

1. How does the tongue-hilt sword help explain the development of the Western Iron Age?
2. Could the same model be applied to the use of iron in other regions?

Lecture Six—Transcript
The Sword Revolution

Welcome back. Last time, we investigated the chariot revolution, and the development of palace-based states throughout the core. In this lecture we will look at another military revolution: the sword revolution. The sword has a long history as a bronze weapon, but it is connected to the adoption of a metal that will transform history: iron.

The term "Iron Age," like "Bronze Age," is a relative one. That is, it refers simply to the time after which a particular culture first used iron. This date differs, of course, from place to place. Thus, the Iron Age in Anatolia is usually dated to around 1500 B.C., when iron tools and weapons are first found there. In China, in contrast, the Iron Age dates to a much later time, sometime between the 8th or 7th century B.C. Indeed, in the Americas, the Iron Age does not arrive until the Europeans come in the 16th century A.D.

Early archaeologists often explained the replacement of bronze by iron in military terms. To them, iron weapons seemed obviously more effective, and the introduction of the new technology was thought to be an important factor, if not the most important factor in the decline of the Bronze Age empires. This theory was discredited by a number of arguments. In the first place, the introduction of iron seemed too early. After all the palace-centered cultures were at their height in 1500 B.C., when the Hittites first used iron. In addition, further study showed that in the first place, the use of iron was very rare for hundreds of years after its discovery. And it was found that iron weapons were really not that much more effective than bronze ones, at least in the case of spears and arrows. In this case bronze, or for that matter, stone points continued to be used, and they are not that much less lethal than iron ones.

In addition, as we have noted in other cases, archaeologists did not believe that a new military technology was capable of causing dramatic political and social change, and they searched for other explanations. The consensus developed that it was the downfall of the Bronze Age empires that led to the Iron Age, not vice versa. To explain the way in which iron weapons replaced bronze, we need to back up and explain the differences between the metallurgy of bronze and the metallurgy of iron. Bronze is a combination of copper and tin, or arsenic, and is a great improvement over copper alone as it is more durable. Both tin and arsenic were rare, and places such as

Mesopotamia and Egypt were dependent on long-distance trade to obtain them. This made bronze expensive, and during the Bronze Age, many—if not most—tools and weapons also continued to be made of stone.

Bronze Age kilns for smelting were no different than those for baking pottery, and were basically simply enclosed ovens. Such kilns produced enough heat for copper and bronze metallurgy, as well as other metals such as silver and gold. Bronze did have some advantages over stone or wood in the making of certain agriculture implements, such as sickles, [but] much less so with others, such as axes. Many simple household tools were much better in metal form than stone, but to a large extent bronze was confined to the wealthy. In general, however, although bronze is a perfectly acceptable metal for the production of weapons, it was not a great improvement over flint or other stone for ax-heads, arrowheads, and spear points. Indeed, stone continues to be used, especially for arrowheads, which might not be retrieved, and thus stone lowers their cost. Bronze did improve certain weapons. A bronze dagger was a big improvement over a stone one, which was liable to break. Stone could not be made into a cutting or slashing weapon larger than a dagger, and with bronze, short swords were possible. The sickle sword, which is a characteristic weapon of the period, could not possibly have been made of stone.

Bronze swords, however, were not very effective, and could not be made longer than over about three feet, as they lost their tensility. Tensile strength is a very important factor in swords, although not very important in most tools or implements. It refers to the ability of a metal to bend without breaking. If a sword blow hits a hard object, such as a metal helmet, the lack of tensility is what causes it to break. Another problem with swords in the Bronze Age was one of design. In almost all cases, the blade was cast separately from the hilt. This created a weakness which also made them liable to break due to the stress generated by the force of a blow. So it is not surprising that spears and bows continued to be the primary weapons of the Bronze Age, whether carried by infantry or charioteers. In fact, once the light chariot had been introduced, there was relatively little weapons development for many centuries.

Let us return to iron. There seems to be in fact, at least one, and perhaps several, independent discoveries of iron, but let's concentrate on the Near Eastern one. While ironworking was discovered by the Hittites around 1500 B.C., the use of iron spread slowly, and it is relatively rare even among the Hittites and their neighbors until about 1200 B.C. Since the military explanation for the adoption of iron had been discarded, it is often assumed that iron replaced bronze because it is obviously a better metal for civilian purposes. In fact, it is only marginally better for most purposes. While iron, unlike bronze does not need the addition of a rare metal such as tin, there does have to be a sufficient demand to justify mining it, and this demand was difficult to generate. As I've said, there was no advantage of iron for most civilian purposes. The fact is that iron is considerably more difficult to produce than bronze, which would have interrupted its introduction.

In order to be worked effectively, iron needs to be heated up to a very high temperature, up to 1500 degrees Fahrenheit. This requires a more sophisticated oven than that used for bronze. Oxygen needs to be introduced to raise the temperature. How this was done in the earliest days of ironworking is unclear, but eventually bellows are developed to force air into the oven and raise its temperature. In addition to a special kiln, both strength and skill were needed to work iron. Iron needs to be worked into effective tools and weapons, and the skills of the blacksmith, as the worker in iron comes to be known, is very important. Later on, we shall see, for example, that by hammering out a blade, then bending it in half, raising it again to red-heat, and hammering again into a single blade, the tensility of the sword was doubled. This process can be repeated over and over again to create very high quality swords. This sort of technique was often kept secret, and it is not surprising that in many cultures the blacksmith is often a hereditary guild or even a caste.

It took many centuries, however, before such skills were learned. Early workers in iron could not make weapons significantly better than bronze ones. If fact, early iron weapons, the Hittite ones for example, seem to be luxury, or even a curiosity item, carried by kings or other important people more for prestige due to their rarity and expense than for their usefulness.

In the centuries before 1200 B.C., one does find some increase in the use of iron in various regions, but in those cases there is usually some shortage of tin, and a disruption in copper supplies, so the turn to iron may have been a way of substituting one metal for another, and was abandoned when the supplies for bronze improved. It is only after 1200—how much after is a matter of great debate among archaeologists—that the situation changes drastically. Iron tools and weapons become more common. From the point of view of weapons technology, at least, the real Iron Age occurs in the first millennium, not the second millennium B.C.

What happened around 1200 that might explain the change from bronze to iron? It turns out, quite a lot, and most of it seems to do with war. In a relatively short period of time the Hittite and Mycenaean empires disappear. Many of the thriving city-states of Canaan are destroyed, the Assyrian and Egyptian empires are shaken to the core, and a host of new people appear in the historical record. The break is so sudden and violent that Robert Drews, who has written a number of important books on this period, calls it simply The Catastrophe. Although there has been much criticism of Drews's use of this term, one can imagine that few of those who actually lived through it would have argued with him.

The catastrophic period of history, running from around 1200 to around 900 B.C., is notoriously complex and puzzling. For one thing, the invasions that wracked the world (at least the Western world) brought an end to much of our written record. In Egypt, the number of hieroglyphic texts taper off after around 1100 B.C. During the invasions, some of the great cultures that used cuneiform documents were either destroyed, like the Hittites, or so weakened that far fewer records were kept, or survived, like the Assyrians. In Mycenaean Greece, where a form of writing called Linear B had been inscribed on clay tablets, the disruption is so great that literacy is lost altogether, and historians call this the Dark Ages. The term might be applied to the entire region.

There are some contemporary sources for this period. The best ones are the Egyptian ones, which date mainly from around 1200 to around 1100 B.C. These both discuss and illustrate the invasion of the so-called Sea Peoples in a number of inscriptions. Although they mention, as an aside, that the Sea Peoples destroyed the Hittite empire, the Egyptians are typically little interested with events outside of Egypt. There is a remarkable Linear B tablet from Mycenaean Greece that refers to an upcoming invasion from the sea, and was apparently written shortly before an attack destroyed the city, and it was left, actually, in an oven where it was left to be baked. And the author apparently died before he was able to do so.

Since we are going to be using the Bible as a source in this and later lectures, let me quickly say something about it from a military historical perspective. The Bible is not a book, but an anthology of books, and they are not put together randomly. The part that we are dealing with in this lecture, the books of Genesis to II Kings, was probably edited together during the Babylonian exile around 580 or so to 530 or so B.C. This part of the Bible, from Genesis through II Kings, is called the "Primary History." It is a historical work, which is not to say that it is necessarily historically accurate, but it was intended to be taken as a history of the Jewish people from the creation down to the destruction of the Kingdom of Judah by the Babylonians in the 6th century B.C. Now, in using this [Primary] History—and I use the word "history" in the ancient not modern sense (it's very important to understand)—is that the earliest parts of this History, the five books of Moses, were the last to be written. The books that contain the oldest material and the most relevant military material are the books of Judges, I and II Samuel, and the books of Kings. The earliest portions of these books may date back (in their written form) down to about the 10th century B.C., perhaps a little earlier.

Most of the Primary History was probably written down sometime between 900 and 750 B.C. It is possible that some of the stories in the earliest biblical books, such as Judges, might go back to oral stories or legends or even possibly written sources as far back as the 12th century. There's a reference, for example, to the Philistines which notes that they have iron, while the Hebrews do not. So this might refer to a period when iron is being introduced. Since at least some of these stories were already several generations old when written down and since the text has gone through extensive editing to be put together in this form, separating fact from fiction in the biblical text and making sense of the events is very difficult. The many mutually contradictory reconstructions of early Israelite history during this period, all based on the same source, is a testament to how confusing it is.

The stories in the *Iliad* and the *Odyssey* may also go back to the same period. There has long been an argument among classicists called the "Homeric Question" on how the text of the *Iliad* and the

Odyssey came to be written down and whether the *Iliad* and *Odyssey* were written by the same person and so forth. Suffice it to say that the texts were probably first written down in the 7th century B.C. But they were based on oral traditions that had developed over the previous century or more. Like the study of the Bible, Homeric studies is very complex and suffers actually from a superabundance of theories. Basically, it has been established that the text that we have contains elements from the Mycenaean period, from the Dark Ages, and from Homer's own time. The problem is that without outside evidence, it is difficult if not impossible to untangle the various elements in most cases.

Despite the paucity and the confusing nature of our sources, it is clear that there were a number of major invasions, or migrations, or both, in the 13th and 12th centuries B.C. The first is a series of attacks by the "Sea Peoples," a term that the Egyptians gave them. This had a dramatic effect. They certainly destroyed the Hittite Empire, and probably the Hurrian empire as well, and probably most of the Canaanite city-states, although a few survived. The Egyptians managed to defeat them, but the attacks of the Sea People are almost certainly a factor in the end of the New Kingdom. The Egyptians name a dozen or more separate groups among the Sea Peoples though what these groups are is not clear. They might have been subgroups of a single people or different peoples allying themselves in large scale raids. We don't know. Indeed, only one of the Sea Peoples can be identified: that is the group called the "Peleset," who in the English translation of the Bible are called the Philistines.

As I mentioned before, the Egyptians not only wrote about the Sea Peoples, but illustrated them in a series of reliefs showing battles. The Sea Peoples wore a distinctive feather or horn or helmet. But more interesting to us is their armament: In addition to bows, they carry swords and round shields. They are almost never shown with spears, which recall was the common weapon of the Bronze Age. Around the same time that the Hittite Empire was being destroyed and the Egyptians attacked, the Mycenaean cities in Greece were sacked. The palace-based culture there disappears. This invasion, which is sometimes called the "Dorian Invasion," was carried out by Greek speakers, just like the Mycenaeans, but their culture was completely different. Some scholars think that the Dorian Greeks were part of the Sea Peoples, but this problem is too complicated to discuss here.

Another invasion we can identify is that of the Aramaeans. These peoples seem to have originated in the arid region between northern Mesopotamia and Syria. They spread both to the southwest, into Canaan, and southeast, into Mesopotamia. They created a number of kingdoms that dominated Syria, and both fight with and ally themselves with the early Hebrews. It is probably the Aramaeans who bring an end to the Middle Assyrian Empire, and they migrate along the Tigris and Euphrates, conquering the old Mesopotamian cities. One Aramaean tribe, the Chaldeans, takes over the region around the city of Ur, thus the Bible speaks of "Ur of the Chaldees." The relationship between the Hebrews with the Aramaeans is unclear. While they appear around the same time, and seem to be doing the same thing as the Aramaeans, that is conquering Canaanites, there is a big problem with identifying the Hebrews with the Aramaeans, that is, that Aramaeans don't speak Aramaic. In fact, Hebrew is a dialect of Canaanite, which has led to much confusion. Without going into this issue, I want to point out that it is not unknown for conquerors to take on the language of the people they are conquering, for example the German-speaking Franks, who adopt French, and the French-speaking Normans, who adopt English.

One of the most interesting and enigmatic features of this period are the people called Habiru in Mesopotamian records or Apiru in Egyptian ones. They have long caught the attention of scholars who saw a connection with the Biblical Hebrews, since the Habiru date back to around 1500 B.C. And a lot of scholars wanted to push Habirus back into the second millennium. There are many problems with this connection, not least of which is that the Habirus do not seem to be an ethnic class, but rather a social class, or rather social outcasts. We see Habiru functioning sometimes as outlaws, sometimes as soldiers, although individual Habiru are seen in all sorts of professions. We shall discuss the Hebrews later, in the context of the development of monotheism, for which they are best known, but we should note that the earliest portions of the Bible to be written are filled with stories of wars and conquests. While the details may be difficult to untangle, there is evidence that the development of the Hebrew peoples, and of the kingdoms of Israel and Judah, occurred in the context of a great deal of fighting. While these invasions are very complicated, the Hebrew and the others, from an ethnic and political perspective, as we've seen, they may be quite simple from a military one.

Let us go back to Robert Drews, whose books have resurrected the military explanation for the fall of the Bronze Age empires. According to him, what may have changed the situation was the development of a new type of bronze sword, which is first seen in the region of modern Austria and Hungary around 1450 B.C. While I like Drews's theory quite a bit, I do not particularly care for his name for this sword. He calls it the Naue II sword, and this is the name that has caught on among military historians. It is so-called because it was identified by a German archaeologist named Julius Naue.

Dr. Naue actually called this sword the *griffzungenschwert*, which literally translates to "grip-tongue sword," which is not much of an improvement on Naue II. Other military historians have called it the "short-slashing sword," which trips off the tongue but doesn't really describe the revolutionary feature of this weapon. With some hesitation, I will call it the "tongue-hilt sword," which is a bit awkward, but gets the message across. The improvement in the tongue-hilt sword is relatively simple: The blade and hilt were cast as a single piece, with the hilt sticking out from the rear of the blade like a tongue. A raised flange or edge around the tongue-hilt portion allowed wood or bone to be added by the swordmaker. For hundreds of years after their invention, the tongue-hilt swords were made of bronze, but the all-in-one casting made them a big improvement over previous swords.

Drews's theory is that the use of this sword made possible the defeat of chariot forces. Swordsmen could get close to the chariots, and cut their reins or stab the horses. There has been a great deal of debate about this. Some have countered that chariots were not used in the close-up fighting that would have put them in touch with the swordsmen and also that the armies of the Bronze Age had plenty of infantry.

The fact is we know very little how war was conducted in the Bronze Age, and especially in this period. The critics of Drew miss the point, I think. The stronger tongue-hilt sword allowed for a new kind of fighting, close and personal. A good analogy is the better documented interaction, that we'll talk about a little later, between the sword-wielding Romans and the spear-carrying Greeks a thousand years after this. The advantages of the short sword in the hands of a skilled and aggressive fighter are obvious, and the same can be said for this earlier period. We should note that the "mighty man" or hero becomes a common type in stories from this period, for example [Goliath] in the book of Joshua in the Bible and Achilles in the *Iliad*. This may reflect the new kind of warfare, in which the individual's courage and skill involved in sword fighting becomes a premium.

The success of the tongue-hilt sword may have had another effect. This new type of weapon, unlike spears or axes, could be considerably improved by replacing bronze with iron. Iron has a much higher strength and tensility, so an iron sword of the same length as a bronze one is considerably more effective and especially more durable. In addition, iron swords could be made longer. The bronze tongue-hilt swords were generally less than thirty inches long. As I said before, no effective bronze sword could be longer than thirty three inches. Iron, however, was another matter. We now have the introduction of the long sword next to the short sword.

Exactly when this switch from bronze swords to iron swords occurred is not clear: It was sometime between 1200 and 900. Once it happened, however, we start to find not only iron weapons but iron implements of all kinds becoming more common. We can speculate that the advantage of the iron sword made both the mining and the smithing of iron much more attractive. Of course, as long as a blacksmith was making swords, he might as well make other tools and weapons as well.

Iron is one of the first technologies where we see the increase of scale bringing down costs significantly. Once there was sufficient demand for iron, and the supply both of ore and of skilled workers was sufficient, iron becomes significantly cheaper than bronze. As we shall see, the lowering cost of individual weapons will have a significant impact on warfare.

As complicated as the Iron Age is in the Near East, it is even more so around the world. Nevertheless, I think that the model developed here can be very useful. In India we find iron around 1200 B.C., and although many archaeologists have argued for an independent development, its proximity to the Near East and the similarity in their military cultures, suggests a second look. There is no question that the quality of Indian ironworking is very high. The Indians were the first to cast arrowheads in iron, although exactly how early has not been determined.

To the south of Egypt, the ancient Kingdom of Meroe, located in what is today Sudan, became a major ironworking center. Whether it got its knowledge of ironworking from Egypt or developed it independently is debated. The adoption of iron in Europe is also a complicated question. We should note, however, that the Europeans like the Indians, become adept at ironworking, especially the Celts, whose spread into Western Europe may be associated with the quality of their iron weapons. In China also, although there is some evidence for early experiments with iron, it is becoming apparent that ironworking was introduced from Central Asia, sometime around the 8th or 7th century B.C., and that its adoption was connected to new weapons.

I would like to suggest that historians of weapons and of metallurgy look not so much at the spread of iron, but rather at the spread of the tongue-hilt or Naue II sword. Does the rise in the use of iron follow the adoption of a more effective sword technology in each region? Perhaps someone will undertake such a study. One factor that might explain the way the Iron Age developed, in regional fits and starts, might have something to do with another factor we shall see in military revolutions. The adoption of a new weapon may increase military effectiveness, but this is often done at the expense of a military caste that has grown due to the previous military technology. We have seen the growth and spread of the chariot nobility, and how the sword, for example, and especially the iron sword, was involved in the decline and fall of the chariot based empires of the Near East.

It is not inconceivable that the spread of the iron sword, and of the ironworking that goes with it, was consciously blocked by some of the very elites whose adoption it would have threatened. Although there are some early examples of iron in Egypt, it is very rare until the 7th century B.C.—although Egypt stood literally next to an Iron Age Palestine. Indeed, Egypt is one of the last places in the Near East to adopt iron. The first evidence for smelting comes from Naucratis, a Greek city founded around 620 B.C. We are not sure why this is so, but it may be related to the reluctance of elites to adopt such culture-transforming weapons and technologies that we shall see in later lectures.

There is one place where we know that ironworking was not adopted in response to a new type of sword, and that is in the case of the Bantu migration. The use of iron was an important factor in the success of the migration of the Bantus, which moved in three great waves southward from the modern Cameroons. This migration pushed the Bushman out of central and most of southern Africa, and Bantu languages are spoken now from Uganda to South Africa. Yet, among the Bantu, iron was used only for spearheads and not for swords. The reason for this is unclear. Bantu, Africa, however, is the exception, and this area remains part of the margin militarily. In most places, iron and the sword are closely connected.

In this lecture we have seen how improvements in the sword may have brought about the Iron Age and its military culture. In the next lecture, we shall explore how another innovation, the horse warrior or cavalryman, affected societies throughout the core.

Lecture Seven
Steppes, Standing Armies, and Silver Trade

Scope:

Cavalry transformed steppe cultures, such as the Scythians and Cimmerians, making them more powerful and dangerous to settled regions. The use of mounted warriors spread east to the Hsiung-nu and Yuëh-Chi peoples, and ultimately to East Asia. Cavalry gradually replaced chariots throughout the remaining Old World. In the 9th and 8th centuries B.C., the Assyrians developed the most sophisticated and expensive military system yet. They adopted cavalry, mainly horse archers, which were made possible by the breeding of larger horses. The greater cost led to taxation based on silver and a provincial structure to collect it, both of which had long-term effects.

Outline

I.   The story of the early development of cavalry is somewhat unclear.

    A. It seems likely that the use of cavalry began in the Near East and spread to the western steppes, but the reverse is certainly possible.

        1. Our first illustration of a horse being ridden comes from Egypt and dates from the 14th century B.C.

        2. The first sign of cavalry appeared in Assyria around 900 B.C. This cavalry functioned like a chariot corps without the chariot.

        3. Eventually, horsemen learned to fire while riding, and this led to the development of a new type of soldier: the horse archer. The lancer did not develop in Assyria for another century.

    B. We turn now to the effect that cavalry had on the peoples of the steppes.

        1. The tribe was the basic political and military unit of nomadic pastoralists, ranging in size from a few hundred to tens of thousands.

        2. Tribes could also form larger units, either in temporary alliances or as more permanent confederations. Confederations sometimes grew large enough to be referred to as kingdoms or even empires.

3. Tribes were divided into clans organized around kinship.
4. Steppe armies were made up almost entirely of cavalry.
5. From an early period, we find the use of decimal organization: units of tens, hundreds, thousands, and eventually ten thousands.
6. The steppe warriors became highly skilled as horse archers and developed the ability to shoot over the horse's back.
7. With some minor exceptions, it is only among the steppe peoples that we find women commonly fighting alongside men. This no doubt derives from the fact that women, like men, were skilled riders and therefore highly valued as warriors.

C. Though there was little sense of land ownership in the steppe culture, territorial rights were important to establish grazing land.
1. The domestication of the Bactrian camel allowed for the development of the Central Asian trade routes, which steppe people routinely raided as a source of income.
2. To supplement their incomes, tribes or clans would serve as allies or mercenaries in the armies of more settled peoples.
3. As the market for warhorses grew, the breeding of horses became another important economic factor in the steppes.

II. In the 1st millennium B.C., most of the steppe people were still Indo-Europeans.

A. One branch, the Iranian-speaking tribes, dominated the western and central steppes, from Ukraine to central China.
1. A group of related Iranian tribes migrated into what is now Iran and Afghanistan. These were the Persians, the Medes, the Parthians, the Sogdians, and the Bactrians.
2. Other confederations of Iranian-speaking tribes started to raid into the Near East and eastern Europe in the 8th century B.C. These tribes included the Cimmerians and the Scythians.
3. To the east of the Scythians, we find other Indo-European steppe people, such as the Samartians and the Kushans (known by the Chinese as the Yuëh-Chi).

B. There was another language family that was present in the steppes in this period: Altaic.

C. There is debate about the date of the domestication of the dromedary, or one-humped camel, in Arabia.

    1. There is some evidence for its domestication around 2500 B.C., but its use did not become widespread until after 1200 B.C.

    2. Unlike the Bactrian camel, the dromedary was used as a military mount. Eventually, desert nomads became skilled at both riding and shooting on dromedaries.

III. Around the 9th century B.C., there was a resurgence of Assyrian power known as the Neo-Assyrian Empire.

    A. Although cavalry was used, the Assyrian army was still dominated by a traditional chariot nobility backed by an infantry force.

        1. One factor in their success was their openness to innovation and their willingness to incorporate foreign military ideas.

        2. The Assyrians also used military intelligence effectively. Careful daily records were kept during campaigns and used partly for intelligence purposes.

        3. In addition to their army, the Assyrians used propaganda, presenting themselves as terrifying and irresistible. They used terror and cruelty as a systematic method of policy.

    B. Around 750 B.C., we find a major change in Assyria. Tiglath-Pileser III reformed both the Assyrian state and its military.

        1. The power of the nobles was repressed, and the chariot force was replaced by a cavalry force made up of archers and lancers.

        2. The most important Assyrian innovation was the establishment of a standing army. This army consisted of settler soldiers, both Assyrian and foreign, all armed in a standard manner. This idea was subsequently adopted by Persia, Macedonia, Greece, Rome, and possibly India.

        3. The Assyrians also introduced permanent arsenals on the frontiers, where weapons and equipment could be stored.

C. Assyria expanded its territories and organized them into provinces. These provinces remained the administrative units in the Near East through Roman times. The most important function of the province was to collect taxes, which were paid in silver.

1. The military and economic need for silver had an important effect on the Near East during this period.

2. Recent discoveries have proven that the Phoenicians set up colonies in the Mediterranean not to flee the Assyrians but to profit by providing silver to the Assyrian economy.

3. This silver trade was carried out in sailing ships, and soon Phoenician settlements were established as far west as Spain.

4. To protect their trade ships from pirates, the Phoenicians developed a new type of warship, the bireme. This was the first ship designed and used solely as a warship.

Suggested Reading:

DiMarco, *War Horse.*

Drews, *Early Riders.*

Postgate, *Taxation and Conscription.*

Questions to Consider:

1. How did the adoption of cavalry impact the steppe cultures?

2. What were the long-term effects of the Neo-Assyrian military reform in the 8th century B.C.?

Lecture Seven—Transcript
Steppes, Standing Armies, and Silver Trade

Welcome back. In our last lecture, we looked at the sword revolution, its role not only in the decline of the palace-states, but also in the introduction of iron. In this lecture, we will look at the impact of the rise of cavalry both on the steppes and in urban civilizations. In addition, we shall see how, in the 8th century there is a military reform in the Assyrian army that changed not only the role of cavalry, but the way that subsequent armies were organized throughout the core.

We shall see that, although the practice of riding on horseback goes back to the middle of the second millennium, it is only after around 1000 B.C. that the use of cavalry begins to spread widely. Once it does, cavalry is adopted all over the core, from Europe and West Africa and east to China, although it only very slowly replaces the chariot. We will have to wait for an important innovation, which we will discuss in a later lecture, to make cavalry into a truly transformative weapons system.

As I mentioned earlier, when they were first domesticated, horses were too small to be ridden. The idea of selective breeding had already been discovered, and gradually horses were bred larger, so that it becomes possible, first to ride on the horse's haunches, like a donkey, and later on its shoulders. As in the case of the chariot, the story of the early development of cavalry is somewhat unclear. Perhaps, and this seems somewhat more likely, the use of cavalry began in the Near East and spread to the western steppes, but the reverse is certainly possible.

Interestingly enough, our first illustration of a horse being ridden comes from Egypt. There is a relief of an Egyptian riding a horse, dating to around 1300 B.C. Written evidence indicates that Egyptian soldiers rode horses to be used as spares for chariots but it never seems to have occurred to them to replace the chariot itself by arming the horsemen. There is no evidence that this Egyptian practice of riding spare horses, led to the use of cavalry, and it seems to have eventually simply disappeared.

The next sign of cavalry appears in Assyria around 900 B.C. The first illustration of horses show them being ridden on their haunches, and the original horsemen operated in pairs. We have an illustration of two Assyrian cavalrymen riding, with one holding the reins of the other while the archer shoots his bow. From a military point of view, the cavalry is operating like a chariot without the chariot, as the same number of soldiers and horses are needed as before. Eventually horsemen learn to fire while riding their horse by clenching the horse's flanks with their thighs. This is the development of a new type of soldier: the horse archer, which will be a very important part of warfare for thousands of years.

The next type of cavalry soldier to develop, the lancer, does not come along in Assyria for another century or so, so let us turn to the effect that cavalry had on the peoples of the steppe and elsewhere. As we have seen the chariot made it possible for pastoral peoples to exploit the grasslands that ran from Eastern Europe through Central Asia. Whether they borrowed horse riding or developed it themselves, the adoption of this practice increased the productivity of the pastoral peoples—think of the difference of herding on a chariot and herding on a horse. And this resulted in not only more populous but also militarily more powerful steppe tribes. From this point forward, steppe tribes and confederations of steppe tribes would become a constant threat to the settled people to their south along the entire length of the core. While peaceful relations, such as trading continued, raiding agricultural settlements became incessant, plundering expeditions into bordering urban regions were more common, and occasionally one or more of these peoples would seize control of cities, states, and even entire empires.

Since the steppe peoples will be such an important part of subsequent lectures, let us look more closely into steppe culture and especially their military culture. The tribe is a basic political and military unit of nomadic pastoralists, and could range in size from a few hundred to tens of thousands or more. All members of a tribe think of themselves as related and as descended from a common ancestor, whether or not this is true. On the steppes we find tribes that were related, using the same tribal name but calling themselves, for example, "western" or "eastern," "left" or "right," "black" or "white," or perhaps divided into several tribes each named after an ancestor. In some cases, there is a royal tribe as well as a common one, as in the case of the Scythians.

Tribes could also form larger units, either in temporary alliances, or in more permanent confederations. These confederations, which sometimes grew large enough to be referred to as kingdoms or even empires, are a constant feature of steppe political organizations. They were led by a chief or king. The Persian word "shah" is often used in early times to refer to this leader in the West. In Chinese sources, the rulers of steppe confederations are sometimes called the "shan-yu." In later times, when Turkish-speaking peoples begin to dominate the steppes, we find the term "khagan" or "khan" being used. (These are simply different pronunciations of the same word being used.)

Tribes were organized into clans, [which were] also organized around kinship. Like agricultural peoples, and unlike hunters and gatherers, there was a strict social hierarchy among pastoralists, with hereditary nobles serving as the leaders of clans. These nobles were often buried with great wealth and ceremony. Horses, and sometimes human beings, were sacrificed and buried with them, along with their arms and armor, and other precious items. A burial mound or tumulus was put over the grave, and the excavation of these tumuli has provided much of our knowledge of steppe life in this period.

Steppe armies were made up almost entirely of cavalry. In contrast to the settled people of the core, who almost universally wore some sort of tunic or robe in this time, the steppe people wore breeches or pants, which certainly developed due to the practice of riding horses constantly. Tall pointed hats were seen already by the 8th century B.C., especially among rulers. And we'll see these tall hats coming back and see perhaps what Genghis Khan and Mickey Mouse have in common. These tall hats were used perhaps to allow rulers and warriors to be recognized in the dust of a horse battle. Originally, these steppe warriors seem to have worn little, if any, armor, relying mainly on the bow, with an ax or sword as a sidearm.

From an early period, we find the use of decimal organization: units of tens, hundreds, thousands and, eventually, tens of thousands. The steppe warriors become highly skilled as horse archers, and developed the ability not only to shoot while riding, but to turn and shoot over the horse's back while riding away from the enemy, a practice that becomes known as a "Parthian shot." This method of firing leads to a common practice of the steppe people, the feigned retreat, in which the steppe warriors would pretend to ride away to lure the enemy into a reckless advance. Then at a signal the retreating warriors would turn on their pursuers.

One of the most interesting features of steppe warfare is the practice of women fighting. Women, of course, will fight and fight quite well, when necessary, and during sieges. Even in ancient times, it is not unusual to find women fighting alongside their men. With some minor exceptions, however, it's only among the steppe peoples that we find women commonly fighting among men in ancient times. The practice no doubt derives from the fact that women, like men, would have spent much time riding, and skilled riders were highly valued in war. Noblewomen who fought were buried with weapons, like men and, in some cases, up to thirty percent of female burials contain weapons. This steppe practice is the origin of the Greek myth of the Amazons, in which all-female tribes of warriors were thought to live on the steppes.

Naturally, given their nomadic nature, there is little sense of land ownership among steppe peoples, either individually or communally, but since grazing land is important, the control of territory is vital. This was usually organized on a tribal basis, so that when territorial rights were threatened, a large enough force could be raised to defend it. The actual herding of animals was often done by children, and much of the other work was done by women, so adult men were more free—one could say more idle—than agriculturalists to develop horse riding and other military skills through hunting and playing games, such as polo or archery contests.

The two-humped or Bactrian camel was domesticated around 2500 B.C. in northern Iran. It was first used for its hair, which can be woven into carpets and garments. The Bactrian camel was not suitable as a cavalry animal, but it could carry a great deal of weight and, thus, once the steppes began to be exploited for pastoralism, the Bactrian camel became the ideal beast of burden. Indeed, it was the two-humped camel that made long-distance trade through Central Asia possible. This Central Asia trade route, which will collectively become known as the Silk Road, is going to be a very important element in world history in our lecture series.

As the Central Asian trade routes developed, tribes began to derive income from either plundering merchants who traveled through their territory (and the right to plunder in a particular region was jealously guarded), or demand tribute from the traders, or serve as guards for the traders or, to put that another way, by practicing a sort of protection racket. Hereditary leaders, such as leaders of clans, gained much of their power from the traditional right to lead plundering war parties as well as the right to receive tribute and pay, which they could then distribute to their followers, building loyalty. Another source of income was to serve in the armies of more settled peoples. Steppe people seldom served as individuals, however, and generally it was as tribes or clans that they served aristocratic leaders, who would take their followers with them, receive their pay, and then distribute it.

As the market for warhorses grew, the breeding of horses became another important factor in the economy of the steppes. In both the plains of northeastern Iran and the Ferghana Valley, which is shared by Uzbekistan, Kyrgistan, and Tajikistan, we find especially large horses being bred. This breed, called Nisaean horses in the west, and "blood sweating horses" by the Chinese, were highly prized, as they were strong enough to carry much more weight and had more durability, without sacrificing speed.

In the first millennium B.C., most of the steppe people were still Indo-European speaking. One branch, the Iranian-speaking tribes, dominated the western and central steppes, from the Ukraine to the Tarim Basin, which is now located in western China. We shall meet many of these peoples in subsequent lectures, so let's get acquainted. A group of related Iranian tribes migrated into what is in now Iran, of course, renamed for them, and Afghanistan. Roughly from west to east, they are the Persians, the Medes, the Parthians, the Sogdians, and the Bactrians.

To the north, in the western area of the steppes, what is now the Ukraine and Kazakhstan, other confederations of Iranian-speaking tribes started to raid into the Near East and eastern Europe starting in the 8th century B.C. We normally call them by the names the Greeks gave them. These peoples were called the "Cimmerians." They were called "Gomer" by the Hebrews (and this is the origin of our name "Gomer"), also the "Scythians," who were also known as the "Saka." To the east of the Scythians we find a number of steppe people speaking Indo-European languages, such as the Sarmatians and even farther east, the best-known tribe are the people known by the Chinese as the "Yuëh-Chi." They are better known in the west as the "Kushans," which is the name of one of their constituent tribes.

There is another language family that was present in the steppes even in this period. They were the Altaic speakers, which included (and includes) both Turkish and Mongolian. The people that the Chinese called the "Hsiung-nu," who lived to the north of China, may well have been the earliest Turkish speakers to adopt the horse and bow and live on the steppes. Their relationship to the later Huns, and other famous steppes people, is hotly debated. But in any case, we'll see that the Hsiung-nu had a dramatic impact on Chinese history. Later on we'll see how both Turkish-speaking and Mongolian-speaking peoples will grow in importance in the steppes, eventually eclipsing the Indo-European speakers.

In addition to the nomadic culture of the steppes, other pastoral economy begins to develop in semi-arid and arid regions: These are the desert nomads. There is debate about the date of the domestication of the dromedary, or one-humped camel in Arabia. There is some evidence for domestication as early as the Bactrian camel, say around 2500 B.C., but the use of the dromedary does not become common or widespread until after 1200 B.C. We find the dromedary being used as a beast of burden, like the Bactrian camel, though in Arabia, Syria, and Palestine. The one-humped camel allowed the nomad pastoralists to penetrate deeper into arid regions and even deserts, to exploit oases and other sources of food for flocks. But this had the effect of opening up new trade routes running along the length of the Arabian peninsula. This route becomes increasingly important for (among other reasons) it allowed traders to avoid both Egypt and Mesopotamia, with their high taxes, in order to gain access the Mediterranean.

Unlike the Bactrian camel, the dromedary was used as a military mount. In an Assyrian relief, we see Arab warriors riding camels in battle. At first, there were two men on a single camel, one to guide the animal and the other to shoot a bow, but soon the desert nomads became skilled enough to both ride and shoot. Remarkably, although the camel is common in ancient Canaan (modern Israel and Palestine) by around 1200 B.C., its use does not spread to Egypt or to North Africa, where it's common today. It was introduced there only in Roman times.

At this point, I would like to turn back to the Assyrians. In the 9th century, around the same time that cavalry is first attested, there is a resurgence of Assyrian power. To distinguish it from earlier Assyrian states it is called the "New" or "Neo-Assyrian" Empire. Although cavalry was used, the Assyrian army was still dominated by a traditional chariot nobility backed by an infantry force. Although the iron sword was used by virtually all Assyrian soldiers as a sidearm, it was not used as a primary weapon. In fact, the spear again becomes the main infantry weapon in this period. This may be a matter of training. The use of the sword requires a more intense drill, both to learn the complex method of killing with a sword and to overcome the fear inherent in such close fighting. Due to the difficulty of it's use, we often find that the sword—although a very effective weapon and common in tribal societies—is replaced by the spear over time, especially in established armies. The Assyrians also used iron armor, mainly in the form of scale armor, in which small plates of iron were sewn onto leather coats. Iron helmets were also common.

Assyrian success in expanding their empire was due to a number of factors. They constantly experimented with different sizes of shields, different roles for the cavalry and chariots, and different types of battering rams. The Assyrians were very open to innovation and borrowing and incorporating foreign military ideas, for example foreign-style chariot and cavalry experts. This ability to borrow is one of the features we'll see in successful military states. The Assyrians also had a series of highly aggressive and capable kings. Another possible factor is Assyrian religion, which we will discuss in a later lecture.

The Assyrians also use military intelligence effectively. Careful records were kept of campaigns, in fact, in some cases it's possible to follow a campaign almost on a day-to-day basis. These reports were dedicated to the god Assur, but their detail indicates that they were used partly for intelligence purposes to aid in later campaigns. Not only battles, but marches were described, and careful attention is given to logistics, such as the number of mules and camels used in the supply train.

In addition, the Assyrians used propaganda very effectively, presenting themselves as terrifying and irresistible. Terror tactics and deportations were used but not necessarily out of a blind cruelty but as a systematic method of policy. The Assyrians actually did use terror and cruelty: They flayed their enemies, taking their skin off. They made piles of heads [and] impaled and burned enemies alive. Assyrians also practiced deportations, moving people from their homelands to distant areas in the empire. Captives were humiliated, for example the Arab king, who was chained like a dog in front of one of Nineveh's gates. These cruelties and humiliations were done especially in the case of rebellion, and they were carefully advertised in palace reliefs and inscriptions. It's interesting to note that these famous reliefs of cruelty are only in the public parts of the palace, where enemy ambassadors or foreigners would come, and they were completely absent in the private chambers of the palace.

In the 9th and early 8th centuries B.C., the Assyrians either incorporated regions into Assyria itself—they thought of this as returning to the rightful size of the earlier Assyrian empires—or they allowed conquered kings to remain on their thrones in return for submission and tribute.

Around 750 B.C., however, we find a major change. The Assyrian king Tiglath-Pileser III reformed both the Assyrian state and its military. The power of the nobles was suppressed, and the chariot was replaced by a cavalry force made up of horse archers and a new type of cavalryman: the lancer. At this point, there are no saddles or stirrups, and horsemen rode with only a saddle blanket. Thus an Assyrian soldier on horseback could not use his lance as the medieval knights did, or he would go flying off his horse. This does not mean that the lancers were useless in war. We find them, for example, being used as scouts, and they could also be used to pursue routed enemies. Eventually, we will find the lancer being armed with a bow to create the prototype of the heavy mounted warrior, although to make this combination effective, we'll have to wait for the development of a new type of saddle, which will take centuries to develop.

This switch from chariots to cavalry may have had as much to do with diminishing the importance of the nobles as any military advantage. It is noteworthy that this is the same period of increased interaction with steppe people, such as the Cimmerians and the Scythians (who I mentioned before), who were used first as allies by the Assyrians and who then launched a series of invasions of both Assyria and other regions of the Near East and Europe. The increasing importance of cavalry among the Assyrians might well be a reaction to this.

The most important Assyrian innovation, from the long-term perspective, was the establishment of a standing army. There was, as in earlier armies, a royal guard and traditional levies provided by provinces and vassal kings. What was new was the practice of using settler soldiers made up both of Assyrian and foreign contingents. These included Aramaeans, Israelites, and even Greeks from Asia Minor. Although these settler soldiers were drawn from different ethnicities, all of them were armed in a standard manner. The settler soldier will become an important feature of ancient war, and needs to be understood. Soldiers received farms in exchange for military service. From each farm, a single adult soldier was recruited, the father until the father became too old, then the son. And then even when he was at war, the farm could be operated by his family and slaves. Technically, then, the farm would be forfeited to the king if they could not provide a male heir. The foreign contingents may have had their origins in deported peoples as the movement of captives from one point of the Assyrian Empire to another became common.

The importance of this model for subsequent militaries is often not appreciated. The idea of using uniformly armed settler soldiers both as garrisons and as the basis of offensive forces is going to be adopted by the Persians, the subsequent Macedonian and Greek dynasties, the Romans, and quite possibly the Indians as well. It is another sort of military revolution, in this case, an organizational rather than a technological one.

The Assyrians also introduced permanent arsenals on their frontiers, where weapons and equipment were stored for the army. This allowed for more rapid mobilization and the movement of soldiers to the border. It was very expensive, however, and the practice was not generally adopted by their successor states.

The areas incorporated into Assyria proper were vastly expanded and organized into provinces. For the most part, the provinces established by the Assyrians remain the administrative units used in the Near East through Roman times. The kingdom of Israel, for example, was incorporated into the Assyrian empire in two different wars: The northern part was first incorporated into the province of Galilee and then, some time later, in another war, the southern part was conquered and made into the province of Samaria. These administrative divisions, which were created by military campaigns, end up defining ethnic groups. In this case, the people who had previously been Israelites, now (because of these arbitrary borders) come to think of themselves as Galileans and Samaritans. We'll mention the most famous Galilean in a later lecture.

As was typical in such cases, the Israelite king and nobility were deported to various parts of Assyria. And at least parts of the Israelite army were incorporated into the Assyrian army, almost certainly as settler soldiers. The kingdom of Judah, to the south, became a vassal state, but managed by judicious groveling and payment of tribute to maintain a precarious independence.

Assyrian expansion was not random but was carefully thought out to control trade routes: the eastern trade route to the mines of Afghanistan, the western trade route to sources of iron and silver, [and] the southern route toward Babylonia that provided access to the Persian Gulf trade. Other areas were conquered to provide resources, for example, northeast Iran, which provided the large Nisaean horses for the cavalry. The first attempt of the Assyrians to drive to the Mediterranean had been blocked in the 9th century by a coalition of kingdoms, including Israel and Judah. Much of the book of Kings, and the prophetic books of the Bible deal with these Assyrian wars. In the 8th century, however, with the new Assyrian army, the resistance is overcome, and these areas are conquered and, eventually, the Assyrians in the 7th century conquer Egypt as well and, for the first time, these two major cultures of the Near East are united in a single state.

The most important function of the Assyrian province was to collect taxes. The new standing army was effective but very expensive. The Assyrians' standardized provincial structure, which was overseen by a central bureaucracy. A governor was installed in each province, who was in charge of collecting silver and sending it to the central government. There were reforms in taxation based on the silver shekel, still a weight but not a coin yet.

This need for silver, partly due to the needs of the Assyrian military and partly because of a healthy economy, had a very important effect. Until recently historians have thought the Phoenicians had set up colonies in the Mediterranean because they were fleeing the Assyrian invasion in panic. This view was supported by the image of the Assyrians in the Bible and in the reliefs in their palaces, showing them razing cities and slaughtering civilians. Recent analysis of Assyrian cuneiform documents, including copies of contracts, now prove that the Canaanites were not fleeing, but seeking profit, by providing silver from Spain to support the Assyrian economy and especially its army.

Starting around 800 B.C., the Phoenicians built a chain of maritime colonies as far west as Spain. These include famous cities such as Gades, now Cadiz, in Spain, and Carthage in what is now Tunisia. Like other Phoenician colonies, Carthage was politically independent, although it sent a ritual tribute to its founding city of Tyre. This was the model that the Greeks used later. There were many other Phoenician colonies in Cyprus, Sicily, North Africa, Spain, and elsewhere.

In part, to protect their trade from pirates, the Phoenicians developed a new type of warship, the bireme, which subsequently was improved as the trireme. These are shown in Assyrian reliefs. They perhaps developed out of the ships used by the Sea Peoples. These were much more sophisticated warships, the first ships solely designed and used as a warship to fight other warships. Its revolutionary weapon was the ram. Since it sinks the other ship, it's not suitable for commerce raiding. The bireme and the trireme were probably specifically designed to sink pirate ships and then, as other naval powers adopt the trireme, to fight them.

In this lecture, we have seen the wide-ranging influence of cavalry, the impact of the Assyrian army and conquests, and its effect on trade in the Mediterranean. In the next lecture, we will see how this trade fostered a new kind of politic and military system: that of the Greek city-state.

Lecture Eight
Pirates and Hoplites

Scope:

The rise of the Greek city-state and its institutions may well have been connected to the "Catastrophe" we discussed before. The Greeks shared some characteristics of the Sea Peoples, and piracy was an important part of their culture. They also, however, had some elements of steppe cultures. This combination, along with the rise of the Assyrians and Phoenician colonization, may have led to the rise of both the city-state and the characteristic Greek hoplite warfare.

Outline

I.   In this lecture, we see how the wealth of the Phoenician trading colonies helped lead to the rise of a new and distinctive type of political unit: the Greek city-state.

    A. The city-state was such an influential phenomenon, both in its own time and in modern political theory, that its origins have long been a matter of investigation and debate among scholars.

        1. Scholarship has focused on the so-called Dorian invasion, which occurred around 1000 B.C.

        2. The timing of the Dorian invasion is very suggestive: The era between 1200 and 1000 B.C. was not only the time of the Sea Peoples, but also of the sword revolution.

        3. Indeed, Robert Drews included the Dorian invasion in his discussion of the Catastrophe that brought down the palace-centered empires.

    B. There is evidence of similarities between the Greeks and the Sea Peoples.

        1. There is a great deal of evidence of the early Greek connection to the sea, and not as peaceful fishermen. The English word "pirate" comes from the Greek word for pirate, and both the *Iliad* and the *Odyssey* illustrate the Greeks in this role.

        2. They used the *pentekonter*, the 50-oared raiding ship mentioned in Homer's poems and other sources. These ships seem very similar to those illustrated in Egyptian reliefs of their fight with the Sea Peoples.

3. In addition, some scholars have argued that the names of certain tribes of Sea Peoples correspond to the ethnic groups and names of early Greek peoples, such as the Achaeans (the name for Greeks used by Homer).

C. However, there are ways in which early Greek culture sharply differed from that of the Sea Peoples.
1. Early Greek culture is in many ways reminiscent of steppe culture. This is especially evident in their use of mercenary soldiers and in their adoption of Assyrian military practices.
2. There also seems to be some military continuity from the earlier Mycenaean civilization. It has been suggested that the Ionians were directly descended from the Mycenaean Greeks.
3. Perhaps the best way of understanding Greek culture, and the rise of the polis, is as a result of a mix of military cultures.

II. Before we discuss the rise of the city-state, we have to describe what a city-state was and what made it distinctive.

A. The city-state, or polis, is distinguished by a number of social and political elements: the idea of citizenship; the existence of an assembly, an aristocratic council, and elected magistrates.
1. City-states were originally ruled by kings.
2. City-states generally lacked a class of hereditary priests; sacrifices and other rituals were carried out by magistrates elected from among the aristocrats.
3. Military command was also held exclusively by aristocrats.
4. Much of a city-state's land was worked by individual families that owned small farms. This "small-holding" was one of the most distinctive economic features of the Greek city-state.
5. The existence of a class of free citizens also seems to be a very early institution in the polis.
6. An empty gathering place, called the agora, stood at the center of the polis, replacing the temple or palace common in other ancient cities.

B. What were the origins of these distinctive institutions in the Greek city-states?

1. The aristocratic clans had much in common with similar institutions in the steppe cultures.
2. Though the common people in Greek society were often treated with contempt by the aristocracy, they had a relatively high economic position based on their ownership of farms.
3. Wealth brought home by Greeks who served as pirates and mercenaries was often invested in land and trading expeditions.
4. Piracy was quite important in early Greek society. After the Assyrians established control over trade routes in the Near East, the Greeks turned their raids toward Phoenician trading vessels.
5. Eventually, piracy and trading mixed, with trading gradually becoming more profitable than plundering.
6. In the 8th century B.C., the Greeks began establishing colonies to compete with Phoenician trading. Unlike the Phoenician settlements, these colonies were politically independent.

C. The Greek practice of serving as mercenaries for wealthier states may have prompted the development of a system of coinage.

1. The Greeks found coinage highly useful. In addition to paying mercenaries, it could also be used to divide loot and trading profits more easily.
2. Coinage also made it easier for individuals to collect the wealth necessary to buy arms and armor.

III. We do not know exactly when the Greeks adopted the hoplite style of military organization, but it probably occurred before 650 B.C., during the development of the city-states.

A. Greek arms and armor were probably borrowed from the Assyrians.

1. Greek hoplites carried a large round shield called the *hoplon* and often wore breastplates, helmets, and greaves.
2. Hoplites did not fight as individuals. They were organized into phalanxes, which could be hundreds or even thousands of men wide.

B. This shoulder-to-shoulder phalanx method created a new kind of military ideology, one that was incompatible with the aristocratic ideologies we have seen so far.

    1. In this ideology, all citizens are equal, whether aristocratic or not, since they all stand together in the line of battle.

    2. In hoplite warfare, loyalty is not to one's class but to one's city-state.

    3. The most interesting and historically significant element of hoplite warfare was its method of recruitment. If one was wealthy enough to buy armor, one was required to buy it and to serve when called upon. Citizens without wealth were banned from service along with slaves and noncitizens.

    4. This recruitment method allowed city-states to field large armies relative to their size and wealth.

C. While the origins of hoplite warfare remain a mystery, let me suggest one avenue of exploration: Greek piracy and trading.

    1. Greek piracy involved raiding coastal towns and villages, where the heavy armor and tight formation of hoplite warfare could be very effective.

    2. The hoplite method of recruiting may have developed as an efficient way of gathering soldiers from Greek colonies, or it may have been an adaptation of the Assyrian soldier-settler system.

    3. Though the Near Eastern kingdoms did not adopt the hoplite system, it was absorbed by the Etruscans, the Latins, and to some extent the Phoenician colonies.

Suggested Reading:

Van Wees, *Status Warriors*.

Wallinga, *Ships and Sea-Power*.

Questions to Consider:

1. What were the military conditions in Greece that led to the rise of the city-state?

2. Why did the Greeks develop the distinctive hoplite system of warfare?

Lecture Eight—Transcript
Pirates and Hoplites

Welcome Back. Last time, we saw how the rise of the Assyrian Empire created the economic motivation for the development of Mediterranean trade and the Phoenician trading colonies. In today's lecture, we shall see how the wealth of this trade helped lead to the rise of a new and distinctive type of political unit—and culture—the Greek city-state. The city-state has been such an important phenomenon in terms of its impact both in ancient times and its effect on modern political theory that its origins have long been a matter of investigation and debate among scholars.

The elements of the city-state developed in the Greek Dark Ages. Scholars have focused attention on the so-called Dorian invasion, which occurred around 1000 B.C. The Dorians were one of the dialect groups into which Greek is divided. It was the form of Greek spoken by the Spartans, for example. There is good evidence that the Dorians, along with other Greek tribes, migrated south from the Balkans after the fall of the Mycenaean civilization. There is an important point here: The so-called Dark Age culture associated with the Dorians certainly led to the distinctive Greek cultures centered around the city-states. Most of the debate on this issue has focused on ethnicity, a reflection of earlier discussions on race and on cultural issues. The issue is a complex one, but, we might gain some insight by looking at changing military technology and the interaction of some of the military cultures that we have discussed in the last few lectures.

The timing of the Dorian invasion is very suggestive: The era between 1200 and 1000 B.C., when the Mycenaean civilization fell, is not only the time of the Sea Peoples but also of the sword revolution. Indeed, Robert Drews included the Dorian invasion in his discussion of the "Catastrophe" that brought down the palace-centered empires. There are certainly some similarities between the Greeks and the Sea Peoples. There is a great deal of evidence that the early Greek connection to the sea was not just as peaceful fishermen. The English word "pirate" comes from the Greek word *peirato*, and both the *Iliad* and the *Odyssey* illustrate the Greeks in this role. They used *pentakonter*, or "fifty-oared" raiding ship, as is mentioned in Homer's poems and other sources. These ships seem very similar to those illustrated in Egyptian reliefs of their fights with the Sea

Peoples. In addition, some scholars have argued that the names of certain tribes of Sea Peoples correspond to the ethnic groups and names of early Greeks, such as the Achaeans, the name for Greeks used by Homer.

In other ways, the early Greek culture has some sharp distinctions from those we see in the Sea Peoples. For example, Greece has some of the earliest evidence for the use of horses by aristocrats. Greek aristocrats long have had a close relationship with horses, especially in war, although their use is increasingly out of step with actual military practice. In Sparta, for example, we even find an elite group of infantry who are called "the cavalry," because the name itself has such aristocratic prestige. Indeed, there is a great deal in early Greek culture that is reminiscent of steppe culture. And many legends, including those of the wars with the Amazons and of wise men among the Scythians, are suggestive of such connections. It should be remembered that the northern Balkans, where the Dorians and others migrated from, is right next to the westernmost portion of the steppes, for example, the Hungarian and Bulgarian plains.

Whereas there is a tendency for historians, including military historians, to look at the development of Greece as an isolated phenomenon, it is in fact a part culturally, of the Near East, just as much in the period of the rise of the city-state as it was in the Mycenaean period. This connection is reflected in the mercenary service that was common among the Greeks. References in the Bible suggest that Greek mercenaries were present there at an early stage, perhaps going back to the 11th century B.C. In fact, it is possible that some of the military forces that King David used to put down his son's rebellion were Greeks. Herodotus writes that after Greek mercenaries helped an Egyptian king take power, that king set up a garrison of Greek settler soldiers on one of the branches of the Nile. This developed into the Greek colony of Naucratis, which was founded in 620 B.C.

Perhaps the best indication of the impact of mercenary service by Greeks in the Near East is the fact that the early Greeks obviously borrowed from the Assyrians certain of the arms and armor, for example, the iron helmet, the round convex shield, the spear as a primary weapon, and the iron sword as a sidearm. As we shall see, the Greeks will make distinctive use of these weapons, but their Near Eastern origin should not be neglected.

Finally, there seems to be a certain amount of military continuity from the earlier Mycenaean civilizations. It has been suggested that the other major Greek dialect group, the Ionians, were descended from the Mycenaean Greeks, and that the Ionians' migration around 1000 B.C. to western Anatolia, subsequently called Ionia, was due to the Dorian invasion pushing them out of Greece. In any case, we know that unlike most Greek cities, Athens, where Ionian was spoken, was inhabited continuously from Mycenaean times through the Dark Ages, although it shrank to the size of a village.

One indication of some military continuity from the previous Mycenaean culture is in a section of the *Iliad* a section setting out the contingents from various Greek regions to the Trojan War. This is called by scholars the Catalog of Ships. What is striking is that the cities that were important in the Mycenaean Age, such as Mycenae itself, provide large contingents, although when Homer was writing, the site was abandoned. On the other hand, places that were powerful states later, but were small in Mycenaean times, are shown with minor contributions.

Perhaps the most significant feature of the Greek city-state that is left over from Mycenaean times is the use of a highpoint as a citadel or, as the Greeks called it, an acropolis. Perhaps the best way of understanding Greek culture, and the rise of the polis, is not to think of "Greekness," that is the cultural features of a particular ethnic group, but that the city-state results from a mix of military cultures: an urban culture left over from the Mycenaean period, the steppe culture from the north, and the elements of the sword revolution, as well as elements borrowed from the Near Eastern empires, such as Assyria.

In addition, we should put the rise of the city-state in the context of the political events of the time: the rise of the Assyrian empire, its demand for silver to pay its armies, and the resulting Phoenician colonization movement that we discussed in the last lecture.

Of course, before we discuss the rise of the city-state, we have to describe what a city-state was and what made it distinctive. The city-state, or *polis* as the Greeks called it, is distinguished by a number of social and political elements: the idea of citizenship, the existence of an assembly, as well as an aristocratic council and elected magistrates.

The Greek city-states were originally ruled by kings. But these kings were not of the Near Eastern type, but resembled more a tribal chief, the hereditary or elected leader of a group of aristocrats who shared power. In early times, the aristocratic clans held a monopoly of political power and also religious authority. The city-states generally lacked a class of hereditary priests, and sacrifices and other rituals were carried out by magistrates elected from among the aristocrats. In the same way, military command was also held exclusively by aristocrats. The aristocrats also a great deal of economic power based on large landholdings, sometimes worked by serfs, and they had large households, with personal retainers and slaves.

One of the most interesting and important features of the city-state is that much of its land was worked by individual families owning small farms. Indeed, small-holding is one of the most distinctive economic features of the Greek city-state. The existence of a class of free citizens also seems to be a very early institution. From very early times there is an assembly of these free citizens, although it had little real power at first.

The city-state also had some distinctive architectural features, or rather the lack of them: Rather than the large temple or palace that stood at the center of Near Eastern (and other ancient) cities, the Greek *polis*, city-state, had an empty space, called the "agora," rather than a temple or palace standing at its center. Traditionally, "agora" is translated as "marketplace." But it was also the site of the gathering of the army, out of which developed the Greek assembly. The Greek assembly actually met in the marketplace. It's possible that its original function might be related to the piracy that we'll talk later about, that it was a place to distribute loot rather than to trade.

But let's get back to this question of origins. The aristocratic clans in Greece have much in common with similar institutions among the steppe people. For example, there is a strict division between the "well-born," as they were called, and the common people. Indeed, Greek aristocrats felt more attachment to aristocrats of other peoples, even of non-Greeks, than of the common people of their own city-state. Now this was not a feature of the urban society of the Near East.

Aristocrats led their clans into battle but also led plundering expeditions, as illustrated in Homer's writings, as well as commanding and leading mercenary units, again probably drawn from their clan and retainers. There was a distinct aristocratic ideology. The *Iliad* and the *Odyssey* were clearly written for an aristocratic audience and reflect its ideas. Many of the features of the aristocratic ideology in Greece are reminiscent of later noble ideologies around the core: the focus on courageous, even reckless, behavior in battle, a focus on the nobility and fame of one's ancestors, the desire to add to this tradition through one's own actions, especially in battle, a disdain for merchants and money-making, and the importance of showing generosity, especially to other aristocrats. Common people are either ignored, or treated with contempt, a constant theme in Homer's writings.

On the other hand, as we have noted, the common people in Greek city-states had a relatively high economic position based on their ownership of farms. We have an alternate vision in the ideology of this small-holding class in the writings of Hesiod, who was a contemporary of Homer, but clearly wrote for the common people. In his book *Works and Days*, Hesiod's attitude towards aristocrats, for example, is quite hostile, and he sees them as self-serving and hypocritical. Another target of Hesiod's criticism is his brother, who he thinks is foolish in investing his money in a trading expedition. This indicates that such investments were not unusual and that trading income was not confined to aristocrats. This brings us to another important point.

Where did the money to buy farms and to invest in trading come from? This was perhaps a function of the income brought back by Greeks serving under the aristocrats as pirates and mercenaries. Although on the steppes, such plunder that was distributed by clan leaders would have been transformed into herds. In Greece the same wealth distributed by clan leaders had to either be invested in land or in trading expeditions.

I have mentioned the importance of piracy in early Greek society. But who were the targets of these raids? Certainly, the Near Eastern states, as well as other cities and even coastal villages would be tempting targets, and this is the sort of raid illustrated in the *Iliad*. Yet, by the 8th and 7th centuries B.C., the Near East was controlled by a powerful, military state, the Assyrians, and coastal raids could be quite risky. Fortunately for the Greeks, another target was available: the Phoenician trading vessels that were bringing silver and other valuable objects from Spain right past Greece to ports in Phoenicia. The contents of these ships no doubt bought many a Greek farm.

The work of David Tandy, an archaeologist and classics professor at the University of Tennessee, focuses on the economics of this period of Greek history. In his book *Warriors into Traders*, Tandy traces how the early Greeks mixed piracy and trading. This is quite a common pattern, and we shall see how seafaring peoples often mix the two, raiding weak settlements and trading with strong ones. Tandy shows how, given the enormous profits to be made from moving goods through the Mediterranean to the Near East, trading gradually became more profitable for the Greeks than plundering.

As a result, in competition with the Phoenicians, in the 8th century, the Greeks began establishing colonies of their own to profit from the trade into Assyria and its successor states, such as Egypt, Babylonia, and others. By the 7th century, these Greek colonies stretched from the Black Sea to Spain, and were especially common in Sicily and Southern Italy, so much so that this region was called "Great Greece." Like the Phoenician ones, Greek colonies were sent out by a mother city (the metropolis), but although the new colony shared political and culture elements with its founder, the new city was politically independent. Of course, these cities needed to feed themselves as well as trade, and distributed land to colonies as small farms.

I have already mentioned the Greek practice of mercenary service in the more advanced and wealthier states of the Near East. Some of these mercenaries served in the kingdom of Lydia, in central Anatolia. While it was the Near Eastern custom to pay mercenaries in silver, since the money went to the aristocratic leader, it could be made in the form of silver bars, or other forms, and then the wealth distributed to individual soldiers in other forms, such as grain or cattle or land. By the 7th century, this model may have started to change, and it is possible that individual Greeks, such as Hesiod's greedy brother Perses, may have looked to mercenary service as well as trading as a source of income. This is only speculation, but a practice of recruiting individual mercenaries, and the need to pay them in small units, may explain the introduction of the first system of coinage by the Lydians, which occurred in the middle of the 7th century B.C.

Whatever its origins, the Greeks found coinage highly useful, given the rather free-wheeling nature of their economy. Coins allowed for not only mercenary pay, but loot, and the results of trading expeditions to be divided up more easily. And as I've mentioned before, this may well have happened in the agora. Of course, it had other advantages that were not related to warfare, but it is striking that coinage spreads rapidly among the Greeks, but is not used very much, if at all, by other, more developed economies, at least in this period.

Coinage had another advantage. It made it easier for individuals to collect the wealth necessary to buy arms and armor. This brings up to another distinctive feature of the Greek city-state: hoplite warfare. We don't know exactly when the Greeks adopted this style of military organization, nor whether it was a slow development or a military revolution of sorts. It occurred sometime before 650 B.C., which places it in this period of the development of the city-state.

As I mentioned before, Greek arms and armor were probably borrowed directly or indirectly from the Assyrians. The name hoplite derived from the Greek *hoplon*, the name for the large round convex shield about three feet across. This protected the hoplite's chest, although they often also wore a breastplate in addition. The head was protected by a helmet: originally just an iron cap, like the Assyrian one. One does see crests of horsehair on some Assyrian helmets, but on Greek models, these horsehair crests grow larger and more elaborate. Especially striking is the way that cheek pieces and a nose protector were added, and these eventually developed into what is called the "Corinthian helmet." This provides a great deal of protection to the face but at the cost of vision and hearing. As we shall see, this development in armor is closely associated with the way the hoplites fought. As if this were not enough armor, however, hoplites wore greaves to protect the lower leg which was exposed under the shield.

Hoplites did not fight as individuals. Another distinctive feature of hoplite warfare is the phalanx, in which hoplites stood in ranks and files, close enough so that the shields of the front rank formed a continuous shield wall. These phalanxes ranged from about six to twelve men deep, but could be hundreds or even thousands of men wide. There is an ongoing debate among military historians on how exactly hoplites fought. Originally, scholars visualized the front ranks of the phalanxes dueling with spears, and then when wounded or exhausted being replaced by a fresh soldier behind. Victor Davis Hanson developed a very compelling theory that the phalanx fought not by such dueling, but rather by pushing against the opposing phalanx, literally trying to break the enemy's line. Which theory is correct need not concern us here.

What is significant for the development of the city-state, however, is that shoulder-to-shoulder fighting created a new kind of military ideology, one that was incompatible with the aristocratic one. As we have seen, aristocrats valued courage, even reckless courage, running ahead of one's colleagues to challenge and fight enemy aristocrats, as is seen and praised in Homer's writings. This was not only useless in hoplite warfare, but counterproductive, as it would create a hole in the line. In part because of the nature of hoplite warfare we have the development of a new kind of Greek ideology, one that is reflected in the writings of Hesiod. Ancient historians call this the "middling ideology," another term I am not very happy with. Let's go with "hoplite ideology," as it is more keeping with the military theme of this series.

We shall explore the ramifications of this new hoplite ideology in a later lecture, but for now let's sketch out its basic features. In it all citizens are equal, whether aristocrats or not, since they stand together in the line of battle. Courage was still an important virtue: However the phalanx fought, whether a duel or a push, being in the front row took special courage, and one could gain prestige by volunteering to serve there. For most soldiers, however, courage was defined by holding fast, not running away, but standing together with one's neighbors and fellow citizens. A very important part of the new hoplite ideology is that one's loyalty is not to one's class but to one's city-state. Citizenship is not just a political status, it is a new way of thinking about oneself and one's relation to the state, and this is due at least in part, if not in large part, to hoplite warfare.

The most interesting and historically significant element of hoplite warfare is its method of recruitment. In virtually every city-state, each and every citizen who was wealthy enough to purchase hoplite equipment had to do so. They had to fight for the state when called upon. Citizens not wealthy enough to buy armor, along with slaves and non-citizens, were not only not required to serve, they were banned from service in the hoplite forces. From an ideological point of view, this is quite remarkable, especially from a 21st century perspective. We are used to the saying "a rich man's war and a poor man's fight" and the idea that not only were the rich required to fight but that only the rich were allowed to fight is difficult to believe. Nevertheless, it is a feature of almost every Greek city-state. Its advantages are obvious. One does not need an elaborate tax structure to get the money from the rich in order to arm the poor. Nor does one have to rely on a system of large landholdings run by serfs but can use the more efficient small farm. In addition, it doesn't matter where the citizen's wealth comes from: It could as easily be from trading or mercenary service as from land.

This aspect of the hoplite system allowed city-states to field large armies relative to their size and wealth. Athens, for example, had a population of some 300,000 in the 5th century B.C., and could raise a hoplite army of 30,000 men. In way of comparison, the army of New Kingdom Egypt was about the same size, although it had ten times the population of classical Athens, about three million. Even very small city-states, and most were small, could raise military forces in this way.

As we shall see in a later lecture, the hoplite system had many political and social ramifications that are important even today. One of the reasons for this is that the hoplite is, to be frank, quite weird. It has a number of features that are difficult to explain, and this is one reason for cultural explanations, such as Victor Hanson's. While I do not pretend to be able to explain the mystery of the origins of hoplite warfare in a few lines, let me suggest an avenue of exploration, and that is, counter-intuitively, Greek piracy and trading. The Greek hoplite system may seem very ill suited for sea-borne expeditions, although it also very ill-suited for the hilly terrain of Greece. Let us consider however, that Greek piracy did not occur, at least originally on the high seas. The Greek pentakonter could not possibly have captured a Phoenician cargo ship by boarding, and we never find a description of this. Rather, piracy involved raiding coastal towns and villages.

In such raids, what is desirable is getting in and getting out of a village without suffering casualties. Here is where the heavy armor and tight formation of hoplite warfare might well be very effective, especially against the sword-wielding peoples along the coasts of Italy, Gaul, and Spain. The same principle would apply in order to defend colonies against attacks by these same peoples. The Greeks were not interested in conquering vast stretches of territory inland, where they could be surrounded, but only in holding on to enough land to feed a trading colony. Defense was more important than attack, and one can see that the hoplite system would have been ideal for this purpose. The Greek-on-Greek battles that occurred between city-states, whatever their nature then, would have been a later development, and not the initial system.

The hoplite system of recruiting, which was highly efficient, may also have derived from the colonial system, where because of the small numbers in the colony, efficiency at recruiting was at a premium. However, it might have another origin. In some respects, it resembles the soldier-settler system used by the Assyrians, with the change that instead of owing service to the king, one owes it to one's own city. It is conceivable that the idea for the hoplite recruiting system was brought back by mercenaries who had served in the Near East.

Despite its efficiency, the Near Eastern Kingdoms did not adopt the hoplite system. They had subjects, not citizens, and naturally were uninterested in allowing them to arm themselves. This might well lead to uprisings and, as we shall see, that's exactly the effect it had in Greece. The kings could easily simply continue to use Greek mercenaries, which they did.

On the other hand, the Greek hoplite system does spread. It is certainly used by the Etruscans in northern Italy and is also adopted by the Latins, including the tiny city-state of Rome, in central Italy. The case of the Phoenicians is a bit more complex. In some respects colonies, such as Carthage, resembled Greek city-states. In fact Aristotle, in his description of city-state constitution, lays out that of Carthage with no indication at all that is not a Greek polis. The Greek and Carthaginian city-states certainly shared some features, like elected magistrates. Although the Carthaginians often used mercenaries, there is some evidence of a hoplite system as well, but this is not at all clear.

As we have seen in this lecture, the development of the distinctive Greek political and military system, the city-state and hoplite warfare, did not occur in isolation from the changes, especially the military changes, occurring in the core. In my next lecture, we will look at the changing political and military institutions that were transforming empires in both the west and the east.

Lecture Nine
Great Empires of West and East

Scope:

After the fall of the Assyrian Empire, a number of independent states developed: The Median Empire, with their Scythian allies, had a steppe-style government. Babylonia took over much of the urban regions and used Assyrian administration and settler soldiers, as did Egypt under the Saite dynasty. Anatolia was controlled by Lydia, which pioneered the use of coinage to pay mercenaries. All these kingdoms were incorporated into the Persian Empire in the 6th century B.C. The Persians successfully combined both the Assyrian and the steppe military systems. Steppe and urban systems were also combined in India and China, and we find the rise of cavalry in West Africa as well. The use of coinage or its equivalent differed in various areas but was an important element in supporting armies.

Outline

I. Before and after the fall of the Assyrian Empire, the Near East suffered a series of devastating invasions of steppe people.

  A. The 50 years after the fall of Nineveh were ones of very intense fighting throughout the region.

    1. The Scythians did not just raid; they migrated into and occupied northern Iran and became important allies of the Medes.

    2. The Babylonians took over much of what had been the Assyrian Empire: all of Mesopotamia and Syria, as well as Phoenicia and the provinces that had been Israel.

    3. The Babylonians adopted the Assyrian use of settler soldiers.

  B. Egypt had only recently been incorporated into the Assyrian Empire, and after the fall of Nineveh it again became an independent nation under the Saite dynasty.

    1. According to Herodotus, who visited the country well over a century later, the Egyptians had a hereditary military class.

    2. We happen to know about two foreign settler-soldier units as well, a settlement of Greek soldiers in the north and one of Jewish soldiers in the south.

3. The final kingdom was Lydia, which seems to have had an army similar to the prehoplite Greeks. Their control of gold mines made them very wealthy, and they used at least some of this money to supplement their forces with mercenaries.

C. Beginning around 560 B.C., an imperial power arose that would reunite the Near East and extend its power into Europe and India. This was the Persian Empire.

   1. Its founder, Cyrus the Great, conquered Media, Babylonia, and Lydia. His son added Egypt to the empire.

   2. A later king, Darius I, created the highly effective Persian imperial system, which ruled the western core for the next 200 years.

   3. Best known for his unsuccessful attack on Greece, Darius led a series of campaigns that pacified the northern frontier and ended the threat of the steppe peoples.

II. Darius and his successors instituted a number of reforms, both in the military and in the administration that supported it.

A. The Persians left the Assyrian provincial system in place and did not insist on standardization among their territories.

   1. The Persians generally allowed members of the local elite to govern the provinces.

   2. There were two types of military forces in the Persian Empire. One was the levy—locals who were conscripted into military service either to repel a local attack or to take part in an imperial expedition.

   3. The real backbone of local defense and of the army in general was the settler soldiers.

B. On top of the Assyrian-style provincial administration, the Persians also successfully incorporated a steppe nobility, with its military advantages.

   1. The Persian king and the royal government were not placed in an urban center; rather, they migrated through a series of palace complexes.

   2. Persian nobles also generally did not live in the cities. They were known for their rural villas, where they could live in luxury and maintain their horsemanship.

   3. The Persians developed a level of government above the province and below the palace, called the satrapy.

4. The satrap was a kind of steppe chieftain placed over the urban population who commanded local levies and settler soldiers, as well regular Persian infantry units.

5. The eastern parts of the Persian Empire were also divided into provinces and satrapies, but actual rule was left in the hands of the local steppe peoples.

C. The Persian system benefited from allowing local autonomy, but central control was maintained in a number of ways.

1. A very important element was the idea of the "king of kings" as a peacemaker, both in rhetoric and reality. He was portrayed to his subjects as a lawgiver and fair arbitrator.

2. The king also sent royal commissioners to take control of localities and employed agents to keep him informed.

3. The Persians retained and improved the Assyrian road and postal systems and introduced a standard system of weights and measurements, all of which fostered trade.

III. The steppe peoples had not only invaded the West; they had also moved into India and China, with results that were similar to those seen in the Near East.

A. India can be seen as part of the same military culture as the western part of the core.

1. The arms and armor were the same: high-quality iron weapons and infantry armed with spears, bows, and swords.

2. The Indians also had cavalry, clearly influenced by the methods of the steppe warriors.

3. We find Indian military units organized as communities or guilds. It is likely that this was the institution of settler soldiers, whether borrowed from the West or developed independently.

4. Toward the end of this period, northern India united under the powerful Nanda Kingdom, which had a large standing army supported by an efficient administration and tax system.

B. In China, the Shang dynasty was defeated and replaced by the Chou dynasty sometime around 1000 B.C.

1. The ritual position of the king was inherited from the Shang dynasty, but like the Assyrians, the Chou dynasty was highly militaristic and expansionist.

2. Like many of the earlier Western empires, the Chou instituted a chariot nobility, called the *shih*.
3. Chou armies were organized into units, often decimal, that consisted of both native and foreign troops.
4. The Chou were very effective at expanding their power, establishing military colonies and districts and forming a civilian administration.
5. Villages were reorganized around five-household units, which were collectively responsible for providing taxes and conscripts for the army.
6. This was also the period of the independent development of Chinese coinage.
7. A "coin line" develops, which persists into early modern times. To the west, gold and silver coins are used; to the east they are not.

C. Gold and silver coins were also absent in the growing civilization in West Africa, along the Niger River.

Suggested Reading:

Head, *The Achaemenid Persian Army.*

Yates, "Early China."

Questions to Consider:

1. How did the Persians integrate the urban and steppe regions?
2. What common elements are seen in all the empires of the core in this period?

Lecture Nine—Transcript
Great Empires of West and East

Welcome back. In last time's lecture, I discussed how the development of the Assyrian Empire, as well as other factors, led to the rise of the Greek city-state. Today, we will look at how after the fall of the Assyrian Empire, and of its successor states, the Persian Empire expands until it not only unites the Near East but incorporates parts of Europe and India into a state for the first time in world history. In the East, in a similar way, the fall of the Shang dynasty leads to the expansionist Chou Empire.

One of our main sources of information about the Assyrian empire is the vast library of Assurbanipal. After this king's death in 627 B.C., a sort of veil descends on the historical record, and even the course of political events in the last decade of the empire is very unclear. Therefore, we cannot really say what internal factors [or] external enemies might have left Assyria so vulnerable. We can say for certain however, that in 612 B.C., the capital of Assyria, Nineveh, was sacked by a combined army of Babylonians and Medes, two subject peoples who had revolted.

Both before and after the fall of the Assyrian Empire, the Near East had suffered a series of devastating invasions from steppe peoples: the Scythians, the Cimmerians, and others. Obviously the steppe populations had grown to the point, and the tribes had become wealthy enough to arm themselves with modern equipment: in this case, iron weapons and composite bows. Clearly they had already developed the tactics necessary to defeat the armies of urban regions. These invasions need to be put in the context of the constant fighting of the Assyrians with their subject peoples and the successor states to them. Thus the 50 years after the fall of Nineveh in 612 were ones of very intense fighting throughout the Near East.

The Scythians, however, the stepped people, did not just raid. They migrated into and occupied northern Iran, very valuable as horse-breeding country. Indeed, they had been important allies of the Medes. After the Medes defeated the Assyrians, they had created a Median empire, but the eastern part of Iran was actually controlled by the Scythians. This fact is important in understanding the later Persian government in that area, and we will return to it.

These allies, the Babylonians, were ruled by an Aramaean dynasty, which had descended from the Chaldean tribe. The New or Neo-Babylonian Empire took over much of what had been the Assyrian empire: that is, Mesopotamia and Syria, as well as Phoenicia and the provinces that had been Israel, Galilee and Samaria. The Neo-Babylonian Empire also adopted the Assyrian manner of administration and, although we have few sources, it seems they also organized their army in a very similar manner, especially in their use of settler soldiers. The book of II Kings of the Bible, which is one of the most historically accurate, tells us that when the Babylonian King Nebuchadnezzar took Jerusalem he deported not only the Jewish king and the Jewish aristocracy to Babylon but also 7,000 soldiers of the Jewish royal army, who were no doubt settled somewhere in Babylonia and were incorporated into the Babylonian army.

There are two other major empires in the Near East in this period. Egypt had only recently been incorporated into the Assyrian Empire when Nineveh fell, and it again became an independent nation. According to Herodotus, who visited the country well over a century later, the Egyptians had a hereditary military class, which again might refer to Egyptian settler soldiers. We happen to know about two foreign settler-soldier units as well: There was a settlement of Greek soldiers in the north in the Delta region and one of Jewish soldiers in the south near the border of Nubia. There were certainly many others.

The fourth kingdom that replaced the Assyrian Empire was Lydia, which we have mentioned earlier in the context of the invention of coinage. The Lydians seem to have had an army in some respects similar to the pre-hoplite army of the Greeks. Aristocrats provided cavalry, who were especially famous for their skill with the lance. Infantry was raised from Lydian cities, and from conquered peoples, such as the Ionian Greeks. Since the Lydians controlled gold mines and were very rich, they used at least some of this money to supplement their forces with mercenaries, Greeks, and others.

Beginning around 560 B.C., we see the rise of an imperial power that succeeds not only in reuniting the Near East in a single empire, but of expanding its power westward into Europe and eastward to the borders of India. This empire will succeed in stemming the tide of barbarian steppe invasions and establishing a 300-year period of relative peace and security. This was the Persian Empire.

Its founder, Cyrus the Great, defeated and conquered three of the successor states in turn: first Media, then Babylonia, then Lydia. Before turning to the wealthy region of Egypt, however, Cyrus led an expedition against the Scythians, which he clearly thought more important. He died in this war, but his son did add Egypt to the Persian realm.

While the Persian Empire is founded by Cyrus, it was a later king, Darius I, who created the highly effective Persian imperial system, which ruled the heart of the western core for the next several centuries. Darius was an usurper. He was a distant relative of the previous king, at best, and probably the murderer of the rightful heir, the king's brother. His propaganda, however, shown on the enormous sculptured relief found at Bisutun, portrays him as the dynasty's savior and the king's brother as an imposter.

Despite these questions of his character, Darius was indeed a brilliant general and politician much like Sargon before him or Augustus and Napoleon after him. He is best known for his unsuccessful attack on Greece, which ended at the battle of Marathon. He did lead a series of successful campaigns that pacified the northern quarter with the steppes. Partly through force and partly, as we shall see, through accommodation, Darius succeeded in ending the threat of the steppe peoples.

Darius and his successors instituted a number of reforms both in the military and in the administration that supported it. The Persians take a revolutionary approach to government, which turns out to be highly successful. They have what is in essence a two-level state. The basis of the empire—the first level—is this highly productive urbanized system that had developed over the past several thousands of years. The Persians left the Assyrian provincial system in place, and generally let members of the local elite, sometimes even local kings, rule not only villages, towns, and cities, but often provinces themselves. The Persians did not insist on standardization but allowed local variation in governing. So while Babylonia was ruled as it had been under the Assyrian Empire, with a Babylonian governor, the Greeks in Ionia retained their city-state system. We know the case of the Jews in the province of Judah in some detail, as the books of Ezra and Nehemiah in the Bible focus on the establishment of a theocratic government there by a High Priest. And that is instituted by, and is loyal to, the Persian government.

Under the Persians, there were two types of local military forces. One was the traditional levy, that is locals who were conscripted into military service, either to repel a local attack, or to take part in an imperial expedition. As had been the case for centuries, in most of the regions of the Near East, men could be drafted either into labor projects or into military service, a sort of tax on labor. These troops could be useful if defending their own homes or districts, but were not very effective otherwise. The real backbone of local defense and of the army in general were the settler soldiers. These were often foreigners, in the sense that they differed in ethnicity from the locals, and were not Persians. But it must be recalled that they lived in a region for generations and so, in that sense, they were locals.

The Jewish military unit at Elephantine, an island in the Nile, is known from a cache of Aramaic papyri, which was discovered there and has given us a lot of detail. This unit was probably established around 650 B.C. and served the Egyptians during the Saite period until it was incorporated in the Persian army in the 5th century. This Jewish unit had its own temple to the Jewish god, and one can guess that this was rather typical. Probably the soldier-settlers had their own religion that they worshiped in their villages. The relationship with the local Egyptians was rather hostile, not least of which over the question of religion but, from the Persian point of view, this was not a bad thing. The unit served partly to guard the frontier with Nubia to the south, but it was also there to maintain Persian control in Egypt. So it was good that relations with the locals weren't that great. The Greek settler soldiers who had served the Saite Egyptians at Naucratis, no doubt continued to do so under the Persians.

This system of local control was fairly successful in most cases, and the Persians suffered far fewer uprising than either the Assyrians or the Babylonians. There were exceptions. One is the Greek city-states in Ionia, which were restive perhaps due to the proximity of the independent Greek states across the Aegean. The other was Egypt, which was in an almost constant state of rebellion. Unlike the Assyrians, and really unlike their normal practice, the Persians really took over the Egyptian religion. The king took over the religious persona of the Egyptian king, that is of a god, and thus the Persians were not only political monarchs, but actually deities in the Egyptian religion. This led to a great deal of unhappiness in Egypt. In addition, the Persians used minority groups, such as the Jews and the Greeks, in both the administration and military. In addition, no doubt due to the wealth of Egypt, we have far more Persians moving to Egypt than elsewhere, taking over as local landowners and administrators, which probably also fed local unhappiness. In any case, there were a series of revolts and, at some points in Persian history, Egypt won its independence sometimes for decades at a time.

Despite these revolts, however, the success of the Persian Empire in controlling the very productive urban areas is indicated by a number of factors: the anecdotal evidence of the Greeks, who were always impressed by the wealth and luxury not only of the Persian nobles, but of the empire as a whole; of archaeology which shows it to be a period of expansion in population and in agricultural production; and in the fact that when Alexander the Great took over the Persian treasuries, he found them full of literally tons of gold and silver. Clearly the Persians were not running a deficit.

The success of the Persians was partly due to the second part of their two-part state. The Persians successfully incorporated a steppe nobility and especially its military advantages, on top of the Assyrian-style provincial administration. The Persians themselves maintained themselves culturally and even physically separate from the urban population to try and maintain their steppe traditions, especially military ones. The king and the royal government was not placed in an urban center, as had been the case with Nineveh or Babylon. Rather the Persian kings had a series of palace complexes built far from the urban areas, and migrated, in pastoral fashion, from summer to winter palaces. The king and nobility also retained a focus on skill in horsemanship and battle. In his royal inscriptions, Darius emphasizes his personal strength, his skill at riding and at shooting the bow. Persian kings, at least in the earlier years, actually led their troops in battle, as we have seen Cyrus was killed fighting the Scythians.

Persian nobles also generally did not live in the cities. They were know for their rural villas, where they could both live in luxury, but also ride horses and hunt, maintaining their martial skills as well as enjoying themselves. Interestingly enough, these rural nobles got quite interested in horticulture, and their enclosed gardens were quite famous for their beauty. Indeed the Persian name for these gardens was "paradise," which we know was not only borrowed into Greek but into Hebrew as well. Gardening might not seem to be the most military of hobbies but, in fact, has been and continues to be quite a popular pastime for military men. There was a training program initiated to introduce young Persians to the steppe military methods and culture. And we find out about this from a number of sources, including Greek one. The Persians were quite concerned that luxury would undermine the discipline and military effectiveness of their youth, an idea that we will run into again and again.

From an administrative point of view, the Persians developed a level of government above the province and below the palace. This was called the "satrapy," and was introduced by Darius. The satrapy was made up from a number of provinces, from a few to a dozen, and was always ruled by a Persian. This innovation is often seen by historians as a way of making the large number of provinces more manageable, but the satrapy was never another level of bureaucracy. Rather it was a kind of steppe chieftainship, placed over the urban population. The satrap could command local levies and settler soldiers, but he also maintained Persian troops. Persian nobles living in satrapy provided both military leadership and the core of the cavalry forces. There were also regular Persian infantry units in garrisons who were placed under the command of the satrap. The Persians introduced the steppe custom of decimal military organization, and units were organized in the hundreds, thousands, and tens of thousands. The king had his own units, for example, the 10,000-man royal guard, which is called the "Immortals."

There was another way in which the Persians successfully combined the urban and the steppe. While most of the focus of scholars is on the western part of the Persian Empire, which is not surprising because our sources are from there, our interest is there in the Greeks, and the Jews, and the Egyptians. Yet the Persian Empire spread to the east as well, covering all of modern Iran and Afghanistan and much of modern Pakistan. The eastern border was the Indus River, and the kingdoms of India were its neighbors. This broad area was also divided into provinces and satrapies, but actual rule was left in the hands of local steppe peoples: the Scythians in Iran, and the Bactrians and Sogdians in what's now Afghanistan. This was one way in which the Persians managed to end the steppe attacks on the urban center: that is by sharing power with them. These semi-autonomous steppe kingdoms in the east also provided much of the cavalry that the Persians used in their campaigns.

The Persian system benefited by allowing local autonomy, but central control was maintained in a number of ways. The steppe notion of kinship and a collective identity as steppe peoples was carefully fostered to help keep the ruling class loyal to the king. A very important element was the idea of the "King of Kings," which was introduced and spread to urban areas. The King of Kings was seen as a peacemaker, both in rhetoric and reality. The king's role as a warrior was emphasized to the internal audience, but he was portrayed to his subjects (such as the Jews) as a lawgiver and a fair arbitrator. Very interesting that King Cyrus, who was called "Koresh" in Hebrew, is the first person in the Bible to be named a messiah.

The king also sent royal commissioners to take control of localities when necessary. The prophet Nehemiah, who has a book in the Bible, was actually a Persian royal official. He worked in the palace and was sent to Jerusalem by the king as a commissioner to rebuild the city walls and also, one guesses, to take control of a restive situation, or some sort of difficult political situation. We don't really know what it was. In addition to such commissioners, there were agents called the "Eyes of the King," who kept the king informed. The Persians retained and improved the Assyrian road and postal system, which Herodotus praises for its efficiency.

The royal roads, and the overall security introduced by Persian rule, fostered trade, as did Darius's introduction of a standard system of weights and measures. Darius also introduced gold coins, which he modestly named after himself. They're called "darics." And these were used all over the empire. A silver coin, called a "shekel," was also produced, but it had a more limited circulation. Along with the Greek circulation of coins to the west, we see the development of a coinage system based on precious metals, gold and silver. The use of gold and silver in the form of coins is going to continue to be a feature of economies in the western part of the core. Although as we shall see, not in the eastern part.

The steppe peoples had not only invaded the west, they had moved into India and China, with results that were very similar to those that we have just discussed. Unfortunately, although we know that there were powerful kingdoms in India at the time of the Assyrians and Persians, we are not very well informed about this period of Indian history. The various kingdoms called Janapadas, in Indian history, vied for power. These kingdoms were ruled by dynasties that claimed descent from the Aryan invaders of the Vedic period, and sometimes they're called Aryan kings.

Much of our information about this period is gleaned from various parts of the Buddhist Pali Canon and the Vedas, both religious texts that are hard to use and, unfortunately, very difficult to date. Some of the military information, especially that which is prior to the Mauryan dynasty, may come from this period, but with like dealing with the Bible or with Homeric texts, it's very difficult to say.

Because of our sources, the vocabulary used in Indian history is quite different than in the West and can be confusing. If we look at India as part of the same military culture as the rest of the core, at least the western part of the core, then it begins to make more sense. And I'm going to avoid using technical Indian terminology and just try to explain it. In the first place, the arms and armor are the same. By this time the Indians are using high-quality iron weapons, their infantry relying primarily on the spear and the bow, but also using the sword, as in the West. The Indian bow had some distinctive qualities: It was made of bamboo and the Indians were the first to use iron arrowheads, but these difference are relatively minor.

The Indians also had a cavalry, although unfortunately we don't know a lot about it. It is clear, however, that like the Assyrians and the Persians, the Indians used both steppe warriors as allies and auxiliaries and also adopted, to some extent, the methods of steppe warriors for their own cavalry. As in the West, and as we shall see in China as well, cavalry did not immediately replace chariots, which continued to be used. Indeed, chariots have a much longer history in India than elsewhere, partly because the Indians "go back to the future" as it were, redesigning the chariot as a four-wheeled heavy platform for archers, reminiscent of the original Sumerian model. These chariots survive in Indian religious customs and are used in the Jaganatha festival, from which our word "juggernaut" derives.

There is one element of Indian warfare that is completely different and that is the use of elephants in war. It is unclear how far back this goes, but by the Janapada period, elephants are definitely being used. Elephants can be quite effective, especially against horses, which hate the smell of them, and inexperienced infantry, which are likely to panic. Elephants are difficult to manage, however, and when wounded can be quite as dangerous to one's own troops as the enemy. They are also voracious eaters, as every army that subsequently adopted them soon discovered.

In our Indian sources we see references to military units and communities that are organized as so-called "sanghas," which literally means "community" or as a "sreni," which means a guild. Exactly how and whether these terms are different and exactly what they mean is a matter of great debate. It seems very likely though that what we see here is the institution of settler soldiers, whether borrowed from the West or independently developed. There is another kind of military sangha, the gana-sangha, which in Indian histories is generally called a "republic" although they sometimes had kings. The complicated question of their political organization aside, these gana-sanghas seem to have been communities of steppe peoples. One is the so-called "Kambojas," an Iranian tribe that lived in northwestern India. The Kambojas retained their steppe culture for centuries, like the Persians did, and provided cavalry for many subsequent Indian dynasties.

Toward the end of the period we are discussing, northern India is united into a single state. First the Magadha dynasty and then the Nanda dynasty that replaces it, expand their powers, defeating and absorbing the Janapada kingdoms, until the Nanda king rules from the Indus Valley down the Ganges as far east as Bengal. The Nanda kingdom had a large standing army, supported by an efficient administration and tax system. Indeed, it is the first of the great empires of India, although it is generally ignored outside of Indian historiography.

Let's look at the situation farther east, in China. The Shang dynasty was defeated and replaced by the Chou dynasty around 1000 B.C. The ritual position of the king was inherited from the Shang dynasty, but like the Assyrians. the Chou dynasty was highly militaristic and expansionistic. Our first Chinese historical narrative to survive, called the *Spring and Autumn Anal*, says that the important affairs of a state are carrying out sacrifices, that is, the ritual part of the king, and carrying on war, that is, the military part of the king.

Like many of the western empires a few centuries later, the Chou instituted a chariot-nobility. A member of this class was called a "shih," which in this period meant a noble, but later on is going to take on the meaning of "gentleman" or "gentry" in the Confucian sense. We will discuss this process later. For now, there was nothing gentle about a Chinese shih or nobleman. In addition to the chariots, the Chinese had infantry, armed both with bronze-tipped spears, bows, and a distinctive Chinese weapon called a "ge," which is a kind of dagger-ax, with a blade attached to a haft. It was also used by charioteers and could be very effective. The third person on the chariot besides the driver and the archer would hold and, when driving by another chariot, would use it to decapitate one of the people on the enemy chariot. Chou armies were organized into units, some decimal, such as the 100-man and 1,000-man unit, and some not: There was a 5,000-man and a 15,000-man unit. We know that there were some Chinese units, both of infantry and cavalry, as well as foreign troops, that included those recruited from steppe people.

The Chou were very effective at expanding their power, establishing military colonies and military districts, as well as using a civilian administration. Villages were reorganized around the five-household unit that was collectively responsible both for taxes and providing conscripts for the army. This system continued to be used for centuries in China. This is the period of the independent development of Chinese coinage. In its earlier form, bronze coins were made in the shape of spades or knives. Although both gold and silver are used and valued in China and the eastern part of the core, with some minor exceptions, precious metals are not minted into coinage. Rather Chinese coinage is fiduciary like our modern coinage. An interesting "coin line" develops, which persists into early modern times. To the west gold and silver coins are used, to the east they are not.

Gold and silver coins were also absent in the growing civilization in west Africa, along the Niger river. This is ironic as the region is a major source of gold, both in antiquity and today. As we shall see, neither silver nor gold, much less coinage, is used at all in this region. Rather salt and cowry shells are used, in the latter case, a fiduciary system like the Chinese and, in fact, we have today.

As I have said before, there has been too little archaeological and historical work done in the early history of west Africa. What we can say is that use of cavalry had spread across the Sahara by this time. Among the remarkable terracotta statuettes of the so-called "Nok" culture of which date as early as 500 B.C. there were horsemen. We will return to west Africa in a later lecture.

We have seen that a number of powerful states arise along the core: the Persian in the west, the Nanda in India, and the Chou in China.

None of these states, however, are very long lasting. Their attempts to merge steppe and urban cultures are more or less successful, but ultimately not sustainable. Both internal strife and external threats will grow and bring them down, which we will discuss in a later lecture.

In the next lecture, I want to stop, indeed go back, and investigate a specific theme: the relationship of warfare and religion.

Lecture Ten
War and the Rise of Religion

Scope:

The new faiths of this period struggled with the moral and ethical dimensions of war. Religious ideas are often ambiguous and contradictory, and they reflect both positive and negative attitudes toward warfare. New ideas of sacrifice and cosmic struggle led to the beginnings of the idea of holy war, and the notion of the war god was one element in the rise of monotheism. On the other hand, war was seen as evil and the one god as a peacemaker. The axial age of new religions and philosophers throughout the core may have been influenced by the dramatic military changes we have been studying. The religions of both the West and the East were affected by military changes.

Outline

I. From very early on, religions did not have a single attitude toward war; they often included different, ambiguous, and sometimes contradictory views.

   A. One of the common features of early religions is that gods were anthropomorphic and lacked moral superiority to humans. They fought with each other and with humans.

      1. Most ancient religions were polytheistic. It is interesting to note that in their earliest mythology, Mesopotamia and Egypt did not have a war god per se.

      2. The earliest mythology of the Sumerians was singularly unwarlike, with the gods interacting in a more legalistic fashion.

      3. As cultures in Egypt and Mesopotamia became militarized, more specific, and more positively viewed, war gods appeared.

      4. It is not until 1500 B.C. that we see the first mythologies of war among the gods, such as the Hittite Kumarbi myth, later borrowed into Greek myth.

B. An element that most early religions share is sacrifice, both human and animal.

    1. One problem for historians is that illustrations of, or even the reality of, human sacrifice can often be mistaken for warfare.

    2. Most early sacrifice was on the principle of "I give in order that you might give." A general might promise a large offering, or even a temple, to a god to ensure victory.

    3. The Canaanite religion included human sacrifice, particularly the sacrifice of children. This was a different, more sophisticated, principle of sacrifice: "I give up, that you might give."

    4. This new definition of sacrifice would eventually lead to the idea of martyrdom, an important element in religious warfare.

C. The origin of monotheism is complex and controversial, but theologians note an intermediate stage between polytheism and monotheism called henotheism.

    1. Henotheistic religions acknowledge that other gods exist but recognize one supreme deity in heaven, who rules over all others.

    2. The Assyrians were henotheistic and worshipped the supreme god Assur.

    3. Detailed reports on the army's progress were written to Assur and deposited in his temple. The idea certainly existed that the expansion of Assyria's empire was not only sanctioned by Assur but done on his behalf.

II. It is striking that this was the same time period in which the Hebrew culture was coming under pressure from the Assyrians.

A. Dating biblical texts is notoriously difficult, but it is in some of the earliest of the books, dating from the 9th and 8th centuries B.C., that we find the first evidence of Hebrew monotheism.

    1. In these and other early biblical texts, God often functions as a kind of general, directing the children of Israel in their wars.

    2. The Hebrew term *Yahweh Tzaba'ot*, often translated as "Lord of Hosts," more accurately means "God of War" or "God of the Army."

    3. This idea may have been influenced by Assyrian portrayals of Assur.

B. Of course, the Hebrew religion is not simply a copy of the warlike cult of Assur. From the earliest datable texts of the Bible, an ambiguity about war is apparent.

    1. The prophets Isaiah and Micah predicted the end of war. The prophet Joel, on the other hand, encouraged warfare, exhorting Israel to fight the enemies of God.

    2. These contradictory ideas are found throughout the Bible: On the one hand, God abhors war and loves peace, and on the other hand, believers will triumph in war over nonbelievers.

C. War represented a special theological problem for monotheistic religions.

    1. In polytheism, war is seen as the earthly reflection of struggles among the gods or as a plague upon humanity sent by the war god.

    2. Monotheistic religions have to explain why one all-powerful god would allow, or even bring, the evil of war.

    3. The idea that war is a punishment for a people's collective sin is a recurring theme among the prophets and an influential notion even today.

III. Around the same time the Hebrew prophets were developing the idea of monotheism (c. 800 to 500 B.C.), there were a number of other religious and philosophical traditions developing across the Eurasian core.

A. The German philosopher Karl Jaspers coined the term "axial age" to refer to the period in which Greek Platonism, Judaism, Zoroastrianism, Buddhism, Confucianism, and Taoism arose.

    1. Jaspers thought the various societies involved in the axial age did not have contact with each other. He explained the similarities in these movements as a sociological response to an increase in warfare.

    2. As we have seen, there was indeed considerable connection between the western and eastern parts of the core in 800 B.C.

    3. In the chariot age, the king was not only an important military and political figure but also the center of religious ritual.

4. Many axial age ideas involve the rejection of older priesthoods and the introduction of a new, more individualistic faith concerned with virtue.

5. The dramatic military changes of the period and the wars involving the steppe people put the axial age theory into context and support its basic premise.

B. While similarities exist, there are also fundamental differences between the Western and Eastern religious traditions. A sort of "soul line" exists, one whose border has ebbed and flowed over time but is nonetheless evident even today.

1. Although these religions have come to define "West" and "East," they did not originate at the extremes of the core and move inward. Instead, they developed near its center and moved outward.

2. Western monotheism (e.g., in Judaism, Christianity, and Islam) is characterized by the notions of an almighty God, an eternal human soul, an afterlife of reward or punishment, and a powerful and evil countergod.

3. Zoroastrianism, the Iranian faith founded by Zarathustra, introduced the most common elements of Western religions, including the idea of the cosmic battle between the forces of good (led by a savior born of a virgin) and the forces of evil.

C. To the east of the soul line, we see the Eastern religious tradition exemplified by Hinduism and Buddhism.

1. In this tradition, souls are constantly reborn on a higher or lower level depending on one's actions (karma) and adherence to the right path of life (dharma) in a process known as samsara.

2. Various traditions have either many gods, one god, or no god, but they all have spiritual beings, either bad ones and good ones.

3. An important Eastern belief is that everything we perceive is ultimately an illusion. It is the recognition of the unreality of the universe that is key to achieving nirvana.

4. Hinduism evolved as a mixture of the native Indus Valley tradition and the religion of the chariot-riding Aryan steppe people who conquered India between 1500 and 1000 B.C.

5. With the development of Hinduism, the high status of the Aryan warrior caste, the Khsatriyas, was replaced by the priestly class, the Brahmins.

D. To some extent, Buddhism developed as a reaction to the religious control of the Brahmins in Hinduism.

1. Though Siddhartha Gautama rejected the life of warfare, there is evidence of the influence of military ideas in early Buddhist thought and organization.

2. One example is the word "sangha," the name for the original community of Buddhists that became the term for a community of monks. As we saw in the previous lecture, sangha referred to communities of settler soldiers in India.

3. In the earliest Buddhist texts, called the Pali Canon, there are many references to the army. Military discipline is used in the Pali Canon as a metaphor for dharma.

4. Like the Western traditions, Eastern religions struggled with the morality—and to some extent the reality— of war.

Suggested Reading:

Kang, *Divine War*.

Niditch, *War in the Hebrew Bible*.

Questions to Consider:

1. What is the role of the war god in the development of monotheism?

2. How is the problem of war dealt differently in the Eastern and Western religious traditions?

Lecture Ten—Transcript
War and the Rise of Religion

Welcome back. In our last lecture, we discussed how Iron Age empires developed throughout the core down to around 300 B.C. Having brought our chronological narrative down to this point, in this lecture I will go back, and look at how religion and warfare have interacted during the several thousand years we have covered.

Even before the rise of the great religions we will discuss in this lecture, the various polytheistic traditions of the core region had developed much more sophisticated theologies and religious ideas, including the idea of martyrdom, celestial war, and of cosmic order, with the king and the social order on earth reflecting or mirroring a heavenly order ruled by a king of the gods.

With the rise of monotheism and the other great faith traditions of the core, we find religions struggling with the moral and ethical dimensions of war. There seems to be a period of time called the "Axial Age," in which this sort of religious questioning is particularly intense, and warfare had a role to play in this. We will find that from early an time, religions did not have a single attitude toward war, but often included different, ambiguous and, at times, contradictory views.

One of the common features that we find in early religions is that gods are anthropomorphic, that is to say, they are like human beings, although more powerful. The gods are not morally better than humans, or even moral at all, so at this point there is no question of war being judged in that respect. In fact, gods can get quite angry with each other or with human beings and fight.

The Mesopotamian, Egyptian and, indeed, most ancient religions were polytheistic; that is, they believed in many gods. It is interesting that neither Mesopotamian or Egyptian religions had a specific war god in its earliest mythology, although in Egypt the falcon god Horus seems to have functioned at least partly in this role. Gods like Nergal and Sekhmet brought war and disease, but they are both seen as plagues, very negative views.

The earliest mythology that we see among the Sumerians is actually quite unwarlike. Civilian government seems to have been the model for the way that the gods ran the world. The Sumerian gods are rather legalistic in the way that they deal with each other and with mankind. As time goes on and the war king takes over the Sumerian city, around 2700 B.C., gods get more involved in war. But even the first war we can follow politically, that between Umma and Lagash, according to our sources, is fought to defend the god Ningirsu's legal rights. The Egyptian religion starts out being more military, with the warlike god Horus associated with the Pharaoh, but he is replaced in the Old Kingdom by Ra, who is a benevolent and peaceful king of the gods.

After 2000 B.C., when both Egypt and Mesopotamia became more militarized, we find more specific, and positively viewed, war gods, such as Montu among the Egyptians and Rapha among the Canaanites (also known as Phoenicians). Even so, war still plays a rather minor role in mythology.

It is around 1500 B.C. that we see the first mythologies of war among the gods. Among the Hittites and Hurrians, the Kumarbi myth describes the overthrow of earlier [gods] by later gods. Around this same time we find the first Egyptian myth of the contending of Seth and Horus. This idea of divine warfare is adopted by the Babylonians in a story about their god Marduk and, ultimately, by the Greeks as referred to by Hesiod. What's interesting to note in this regard, however, is that a myth and reality are often not connected. While changes in the way warfare really is can have an effect on ideas and vice versa, I think this is something cultural historians need to keep in mind.

An element that most early religions share is sacrifice, both human sacrifice and animal sacrifice. One problem for historians of early war is that illustrations or even the reality of human sacrifice can often be mistaken for war. Indeed, war is a kind of human sacrifice, and so the concepts often blend into each other, an ambiguity that existed for the ancients as well as for us. Both human and animal sacrifice, however, can have different motivations, and thus different, or no, relationship with war. In the early Sumerian concept, for example, the gods are thought to feed off the life force of the sacrificed animal. Since the entire city is seen as a sort of household of the gods, particularly the city god, who owns not only all the land, animals, and crops, but the people as well—who are the slaves of the god. Then sacrifice is done as a duty, simply because that is why humans were created, in order to feed the gods.

There is another notion of sacrifice however. This is the idea that the sacrifice is a sort of bribe to the god. The Romans referred to this as "I give in order that you might give. " Thus in order to ensure victory in battle, a general might sacrifice a large number of especially valuable bulls. Or if he is really clever, he will promise to sacrifice the bulls if he wins, or build a temple, or please the god in some other way.

The Canaanite religion included human sacrifice, in particular the sacrifice of children to the gods. Human sacrifice is actually quite common in religious traditions around the world, but it is usually tied to the idea of keeping cosmic order, appropriating the power of enemies or keeping away evil. In the case of the Canaanites, the offering up of one's own children to the gods, although we see this as a barbaric act, did lead to a more sophisticated notion of sacrifice. The previous notion of "I give, in order that you might give," in other words a sort of divine bribery, became "I give up, in order that you might give," where faith is proven by one's willingness to give up what is dear for the sake of the gods. This notion will ultimately lead to the idea of martyrdom, an important element in religious warfare.

As I mentioned in my lecture on the sword revolution, the Hebrew language is a dialect of Canaanite, a fact confuses both their early history and also their religious connection to the Canaanites. Part of Canaanite mythology is the war between Baal Hadad , the storm god, and Yamm or the Sea, which is borrowed into the Bible as the struggle between God and Leviathan. This mythology develops into the idea of the struggle between Order and Chaos, and religious war develops in part as an earthly version of this universal struggle. There is no question that there are many Canaanite elements in the Hebrew religion, but monotheism is not one of them.

The origin of monotheism, that is, the idea of a single god, is complex and controversial. But theologians note an intermediate stage between polytheism and monotheism that is called "henotheism." The way the Assyrians viewed their god Assur was henotheistic. Although they recognized that other gods, including the gods of other peoples, existed, Assur was considered the supreme deity in heaven, who ruled over all the others. In contrast to other ancient deities worshiped in Assyria, there was only a single temple to Assur.

It was the Assyrians' duty to see that Assur's supremacy in heaven was mirrored on earth, and they fought on their god's behalf. Illustrations of war, found on the palaces of Assyrian kings, show Assur fighting—and leading—the Assyrian army. As I said in my lecture on the Assyrian empire, detailed intelligence reports on the army's progress were written to Assur and deposited in his temple. The idea certainly existed that the expansion of Assyria's empire was not only sanctioned by Assur but done on his behalf.

Now turning to the Hebrew, the difficulty of dating biblical texts is notorious among religious scholars. But the prophets, such as Amos and Micah, are the earliest biblical texts we can date with certainty, to the 9th and 8th century B.C. And it is in these books that we find the first evidence of Hebrew monotheism. It is striking that this was the same time that Hebrew culture was coming under pressure and influence from the Assyrians. Other early books include the book of Judges and the books of Samuel and Kings. A major theme that runs through all of them is warfare. Indeed, God, called either El or Yahweh, often functions as a kind of general, directing the children of Israel in their wars.

It is in the early prophetic books of the Bible that we find the most common use of the term "Lord of Hosts." The common English translation of this title, used both in the King James and Revised Standard version, masks the military connotations of the Hebrew *Yahweh Tzaba'ot*. Yahweh was the personal name of God, becoming our word Jehovah, and *Tzaba'ot* can mean either "army" or "war" and derives from the Assyrian word for "soldiers." So "Lord of Hosts" actually means God of War or God of the Army. It is highly suggestive that this name for God is used at the very time of the Assyrian portrayal of Assur as a "God of the Army" and may well be related to it. The move to have a single temple of God in Jerusalem, which is also a theme in the Bible, may also be in imitation of Assur. Of course, the Hebrew religion is not simply a copy of the warlike cult of Assur. From the earliest datable books of the Bible, an ambiguity about war is apparent. One sees different views expressed by the prophets.

For example, both Isaiah [2:4] and Micah [4:3] predict that at the end of times: "They will beat their swords into plowshares and their spears into pruning hooks. Nation will not take up sword against nation, nor will they train for war anymore." The prophet Joel [3:10], however, says just the opposite, exhorting Israel to fight the enemies of God: "Beat your plowshares into swords," he said, "and your pruning hooks into spears: Let the weak say 'I am strong.'"

These two different ideas are found throughout the biblical text. On one hand, god abhors war and loves peace, and on the other those who believe in him will triumph in war over nonbelievers. War represented a special theological problem for monotheistic religions. In polytheism, war can either be seen as the earthly reflection of conflict between gods, as it is in the *Iliad*, or simply as something inflicted on humanity by a war god, just as storms are brought by a storm god. In a strictly dualistic religion, which we will discuss in a moment, terrestrial war can be seen as the counterpart of the ongoing celestial battle between a good god and an evil god.

Yet, when god is considered all-powerful and perfectly good, as in monotheistic religions such as Judaism, and later in Christianity and Islam, then the problem arises: Why does he allow, or even bring, the evil of war? One common answer is that war is a punishment for a people's collective sin, and this is a recurring theme among the prophets. When Israel strays from the worship of God, foreign peoples, such as the Assyrians, are given victory over them. This is an influential notion even today. What is striking is at the same time, around 800 to 500 B.C., that the Hebrew prophets were developing the idea of monotheism and struggling with the theological issues of warfare, there were a number of other religious and philosophical traditions that were dealing with the very same issues across the core.

The German philosopher Karl Jaspers coined the term "Axial Age" to refer to a period between 800 and 200 B.C., in which revolutionary new types of thinking, Greek Platonism, Judaism, Zoroastrianism, Buddhism, Confucianism, and Taoism occur across Eurasia. To be honest, referring to a 600 year period as a turning point is stretching things a little, even for a philosopher. Let's focus on something a little more manageable for a historian, say 300 years. We will focus on Judaism, Zoroastrianism, and Buddhism, and leave Platonism, Confucianism, and Taoism for later lectures. Jaspers felt that the various societies involved in the Axial Age did not have contact with each other, and he explained the similarities in these movements to the sociological response to a period of warring small kingdoms. As we have seen there was actually considerable connection between the western and eastern parts of the core in 800 B.C.

Nevertheless, I think Jaspers was on to something. What is the connection between warring states and religions? We have seen how in the chariot age the king was not only an important military and political figure, but also the center of religious ritual. The relationship between the gods and the king were very important. A priesthood played an important role in all of this. When the kingships began to break up however, as it happened during the sword revolution, there was a split between the new military nobility and the hereditary priesthood in many cultures. Much of the Axial Age religions and ideologies involves the rejection of older priesthoods and the introduction of a new type of faith, one that is more individualistic and concerned with virtue.

Our survey of the dramatic military changes of the period , for example, the sword revolution, the introduction of cavalry, the impact of standing armies and settler soldiers, and especially the wars involving the steppe people which affected the entire core, puts the Axial Age theory into context, and supports its basic premise. While there are similarities, there are also fundamental differences between the western and eastern religious tradition. We have seen that, although many technologies rapidly spread across the core, there were in some cases lines of cultural division between east and west. For example, there was the coin line, with gold coins used to the west but not to the east, and the "bow line," with mounted armored warriors carrying a bow to the east but not the west. This line was different in every case, but it was definitely there. Likewise, there is a sort of "soul line," one whose border has ebbed and flowed over time, but is nonetheless evident even today. Although these religions come to define "west" and "east" they do not originate at the extremes of the core and move inward. Instead, they develop near its center and move outward.

In the west, there grew a monotheistic tradition that eventually will include Judaism, Christianity, Islam, and related faiths. These religions share the notion of the almighty and perfectly good god, who is the king of both heaven and earth. They all believe that human beings are born with souls, that after death [they] are rewarded in Heaven or punished in hell as they choose the side of good or evil in life. God is opposed by a powerful and evil counter-god, or Satan. History moves in a definite direction, beginning with creation and climaxing in a battle, a literal battle, between good and evil, known in Christianity as Armageddon. This final battle ushers in a kingdom of heaven on earth. All the religions incorporate gods from previous traditions, either as angels, demons, or saints.

The Hebrew monotheism that is reflected in the biblical text, that we have been discussing, developed by around 600 B.C. Most of the ideas found in the books that become the Bible were brought to Babylon when the Jewish king and aristocracy were deported there in the 6th century B.C. What is striking is that most of the elements that one associates with modern Judaism and with the religious traditions of the West are absent from most of the Hebrew Bible: the idea of heaven, for example, of Satan, the end of the world and the Messiah. It was Zoroastrianism that introduced most of the common elements of western religion. And this Iranian faith was founded by Zarathustra.

Zarathustra was born around 600 B.C. in Sogdia. As we have seen, the Sogdians were one of the many Iranian steppe peoples who had such a dramatic impact on the Eurasian core. This is the time in which cavalry is being widely adopted and that iron weapons were becoming cheap and widespread. And it's interesting that it's exactly in the region of Sogdia and also Bactria, where Zoroastrianism arose. This is where the heavy Nisaean or "blood-sweating" horses, whom we met in a previous lecture, were bred. As we have seen, it was Iranian steppe peoples, who overthrew the Assyrian empire and ultimately formed the Persian Empire, whose official religion was Zoroastrianism.

In Zoroastrian belief, as expressed in its holy book, the *Avesta*, there is a good God, Ahura Mazda, and an evil God, Ahriman. These two deities are constantly fighting over the earth, which is a spiritual battleground, with humans free to choose sides. While on earth both Ahura Mazda and Ahriman can operate and battle each other freely. After death Ahura Mazda's followers are rewarded with an eternity in paradise; those of Ahriman are cast into a pit. Zoroastrianism teaches that there will ultimately be a cosmic battle between the forces of good and evil. The army of good will be led by a savior figure, who will be born of a virgin who has bathed in a sacred lake.

These elements were added at some point after Judah became part of the Persian Empire. Although the royal family and Persian nobility were devout Zoroastrians, they did not try to impose their religion. They were not only tolerant, but actively supported local cults, giving money to rebuild the Jewish temple in Jerusalem and the temple of Marduk in Babylon. It is striking that the title "messiah" is first given in the Bible to the Persian king Cyrus, and the biblical prophet Nehemiah was a Persian official sent to Judah not only with royal authority but with the backing of Persian troops as well. This tolerance and support may be what attracted the Jews to Zoroastrian ideas such as that of a good and evil god (or god and anti-god). It is at this point we can speak of Judaism developing, as opposed to Hebrew monotheism. We will discuss the continuing interaction of warfare with Judaism, and its daughter religion, Christianity, in later lectures.

To the east of the "soul line" we see the eastern religious tradition exemplified by Hinduism and Buddhism and other faiths. In this tradition, souls are born not to spend an eternity in heaven or hell, but are constantly reborn in a process known as "samsara." One's soul is reborn on a lower or higher level depending on one's actions or karma and adherence to the right path of life, or dharma. One is not trying to achieve heaven but to escape this cycle of birth and death, a state called "nirvana." Various traditions have either many gods, or one god, or no god, but they all have spiritual beings, either bad ones, or demons, and good ones or, rather, enlightened ones, called "boddhisatvas." An important belief is that everything we perceive is ultimately an illusion. It is the recognition of the ultimate unreality of the universe that is key to achieving nirvana.

In a way similar to that in the Near East, in which the western religious tradition arose, India had gone through the upheaval of the chariot invasions of the steppe peoples. As we have seen in a previous lecture, it was a steppe people collectively called "Aryans" who conquered India between 1500 and 1000 B.C. The original Aryan religion was based on animal sacrifice and ritual and resembled the Iranian steppe religion that was replaced in the West by Zoroastrianism. After conquering the Indus Valley civilization, Aryan belief changed dramatically. Ideas such as reincarnation were probably borrowed from the Indus Valley people whom the Aryans had conquered. It is this mixture that ultimately evolves into Hinduism.

In the original Aryan social hierarchy, the warrior caste, the Khsatriyas, who probably evolved out of the chariot nobility, were above the priestly class, called the "Brahmins." With the development of Hinduism, we see the Brahmin class taking priority.

They held their primary position in large part due to their control of religious ritual. To some extent Buddhism was a reaction against the Brahmin's control of religion.

Siddhartha Gautama, known as the Buddha, was born in a Khsatriya caste in a tribe called the "Shakyas." He was the prince of a small kingdom located in what is now Nepal. It is interesting to note that the founder of Jainism, a closely related religious movement, lived around the same time was also a prince, and a Khsatriya.

The date of the birth of the Buddha is unknown, but estimates range from around 580 to around 480 B.C. Some scholars have connected the Shakyas to the Saka or Scythians, the steppe people we've seen in previous lectures. It may well be that Scythians, in addition to invading the West and Iran, also invaded northern India, the Nepal, and had become the ruling class there. We've already seen the importance of the steppe people in the rise of Zoroastrianism. And the Buddha's possible connection to the Scythians may not be coincidental. The idea of the Buddha's connection to the steppes or to Iranians has been rejected by most scholars of Buddhism. Far be it from me to disagree. But the widespread influence of the Iranian steppe peoples in military and social arenas, I think does make a possible religious influence, at least worth a second look. In any case, while the Buddha rejected the life of warfare and politics into which he was born, there is evidence of the influence of military ideas in early Buddhist thought and organization.

One example is the "sangha," the name for the original community of Buddhist followers that becomes the term for a community of monks. As we've seen, the term "sangha" was specifically used to refer to communities of settler soldiers in India.

In the earliest Buddhist texts, called the "Pali Canon," there are many references to the army. Military discipline is used in the Pali Canon as a metaphor for dharma. The early Buddhist sangha, like the later western monastery, may well have used the discipline of the military as a model for religious behavior. As in the western tradition, eastern religions faced a problem: Is killing in war, or waging war, good or evil or, in this case, good or bad karma?

On one hand, since both good and evil are illusory so is the destruction of war, as was explained by Lord Krishna in the Hindu epic, the *Bhagavad Gita*. Buddhism has a stronger pacifistic element than Hinduism, yet war and military service are certainly part of the Pali Canon and other early Buddhist writings. While all killing is condemned, service in the army is no different from any other earthly activity. War is both condemned and praised in these texts, an ambiguity similar to that seen in the Hebrew prophetic tradition. War is evil, yet the battlefield is a place where one can perfect one's dharma or righteous path. In a very similar way we also find the Buddhists adopting local pagan gods as bodhisattvas. In this form they are known as dharma protectors, a similar process that we see in the West.

Buddhism has the same transformative impact on the East as Zoroastrianism in the West. In later lectures we'll see its transformation into a state religion, follow its influence on Hinduism, and discuss its impact in East Asia.

In this lecture, we have seen how religion has played a role in warfare, and what a complicated role warfare has played in religion as well as in the Axial Age. In our next lecture, we will discuss another ideology Jaspers included in his Axial Age: Greek philosophy. We will see how important the Greek style of warfare was to the development of this, as well as other elements of Greek culture.

Lecture Eleven
The Greek Way of War

Scope:

The hoplite class resented aristocratic privilege, and tyrants overthrew many aristocratic oligarchies on its behalf. In Athens, the reforms of Solon failed to stop a tyranny. When this was overthrown, a new type of constitution—the democracy—was established. Three groups—the aristocrats, the hoplite class, and the landless poor—vied for political power in democratic Athens. In Sparta, a highly militarized culture developed in order to prevent a hoplite takeover. Greeks aristocrats had developed means of passing on military culture, such as poetry, athletics, and higher learning. These were adopted by the hoplite class, with important effects on Greek culture, but both philosophy and history were dominated by aristocrats. The Greeks developed distinctive military features, such as the homosexual relationship between older and younger men.

Outline

I. The empires of the Near East did not adopt the hoplite system, because it held the potential for revolt.

   A. It is not clear why the aristocratic class of Greeks did so, but they must have considered the military advantage worth the risk of social unrest.

      1. As the hoplite class grew wealthier, they became increasingly dissatisfied. They were doing the fighting but were barred from military command, not to mention religious and political posts.

      2. A special cause of complaint was the court system, which favored the aristocracy.

      3. In the 7th century B.C., revolts against the aristocracy broke out all over the Greek world. Tyrants, acting on behalf of the hoplites, replaced many aristocratic oligarchies.

B. The development of tyranny into democracy is complicated. We will begin by looking at the city-state about which we know the most: Athens.

    1. In the 7th century B.C., Athens was ruled by an aristocratic oligarchy, but around 594 B.C., frightened by the success of tyrants in other city-states, the city's rulers appointed an aristocrat named Solon to create a constitution that would maintain aristocratic power and prevent revolution.

    2. Solon created four wealth classes. He only gave real power to the highest class, which was dominated by rich aristocrats.

    3. He replaced Athens's kinship-based tribes with new artificial tribes, with the primary purpose of providing soldiers to the army.

    4. Solon's reforms did not solve the basic social problem: Athens relied on the propertied classes for military service without giving them any power within the society.

C. In 546 B.C., tyranny came to Athens in the form of Peisistratus.

    1. He held sole power and introduced many reforms that benefited the hoplite class.

    2. He abolished serfdom in Athens and confiscated land from the aristocrats to distribute to landless Athenians, giving them enough property to become hoplites.

    3. Under Peisistratus and his sons, the propertied classes became larger and more self-confident.

II. Around 510 B.C., a group of aristocrats supported by the hoplite army overthrew the tyranny in Athens.

A. Instead of reinstating the aristocratic oligarchy, the Athenians replaced tyranny with a new form of government: democracy.

    1. Athenian democracy differed in many respects from our own: It was direct, not representative. Most leaders were chosen by lot, not by election.

    2. While most sources speak of two parties in Athens—the aristocratic (or oligarchic) party and the democratic (or popular) party—there were actually three groups competing for power: the wealthy, landowning aristocrats; the propertied classes, who generally were merchants or craftsmen; and the poor, who worked for wages.

3. In 411 B.C., the aristocrats seized control and reestablished a brief oligarchy. The democratic government was only restored by force of arms.

B. To understand the growing power of the landless poor in Athens, we have to take a look at the change in naval warfare.

1. Almost every city-state had at least a trireme or two, and the larger ones (like Athens) maintained permanent fleets of warships.

2. The ships were paid for by the wealthy and rowed by the poor.

3. The Athenian fleet was vital in the rise of Athenian power. It is not surprising, then, that the landless class began demanding more rights and power.

4. By 400 B.C., the Athenians had the most democratic system in the ancient world—and in fact, one might say, the most democratic system that has ever existed.

C. We should note that democracy did not bring peace. In fact the democratic factions in Athens were often the most imperialistic, a phenomenon we shall see later.

1. Because political legitimacy could not come from ancestry, it had to come from military success, and that could only come in wartime.

2. Courage and skill in military affairs became important elements in politics. This led to a new type of democratic leader.

3. The office of general, or strategos, elected from each tribe became the most important political position in Athens (held most famously by Pericles).

D. During the same period, Sparta developed a completely different political, social, and military system.

1. Sparta's militaristic society was probably the result of the tension between the aristocrats and the hoplites.

2. The Spartan code did not apply to all citizens, only to the Spartiate class—a kind of aristocracy based on elite military training.

3. The Spartiates were taken from their parents and raised by the state in an especially brutal training program.

4. Most of the Spartan army, however, was made up of the regular hoplite class.

5. During the rise of tyranny and democracy, Sparta was a strong supporter of aristocratic oligarchies. This issue certainly contributed to the tensions between Sparta and Athens.

6. While the origins of the Peloponnesian War are complex, one issue was whether political control should be exercised by the hoplite class through democracy or the aristocratic class through oligarchy. Thus in Greece we find the first ideological wars in history.

III. The struggle between aristocrats and hoplites was played out in the cultural arena as well as in politics.

   A. Aristocrats trained their children for war through epic and lyric poetry, such as that of Homer and Archilochus, and stories told at banquets, called symposia.

      1. The symposium (literally, "drinking party") was not only a central part of the entertainment of the aristocratic class, but also of the spread of ideas.

      2. The symposium served as a kind of school, in which young aristocrats were taught about military and political leadership through songs, poems, and the experiences of their elders and ancestors.

      3. Painting and sculpture, part of aristocratic culture, often illustrated war and athletic games.

   B. As they gained power, the hoplite class adopted these methods.

      1. Athletic events began to become popular among nonaristocrats, and gymnasia were built where the members of the hoplite class could go exercise.

      2. Nonaristocratic military and political leaders needed a higher education. This was provided by the Sophists.

      3. Socrates, a student of the Sophists, is an example of a supporter of aristocracy who came from the hoplite class. He was a stonemason and had served as a hoplite soldier in many battles.

      4. Socrates believed that most people lacked wisdom and that allowing the ignorant majority to rule over the intelligent minority was foolish.

      5. In the philosophy of Socrates and his student Plato, the world is only a shadow or copy of the real world, the world of ideas. Thus war in the world is only a representation of the idea of war in the higher realm.

6. Plato built upon Socrates's antidemocratic notions. He believed in the idea of the philosopher king, who would hold absolute power over everyone in the city-state.

7. Aristotle was more sympathetic to democracy. He saw it as something that needed to be controlled through a mixed constitution.

C. As the aristocratic class became less important militarily, it turned to scholarship—a process that we will see repeated through time.

1. This led to a debate over the meaning of the word *arête*, literally "manhood" but increasingly meaning "virtue."

2. Greek history writing, a new development, became a means not only of communicating important military ideas but also of debating the value of aristocratic and common military leadership.

3. Many early historians, such as Thucydides and Xenophon, were aristocrats and had attitudes to democracy that ranged from lukewarm to hostile.

D. The Greek convention of homosexuality was an important part of aristocratic culture and was probably closely tied to military developments.

1. The conventional relationship was between an adult man and a youth. The older man was expected to mentor his young lover.

2. Ritual homosexuality seems to have been a part of the Spartan training system and was present in democratic Athens as well.

3. Thebes raised an entire unit, the Sacred Band, made up of 150 pairs of lovers.

E. War was a basic feature of interaction between Greek city-states. Indeed, the Greeks considered war to be the normal state of affairs.

1. Peace was sometimes made, but only temporarily.

2. The Greeks developed rules and conventions for war, which distinguished them from "barbarians."

3. The distinction that the Greeks made between Greek liberty and foreign barbarism was solidified during the Persian War.

Questions to Consider:

1. What were the political effects of the introduction of the hoplite system of warfare into the city-state?

2. What were the social effects of the new military class challenging the traditional supremacy of the aristocrats?

Lecture Eleven—Transcript
The Greek Way of War

Welcome back. In the last two lectures, we have looked at developments in the larger empires in the core, both political and religious. In this lecture, I would like to return to Greece, and the Mediterranean region to discuss the impact of the rise of the city-state and the adoption of the hoplite system. We are going to be unabashedly western here, but as we will see in subsequent lectures, what happens in the classical Greek will have an enormous effect on the whole world, not just in antiquity but in modern times as well.

We have already seen how the development of hoplite warfare not only changed the way the Greeks fought but developed an entirely new ideology, the hoplite ideology, that challenged the aristocratic ideology that continued to be held by the elite in the new city-states.

The tension between the hoplite class and the aristocrats, and the hoplite ideology and the aristocratic ideology, is going to play itself out in many different ways in Greek society and culture. As we shall see, many of the elements we associate with classical Greeks, such as democracy, philosophy, and even homosexuality, develop from the interaction, usually hostile of these two groups and traditions.

As I mentioned in a previous lecture, the empires of the Near East did not adopt the hoplite system, despite its effectiveness in raising soldiers, exactly because it held the potential for revolt. It is not exactly clear why the aristocratic class in Greece did so. They must have known it was dangerous to arm a class of people with no political rights or privileges, but for the relatively poor states of Greece, and for the colonies, the advantages in military force must have outweighed the dangers. No doubt the aristocrats of the 7th century B.C. thought that they would be able to maintain control.

The military and political success of hoplite warfare, however, led to exactly the sort of social unrest the aristocrats feared. As the hoplite class grew wealthier, in large part due to the success of the colonization movement and the growth of the economy through the spread of coinage, they grew increasingly dissatisfied. After all the hoplites were doing the fighting, but they were barred from military command, not to mention religious and political posts. A special cause of complaint were the courts. Increased wealth meant more legal disputes, often between wealthy members of the hoplite class—

recall all members of the hoplite class were wealthy to an extent—and wealthy aristocrats. All the judges were aristocrats so you can imagine the anger that this generated over time.

In the 7th century B.C. we start to see revolts all over the Greek world that removed the aristocratic oligarchies from power. They were replaced by tyrants, who were popular figures who ruled dictatorially but on behalf of the hoplite class. Tyranny and its development into democracy is a complicated subject. So let us follow them in the city about which we know the most: Athens.

Like other city-states in Greece, in 600 B.C., Athens was ruled by an aristocratic oligarchy. There was an assembly, which contained all the male citizens, but it had no power. All the magistrates or city offices were held by aristocrats, who were elected to one-year terms. Only aristocrats could serve in the city council, which functioned as an aristocratic oligarchy, or rule of the few. The army was organized into what are called "tribes," but in Athens these were kinship-based groups, made up of clans, which were led in battle by their aristocratic clan leaders and by aristocratic generals.

Athens, however, faced increasing internal stresses, and frightened by the success of tyrants in other city-states, around 594 B.C., they decided to allow one of their number named Solon, to try to create a constitution which would maintain aristocratic power while preventing revolution. What Solon decided to do was to create four wealth classes. [From] an entire citizen body (their property was counted in a census), four classes were made. The top three classes were eligible for military service. The citizens of the fourth class were too poor to serve in the hoplite class. Solon only gave real power to the highest class, the first class, that is, those with tremendous wealth, and this was a class obviously dominated by the aristocrats. Solon did something else. He replaced the kinship-based tribes with new artificial tribes—there were 10 of them—whose primary purpose was to provide soldiers for the city's military forces. These 10 tribes became the primary mechanism for keeping the rosters of citizens and, while there is no direct evidence of this, it is probably that these citizen rosters arose out of the rosters kept for the army.

Solon's reforms did not solve the basic social problem: that Athens was still relying on the hoplite class for military service without giving the vast majority of them any power within the society. It's true that many scholars in ancient times thought it was Solon who introduced democracy into Athens because power was now based on wealth and not birth. But still most of the hoplite class lacked power.

So it's not a surprise, like in other Greek city states, tyranny came to Athens in 546 B.C. Peisistratus became the tyrant of Athens. He held sole power, like all tyrants and, like tyrants, he supported the hoplite class. So he introduced a series of reforms. For example, he abolished serfdom. And since many aristocrats opposed Peisistratus and had been exiled for their opposition, he confiscated their land but, instead of keeping it, he distributed it to landless Athenians, including the serfs who had just been freed. This gave them enough property to become hoplites. So this increased the size of Athens military force, not to mention making a lot of happy new hoplites who were loyal to Peisistratus. Under Peisistratus, and his two sons who succeeded him as tyrants, the propertied class became larger and more self-confident.

In 510 B.C. a group of aristocrats, who were helped by the Spartans (whom we will talk about in a moment), organized a plot which assassinated one of the tyrants, one of the two brothers who ruled Athens, and overthrew the tyranny. However, instead of reinstating an aristocratic oligarchy, the Athenians who took over from the tyranny organized a new form of government: a democracy. This was a great surprise to the Spartans, and it was only internal Spartan politics that prevented them from intervening again. The Athenian democracy differed in many respects from our own: It was a direct democracy, not a representative one. All the power was in the assembly, at which every male citizen could vote, speak, and propose laws. The Athenians did not, with very few exceptions (one of those exceptions was the generals of the army), elect any officials or magistrates. Rather they chose their leaders by lot for one-year terms. One might ask if this wouldn't improve our own political system. Trials were also democratized: Juries replaced judges, and these juries could have hundreds or thousands of members.

While historical sources, both ancient and modern, often speak of two parties in Athens: the aristocratic or oligarchic party and the democratic or popular party, there were actually three groups competing for power in the city. There were the wealthy landowning aristocrats, who still held a great deal of power. There were the propertied classes (the hoplite class) made up of merchants or craftsmen, and these were the sort of people who had just gotten political power. And then there were the poor class, who were too poor to serve in the hoplite army. They worked for wages. And they really had still been left out of the early democracy. And so it was the struggle for power between these three groups that stood behind many of Athens' political changes.

Most aristocrats participated in the democracy. For its first hundred years, every major Athenian leader came from the aristocracy. There were those, however, who tried to reinstate an aristocratic oligarchy. For example, in 411 B.C. aristocrats seized control of the government, with the support of the hoplite class, which at the time feared too much power was being given to the poor. During this period, the oligarchs used force to maintain power. Many of the democratic leaders were executed and their property seized. This resulted in the democratic government being restored by force of arms, mainly because the propertied classes now realigned themselves with the poor.

To understand the growing power of the landless poor in Athens we have to look at the change in naval warfare among the Greeks. We have already mentioned the Phoenician development of first the bireme and then the trireme. Both are adopted and used by the Greeks and others in wars over trade routes. Sometime around 540 B.C., there was a naval battle off the coast of Corsica between a Greek fleet on one hand and an allied fleet of Etruscans and Carthaginians. It involved over 200 triremes and was fought over control of the northwestern portion of the Mediterranean trade routes. The Greeks lost that battle, but it illustrates the increasing sophistication of naval warfare in the Mediterranean.

Soon every Greek city-state had to have at least a trireme or two and the larger ones, like Athens, maintained permanent fleets of warships. The Greeks relied on their wealthier citizens to pay for triremes. Indeed, by lot, a wealthy citizen was given a responsibility to build a trireme. Imagine demanding a millionaire to build a battleship. They could say no. But if they said no, I'm too poor to do that, then any citizen can exchange property with them and take their property in return for building the triremes. Those were real incentives to be honest with your tax returns.

As the wealthy built these triremes, it was the poorest citizens who rowed them. Contrary to movies and popular belief, slaves were never used in Greek [ships]—or for that matter Roman ships—to row. To effectively row an ancient warship (remember they used rams), you had to have a lot of skill and a lot of courage. And also rowers were needed to be used as marines to fight if boarding was involved. In around 490 B.C., in the course of an increasing threat to Greece from the Persians, the Athenians used income from a newly discovered silver mine to build a fleet of 200 triremes. From this time forward Athens had an enormous war fleet.

Warfare continues to influence the economy of Greece, which grows to a sophistication out of proportion to its size and wealth. Coinage leads to monetization of the economy. There's a much more efficient flow of capital, and the Greek economy grows. Although the Greek hoplite system was largely self-arming, soldiers were required to buy their own supplies when on campaign. This is one reason that the Greeks adopt coinage on such a large scale. The use of coins led to more liquid capital and encouraged consumer spending which led to more growth in the economy. Monetization also encouraged the growth in manufacture such as pottery and cash crops, such as olives for oil and grapes for wine. Athens actually imported substantial amounts of grain from what is now the Ukraine because their land was mainly planted in cash crops. Pottery was exported on a large scale, especially to Italy, but also to the Near East.

The Greeks built on their monetized economy to develop credit institutions, such as banks and a primitive type of maritime insurance. The larger number of cargo ships and the navies that the city-states could afford to build and needed to protect their trade led to the ability to move large forces by sea, such as in the Athenian invasion of Sicily in 415 B.C. The Athenian fleet played an important role in defeating the Persian invasion of 480 B.C. and was very important in the subsequent rise of Athenian power and in its struggle with Sparta in the Peloponnesian War. It is not surprising then, that the fourth class, the landless, who made up the rowers, began demanding—and getting—more rights and power in the Athenian democracy. By 400 B.C., the Athenians had the most democratic system in the ancient world and, in fact, one might say, the most democratic system that has ever existed.

We should note that democracy did not bring peace. In fact the democratic factions in Athens were often the most imperialistic. This is a phenomenon we shall see later. This is partly because nonaristocrats often benefited the most economically from expansion, but also because their political legitimacy could not come from ancestry so it had to come from military success. And that could only happen in wartime. Courage and skill in military affairs became an important element in both politics and law, leading to a new type of democratic leader. It is noteworthy that the office of general, or strategos, was elected from each tribe, becoming, the most important political position in classical Athens, being held most famously by Pericles.

In the same period, the city-state of Sparta developed a completely different political, social, and military system. It had long been thought that the Spartan system was a relic of the Dark Age past, after all the Spartans kept their kings, who functioned as military leaders, long after the monarchy was abandoned by other Greeks. The Spartans attributed the founding of the system to Lycurgus. On the other hand, the Spartan poems from the 7th century B.C. reveal a society little different from the other Greeks of the time. This suggests that the specialized military society in Sparta was probably a result of the same tension between an aristocratic class and a rising hoplite class that we saw in Athens.

The Spartan Code, and its distinctive training system, did not apply to all citizens, but only to the Spartiate class, a kind of aristocracy. This was not an aristocracy of wealth, as all the Spartiates were supposed to be equal. In fact, technically, they didn't have wealth at all. There was no coinage allowed. They were supposed to use only iron bars to account for wealth. They were supposed to live without any property. In fact, they lived very nicely. But this idea that there was no wealth wasn't just a fiction. It's interesting that Spartan women of the Spartiate class were able to have sex openly outside of marriage with anybody as long as they were of the Spartiate class because property was not an issue for the children. The only issue was that the children were members of the Spartiate class. To be a Spartiate you had to be born a Spartiate.

The Spartiate class didn't work. They only fought, and only trained and fought for war. They were supported economically by helots, who although were not technically slaves, might as well have been. Spartiates had to be born in that class, but that didn't automatically make them a member of this class.

When they were still young, about six years old, boys were taken from their parents and they were raised by the state in an especially brutal training program that involved really brutalization by older boys and involved living outside and starving the youth. It involved very intense training and discipline. And it ended with a kind of initiation, where Spartan youth were whipped until actually some of them even died. And if they cried out during this whipping they were then expelled. After the Spartiate training they still weren't Spartiates. They had to be accepted into one of the communal eating societies that the Spartans had. They weren't allowed to eat at home. They had to eat and, in fact, live with their fellow Spartiates. They had to be elected into one of these eating societies. And it was only after they were retired from the army that they were actually able to go home and live their lives. So their entire lives were spent in the army, in a militarized society.

Of course, this made the Spartiates almost unbeatable as hoplites because they simply would not run away. And as we've seen that was the key in beating the hoplite forces, making the other side run away. But it's worth remembering that most of the Spartan army was made up of the regular hoplite class, which were raised, recruited, and they fought just like those in other city-states.

During the period of the rise of tyranny and democracy, Sparta became a strong supporter of aristocratic regimes. We have seen already that they intervened in Athens. While the reasons for the growing conflict between Sparta and Athens that led to the Peloponnesian Wars are many and complicated, certainly one of the issues was the question of whether political control should be exercised by the hoplite class through democracy or the aristocratic class through oligarchy. Thus in Greece we find the first ideological war in history.

The struggle between the aristocrats and the new hoplite class is played out in the cultural arena as well as in politics. The aristocrats used various areas of culture as methods of passing on the aristocratic ideology and methods of fighting. All are adapted to hoplite warfare and the new society, but not without conflict.

Aristocrats had trained their children for war through epic and lyric poetry, such as that of Homer and Archilochus, and stories told at banquets, called symposia. Symposium literally means "drinking party," and it was not only a central part of the entertainment of the aristocratic class, but also key in the spread of ideas, including ideas about war. Every aristocratic house had a room called an "andrea"— the men's room—which was specially designed to hold the couches on which aristocratic men feasted and drank. The mixing of wine with water—it was almost never drunk straight—was an important ritual function carried out by the host. The recitation of poetry was a major element and was, in addition to conversation, an important way of passing on ideas and ideology. The symposium served as a kind of school, in which young aristocrats could be taught about military and political leadership through songs, poems, and the experiences of their elders and ancestors.

Written versions of these poets were also very popular, and must have inspired the hoplite class as well. The distinctive Greek painting and sculpture, which often features illustrations of war, were another element of aristocratic culture that was adopted by the hoplites. Athletic games, such as running, chariot racing, and javelin throwing, started as ways of aristocratic methods of combat, and was adopted by the hoplites.

The inclusion of the hoplite classes in political and military power, though, introduced a problem. How were these new leaders, who lacked the informal aristocratic training, to learn what they needed to know, not only the skills but also the culture of leadership? For one thing, we see the andrea, or men's room, being built in non-aristocratic houses, and soon almost everyone in the hoplite class had one. We see athletic events, such as the Olympic games, began to become popular among non-aristocrats, and gymnasia were built, where members of the hoplite class could go and exercise, as well as take a bath, which is a remarkable new Greek custom. But the newly elected hoplite leaders needed a higher education, which was provided by the so-called "sophists." Learning was not only learning how to read and write, but also about the nature of the universe, the history of the world and, especially, how to make a speech in court. Thus, like law schools, the sophists taught how to argue both sides of the case.

This is what appalled the brilliant young student Socrates. Socrates himself is an interesting example of the fact that just as many proponents of democracy were aristocrats, both in Athens and later, there were supporters of aristocracy who came from the hoplite class. Socrates was one of these. He was a stone mason and had served as a hoplite solider, bravely it is said, in several battles. He was also a life-long opponent of the idea of democracy. He believed that the majority of people lacked wisdom, and allowing these ignorant people to rule over the minority of intelligent people was foolish. Many of Socrates's aristocratic students such as Alcibiades and Xenophon, as well as Plato, indeed participated in the aristocratic plots to overthrow the democracy (I shouldn't say Plato did but Alcibiades and Xenophon did) and used philosophy as a justification. It is not surprising, therefore, that Socrates was unpopular among those who supported democracy, and not surprising that he was ultimately executed.

Before we go on let's talk briefly about Socrates and his student Plato's idea about truth and idea about war. In the first place we have to understand that the idea that there were different approaches to truth was absolutely against Socrates and Plato's notion. In Platonic philosophy there's only one truth. But the truth is not of this world, not a truth you can see. This world is only a shadow or copy of the real world, the world of ideas. To explain this, there's a table behind me, and this table is a table because, according to Plato, it has "tableness." And I'm standing at a podium, which has some "tableness" but less "tableness" than that table. So if there's less "tableness" than most tables, then it's the idea of table. In war too, there's a war that's fought between two states that has a lot of "warness." And then there's a gang fight that has some "warness" but less "warness." So we have less "warness" and we have more "warness" so there must be most "warness," which is the idea of war.

Thus war in the world is only a representation of the idea of war in the higher realm. Plato continued and built on Socrates's anti-democratic ideas. While we are sure that Socrates criticized democracy, we do not know what he would have replaced it with. Plato's political views are well-known through many of his dialogues and his *Republic*. In many way they were more radical than the aristocratic oligarchs: He believed in the idea of a philosopher king who would hold absolute power over everyone in the city-state. For Plato the excellent soldier had to be trained, but he had to have innate abilities, as he pointed out in his discussion of guardians in the *Republic*.

Plato's student Aristotle was more sympathetic to democracy, although perhaps because it was disappearing at the time. He saw it as something that needed to be controlled within a mixed constitution, an idea that influenced our own founding fathers. Aristotle, by the way, disagreed with Plato about the nature of truth. You understood things through experience. And with Aristotle we have the important idea that will come back to you, that something either is or it isn't. That in logic there can be nothing but existence or nonexistence. And I'll return to this idea later.

As the aristocratic class becomes less important militarily, nobles begin to turn to scholarship, a process that we will see repeated through time. This led to a debate over the meaning of the word "arête," which means literally "manhood" but increasingly means "virtue." (Remember when we talked about the Chinese word "shih"? Well exactly the same shift is going to happen.)

History writing, a new development, becomes a means not only of communicating important military ideas but, like philosophy, of debating the value of aristocratic and common military leadership. It is noteworthy that many of the early historians, such as Thucydides and Xenophon, were aristocrats, and that they had attitudes to democracy that ranged from the lukewarm to the hostile.

The Greek custom of homosexuality was an important part of aristocratic culture, and it was also closely tied warfare, though in what way is controversial. Most Greek love poetry concerns the relationships between men or, more accurately between men and boys. The Greek homosexual relationship was a conventional one between lovers that matched an adult with a boy who had not yet grown a beard. It's a relationship that we would actually call child molestation. It is important to understand that the ancient Greeks did not see these relationships, sexual and romantic, as substituting for heterosexual ones. Men carried on sexual relations with women—their wives and others—simultaneously with those with boys. The point was the older man was expected to mentor the young lover, and this included mentoring him in the ways of becoming a warrior in the aristocratic sense and, later, in the hoplite sense.

Ritual homosexuality seems to have been part of the Spartan training system, and there's some idea that all Spartiate boys had to go through a ritual homosexual relationship with an older boy to become a Spartiate. It was present in democratic Athens as well. Although there seems also to be an ambiguous relationship of homosexuality as a hoplite class. There's some evidence that it was considered an aristocratic feature and was opposed.

The Thebans, another democratic Greek city-state, raised an entire unit called the "Sacred Band," which was made up of 150 pairs of lovers. According to the Greek historian Plutarch, when the Theban army fled from the Macedonians at the Battle of Chaeronea in 338 B.C., this Sacred Band held their ground and were all killed in place.

War was a basic feature of the interaction of Greek city-states. Indeed, the Greeks considered warfare to be the normal state of affairs. Peaces were made between city-states but they were limited, for example a "Ten Years Peace" or a "Thirty Years Peace." The Greeks also, interesting enough, developed rules and conventions of war, which were different for Greeks and for barbarians.

The attempt by the Persians to conquer Greece was an important event, especially in how it led to an idea of Greek liberty verses Persian barbarism. There is no question that the Greeks developed a sense of their own culture as well as military superiority. Victor Davis Hanson has developed a theory that the western way of war arose during this period, and is not only distinctive to Greece, but to the western culture that arose from it.

While in this lecture I have discussed many of the distinctive features of Greek culture, and Greek military culture, I think it is better to talk of these distinctions stemming from their style of fighting, rather than their style of fighting stemming from their warfare. In our next lecture, we will see that due to the various changes we have discussed in the last few lectures, the entire core plunges into a veritable age of warfare.

Lecture Twelve
An Age of War throughout the Core

Scope:

The 5th to 3rd centuries B.C. saw an age of war throughout the core. The Chinese Chou dynasty collapsed into the Warring States period, and in India the warring Janapada states were united into the Nanda dynasty. In the Central Asian steppes, powerful and warlike tribal confederations arose. In the West, the Persian Empire was succeeded by mutually hostile Hellenistic kingdoms and Greek federal states. In the western Mediterranean, there was war between Carthaginians, Etruscans, Greeks, and Celts—and the rise of Rome. Warfare was fed by technological advances in weaponry as well as by economic improvements, and by the spread of writing, which improved administration and military science.

Outline

I. The fall of the core empires led to a period of intense warfare that I call the age of war.

   A. Let's briefly survey some of the political changes that led to this period of intense violence.

      1. In the 8th century B.C., invasions from the steppe weakened China's Chou dynasty.

      2. By around 400 B.C., the Chou period had ended, and China entered what is called the Warring States period.

      3. Around the same time, India was entering the so-called Janapada period and was divided into a dozen or more warring states.

      4. In the 5th and 4th centuries B.C., the powerful Nanda dynasty conquered most of the northern part of India. It was the first Indian dynasty ruled by someone outside the hereditary *Kshatriya* warrior class.

   B. An important development in the age of war was the establishment of a series of powerful tribal confederations in the steppes of eastern Europe and Central Asia.

      1. These included, from west to east, the Scythians, the Sarmatians, the Saka, the Yuëh-Chi, and the Hsiung-nu.

2. Around 250 B.C., a steppe people called the Parthians took over Persia. The Parthians worked hard to keep Hellenistic kingdoms, and later Rome, from interacting with China directly.

3. Pastoral steppe people became wealthy through their control of metals, such as iron and gold; their establishment of trade routes; and mercenary service to warring states.

C. Although the Greek city-states had briefly unified to defeat the Persian forces in 480 B.C., they continued to fight each other.

1. The tensions between aristocratic Sparta and democratic Athens intensified in the 5th century B.C., culminating in the Peloponnesian War.

2. Some historians argue that Athens tried to use an economic boycott as a weapon against Sparta's Peloponnesian League. If true, this was a remarkably sophisticated means of waging war in antiquity.

3. By the 4th century B.C., the Greek city-states were in a state of almost perpetual war, which led to many of the military and cultural innovations of the period.

II. By the middle of the 4th century B.C., the Persian Empire itself was on the verge of dissolution.

A. The satraps had gained more power, essentially setting up de facto independent states.

1. Egypt, the wealthiest part of the empire, was in a state of more or less permanent revolt, and the monarchy itself was very shaky.

2. Between 336 and 323 B.C., Alexander the Great conquered the Persian Empire.

3. The combination of Near Eastern and Greek economic, political, and military systems had a great impact, both in the Near East and farther east.

B. After Alexander's death, his empire splintered into the so-called Hellenistic monarchies. These successor states— the Seleucids, Ptolemies, and Antigonids—were also constantly at war.

1. Eventually these kingdoms began to break apart, generating even more fighting.

2. The Greeks formed federal leagues of city-states, such as the Achaean and Aeolian leagues, with a common assembly and army.

3. The federal leagues gained enough military power to throw off Macedonian rule.

C. There was also a lot of fighting in the western part of the core.

1. Greeks and Carthaginians were fighting over Sicily and the Western trade routes.

2. In Italy, the Etruscans, Greeks, and Latins (including the Romans) were vying for power.

3. The Celts were expanding into Spain and northern Italy, even conquering parts of what is now Turkey.

III. What were the factors that led to this period being one of such intense fighting throughout the core?

A. The increased demand for iron weapons and tools spread the skill of blacksmithing and the opening of more iron mines, lowering the overall cost of iron weapons.

1. An often-overlooked factor is the technological contributions of the Celts, who introduced a more effective sword and a revolutionary type of saddle.

2. During this period, there was much experimentation with new types of warfare. This occurred across the core, but we know the most about the process in the West.

3. By 400 B.C., the cavalry had replaced chariots in most of the western core.

B. In Bactria, this period saw the rise of a new type of cavalry: the armored horseman, or cataphract.

1. The heavy horses, bred in the Ferghana Valley between modern Kazakhstan, Uzbekistan, and Kirghizstan, were large enough not only to carry an armored man but to support armor on the horse as well.

2. The cataphract carried a bow and sword, but his main weapon was the lance. The cataphract was adopted by the steppe people and gradually by the sedentary armies that imitated them, including the kingdom of Chao in China.

C. In both the western and eastern parts of the core, new types of weapons were developed using torsion, the energy in twisted rope.

   1. In around 400 B.C., the ruler of the city-state of Syracuse in Sicily invited engineers from around the Greek world to create a practical torsion weapon. The result was the invention of the catapult and the ballista.

   2. Western engineers came up with handheld versions of catapults, called crossbows. Overall, however, torsion artillery remained quite large.

   3. China independently invented a more effective crossbow in the 4th century B.C. and also developed a weight-driven siege weapon, the trebuchet.

IV. There had also been many developments in the civilian world during the age of war that were important in improving the ability to wage war.

   A. Greater sophistication in taxation, driven by the needs of larger and more expensive armies, led to larger government.

   1. The provincial system was adopted by the Hellenistic kingdoms and systems established in India and China.

   2. In the West, coinage spread through conquest and the need to pay armies. China developed a coinage system independently.

   3. With the spread of coinage, economic systems improved and higher literacy led to better contract and credit systems—even banks.

   4. Trade became increasingly sophisticated, as did shipping. The increase in shipping trade led to the development of war fleets to combat piracy.

   5. With the improvement of trade, food began to be transported, allowing large armies to operate over greater distances.

   B. The surge in both trade and military conquests facilitated the spread of writing. This prompted the establishment of official government languages and systems of writing.

   1. The Phoenicians lent their alphabetic writing system to both the Greeks and the Aramaeans.

   2. In turn, Greek colonization led to the adoption of the Greek version of the Phoenician alphabet by the Etruscans, Romans, Celts, and others.

3. The Persian Empire adopted Aramaic for official purposes, and it was used from Egypt to Afghanistan.
4. In China, an official dialect of Chinese developed, written in the script invented in the Shang dynasty.

C. Writing allowed for better administration of military forces and better communication of strategies and intelligence.
   1. It is during this time that we see the first specialized military manuals.
   2. Aeneas Tacticus and Xenophon wrote in Greek.
   3. Kautilya's *Arthashastra* appeared in India.
   4. The treatises of Sun Tzu and Sun Bin were written in China.

Suggested Reading:

Anderson, *Military Theory and Practice.*

Lloyd, "Philip II and Alexander the Great."

Roth, "War."

Questions to Consider:

1. What factors might have led to the series of military innovations across the core?

2. What was the effect of the spread of new weapons and ideas about war in the core?

Lecture Twelve—Transcript
An Age of War throughout the Core

Welcome back. In the last several lectures, we have discussed the rise of a new style of empire throughout the core, such as the Persian Achaemenids in the West and the Chinese Chou dynasty in the East, as well as the Greek city-states. In this lecture, we shall see how both cultural and political developments led to the fall of these empires and city-states and a period of intense warfare throughout the core, what I am calling an "Age of War."

This Age of War not only saw intense fighting, but technological and methodological changes in warfare. We see a sort of military science developing, and some of our earliest discussions of military theory date to this period. Before talking about some of the general features of the Age of War, let's take a brief survey of the political changes that led to such an intensive period of warfare.

Already in the 8th century, an invasion from the steppes had caused the China's Chou dynasty began a period of decline. Civil wars also broke out among the Chou dynasts and eventually, in many regions, a leading noble, called a *gong* in Chinese, usually translated as Duke, gradually gained autonomy, then independence, and a number of them took the title of *wang* or king. By around 400, the Chou period had ended, and China entered what is called the Warring States period. Some of these new kingdoms of the Warring States, which we will return to later, were Ch'in, Han, the Chao, and the Wei.

Around the same time that the Chou dynasty was beginning its decline, in the 8th century, India was divided into a dozen or more warring states, during the so-called Janapada period. In the 5th and 4th centuries B.C., the powerful Nanda dynasty was able to conquer most of the northern part of the subcontinent, though central and southern India remained under the control of a number of warring kingdoms. Nanda was the first Indian dynasty to be ruled by a non-*kshatriya*, that is someone not from the hereditary warrior caste of India or, in world historical terms, not a noble.

Nevertheless, the traditional nobilities still held control of most of India. Incidentally, the Nanda were apparently the first Indian state to raise what would become the traditional Indian "four-fold army" made up of chariots, elephants, cavalry, and infantry. India retained the chariot far longer than other regions, mainly as they reverted to a large four-wheeled version, typically of the type we saw with the Sumerians, that served as a platform for archers.

A very important development in the Age of War was the establishment of a series of powerful tribal confederations in the grasslands or steppes running across Eastern Europe and Central Asia. Most of these were Iranian-speaking people, the Scythians, in what is today the Ukraine, the Sarmatians in southern Russia, and the Saka in Kazakhstan. The Yuëh-Chi, despite their Chinese-sounding name, were also Iranians. They rose in western China and the Hsiung-nu, whose language is a bit of a mystery, had a kingdom in Mongolia.

A steppe people called the Parthians took over Persia, what is now Iran. This would have an important impact, as when the Silk Road develops, as we will see, the Parthians work hard, and fairly successfully, to keep the Hellenistic kingdoms and later Rome from interacting with China directly.

These pastoral peoples not only provided raw materials, such as wool, to agricultural states, but also established trade networks, particularly as the use of the camel spread. Pastoral peoples often also controlled sources of metal, including not only iron, but gold and silver as well. The Scythians, for example, grew rich from the gold mines they controlled in what is now the Ukraine. Increasingly pastoral groups gained wealth also by raiding trade caravans, or extorting protection money not to raid them. In addition, money was earned by selling their military services to the warring states to their south. The rise of these powerful steppe kingdoms during the Age of War is often not recognized for its importance. We shall see how important they were in upcoming lectures.

In Europe, the Greek city-states, although briefly unifying to defeat a Persian invasion in 480 B.C., continued to fight each other. The rivalry between aristocratic Sparta and democratic Athens, intensified in the 5th century, conflict culminating in the Peloponnesian War.

We shall discuss the role of the more sophisticated economy of this period, but some historians have argued that the Peloponnesian War itself broke out because Athens tried to use an economic boycott as a weapon against Sparta's Peloponnesian League. If true this was a remarkably sophisticated means of waging war. In any case, it is certain that the Persians used their vast wealth to influence the course of the Peloponnesian War, and it was they who enabled the Spartans to win. The Spartan stand at Thermopylae is well remembered, and movies are made about it, but not their accepting Persian money to defeat fellow Greeks.

By the 4th century, the Greek city-states were in a state of almost perpetual war, not only with each other but with the Carthaginians and Etruscans in the western Mediterranean, and the Thracians, Macedonians, Persians, and others in the East. This constant fighting led to the many of the military and cultural innovations of the period, but also was one factor that led to the conquest of by the Macedonian kingdom in 338 B.C.

By the middle 4th century, the Persian Empire itself was on the verge of dissolution. The satraps had gained more power, and some of them had forced the king to make their posts hereditary, in effect, turning them into de facto independent states. This is a fact that is often overlooked, making Alexander the Greats' conquest of Persia more impressive. The fact is that in many parts of the empire, satraps ruled as virtually, or actually, independent monarchs, much like the Chinese dukes of the late Chou period.

Egypt, the wealthiest part of the Persian Empire, was in a state of more or less permanent revolt. When Darius III took the Persian throne in 338, Egypt had just been taken after decades of independence. The monarchy of Persia itself was very shaky: Darius was the third Persian king to rule in 338, his two predecessors having been assassinated. So it's not very surprising that starting in 336, Alexander the Great was able to conquer the Persian Empire. My own view is that Alexander was less "great" and more lucky than is generally thought, but the importance of his conquest is undeniable. Alexander's conquest of the Persian Empire led to a combination of Near Eastern and Greek economic, political, and military systems. The impact of Alexander's campaign also had an impact farther east.

After Alexander's death, his empire splintered into the so-called Hellenistic monarchies as well as a steppe kingdom, the Parthians, in Persia. The Macedonian Successor States: the Seleucids, Ptolemies, and Antigonids, were also constantly at war. Eventually, the large Hellenistic kingdoms started to break up, themselves, generating even more fighting. The Ptolemies remained wealthy but lost their territory outside of Egypt itself. Judea and other small kingdoms won independence in revolts. The Greeks formed leagues made up of groups of city-states, and gained enough military power to throw off Macedonian rule. The Achaean Aetolian Leagues had federal governments, council made up of representatives, assembly made up of citizens, and a common army with a general elected each year. The similarity to the United States constitution is not coincidental, as we shall discuss in a later lecture.

In the 5th and 4th centuries, there was also plenty of fighting at the western end of the core. Greeks and the Carthaginians were fighting an intense war over Sicily and the western trade routes. In Italy, various powers, the Etruscans, Greeks and Latins, were vying for power. At the same time, the Celts or Gauls were expanding, conquering parts of Spain and northern Italy, attacking Greece, and even conquering part of Anatolia, now Turkey. This becomes the region known as Galatia. The Romans, one of the Latin peoples, were involved in almost constant warfare with their neighbors. We will discuss Rome's rise to empire in our next lecture.

What were the factors that led to this period being one of such intense fighting throughout the core? The increasing demand for iron weapons and tools had spread the skills of blacksmithing and had led to the opening of many new iron mines, lowering the overall cost of iron weapons, such as swords. Every region of the core now had access to relatively inexpensive iron swords, spearheads, and iron scale armor. Although arrowheads were still primarily made of bronze, except in India, high quality bows, both compound and simple, were being used all through the core. And skilled archers, while still specialists, were found in virtually every military force. The equipment of slingers was very inexpensive, but certain groups became known for their expertise, often islanders, such as those from Rhodes and the Balearic Islands, now Minorca and Majorca, off the coast of Spain.

An often overlooked factor in the development of military technology, especially in the West, is the contribution of the Gauls, or Celts. The Celts took advantage of the iron deposits they found in the regions they had taken over and developed a very high level of ironworking. They introduced a new and more effective kind of sword, a short sword that we will see being used later by the Romans, as well as, possibly, a revolutionary type of saddle.

This saddle was reconstructed by an English equestrian named Ann Hyland, based on reliefs of Roman cavalrymen of a much later period. It had four leather bumps or protrusions, two in front that sat against the rider's thighs, and two in the rear, holding his backside. Recent experiments have shown that such saddles are almost as effective as stirrups in holding a rider on a horse. While there is no direct evidence of its existence as early as the 4th century B.C., this date makes sense due to the changing nature of the use of cavalry that we find in our historical sources. In addition, an origin among the Celts, known for their cavalry and for their innovation in weaponry is a good guess. The idea of this Celtic saddle is based on circumstantial evidence, but is gaining acceptance among military historians.

There was much experimentation with new types of warfare. Due to our sources, we know more about this process than in the western part of the core, so we will discuss these in greater detail, though equally dramatic changes are apparent in the Indian and Chinese military cultures, as well as on the steppes. Macedonian success resulted from a series of military reforms introduced into its army by King Philip II. One was the lengthening of the six to eight foot hoplite spear into a sixteen foot pike called a "sarissa." This sarissa allowed for the elimination of most of the hoplites' armor, as the long pikes provided a sort of hedgehog or porcupine defense against both enemy spears and arrows.

It also meant that the army could be recruited from peasants while retaining many of the advantages of the hoplite phalanx. Philip also had his soldiers grind their own grain and carry their own equipment, which cut down on the number of slaves and mules in the army's train. It is in Philip's army that we first find cavalry operating as shock troops, that is charging cavalry or infantry forces directly— shock troops with lances. This was probably made possible by the adoption of the new style saddle, borrowed from the Celts.

By 400 B.C., cavalry had replaced chariots in most of the western core, although they continued to be used in the far west, for example in Britain and in India. China lagged somewhat behind the rest of the core. While iron weapons were now common, the Chinese were still using chariots, but cavalry had mainly replaced them by 200 B.C. The spread of the horse culture meant that large warhorses were now being bred in many different parts of the core, and the skill of taking care of them was also now more widely available. Although, as we shall see, China has an ongoing problem with breeding sufficient horses. The steppe peoples still provided the best cavalry, but many agricultural regions in the West, such as Gaul and Macedonia, we find horse-riding aristocracies supported by mainly agrarian states.

In Bactria, today northern Afghanistan, sometime around the 4th century B.C. we find the rise of a new type of cavalry: the armored horseman or cataphract. Some of the elements of the cataphract had already been present in the steppes for some time. The Sarmatians, the Iranian-speaking peoples I mentioned before, had used shaved horses' hooves to make armor for themselves and their horses, and these were eventually replaced by small plates of iron, called scale armor. The heavy horse that was bred in the western steppes was large enough to bear this weight. This is what the Chinese called "heavenly horses" or "blood-sweating horses," [which were] bred in the Ferghana Valley, now located between modern Kazakhstan, Uzbekistan, and Kirghizstan. These were large enough not only to carry an armored man but to support the armor on the horse as well. The cataphract carried a bow and sword, but his main weapon was the lance. This lance was perhaps borrowed from the Greek cavalry pike, the *kontos*, the counterpart to the sarissa, introduced into the region by Alexander the Great. It is also possible that the Celtic saddle was also introduced into the region by the Macedonians, giving the cataphract the stability needed in the saddle to charge on horseback. Again, all of this is rather speculative, but it makes sense in a world historical perspective.

The cataphract joined the horse archer in the cavalry of the steppe peoples and gradually by those sedentary armies that imitated them. In China, the kingdom of Chao, for example, originally was one of the weakest of the seven kingdoms that divided China at this time. King Wu Ling, of Chao, ordered his nobles to give up their chariots, and not only adopt the horse and bow, but to dress and act like the barbarian Hsiung-nu people. Chao quickly became the most powerful of the warring states, and the other states hurried to copy its military reforms.

While stone had long been used for fortification, the Greeks developed a very high quality stone fortifications in the 4th century B.C. The improvement in iron tools, the accumulated skill of masons, allowed stone to be worked more effectively and less expensively. In China, stamped earth continued to be used instead of stone or brick, but it also reached a very high degree of sophistication. Improvements in fortification led naturally to innovations in siege warfare.

In both the western and eastern ends of the core, new types of weapons develop, using torsion, that it the energy in twisted rope. These weapons used various types of pulleys to draw back the rope, creating much more energy than could be stored in a hand-pulled bow, and then a trigger mechanism was used to release a stone, a bolt, or an arrow with great force. In an incident reminiscent of modern military contracting, Hiero, ruler of the wealthy city of Syracuse, invited engineers from around the Greek world to create a practical version of this type of war engine. These anonymous inventers came up with two basic models called the "catapults" and the "ballista," both of which remained the basic types of torsion throughout western antiquity. Oddly enough, the ancient and modern meanings of catapult and ballista are different. In Greek and Latin, a catapult shot a bolt, in other words, a bolt going through a shield. And a ballista hurled a stone ball, in fact that was ballista means, to hurl a ball. In modern English, however, it is exactly the opposite: A catapult shoots a ball, and a ballista shoots an arrow or bolt.

Although ultimately western military engineers come up with smaller and even handheld versions of catapults, called crossbows, western torsion artillery always remained very large, as they were complicated devices and expensive to build. The primary purpose of western torsion artillery was to fire at defenders of walls, to keep them from interfering with the building of a siege ramp or the use of siege towers or ladders.

The first evidence for the Chinese crossbow is in the 4th century B.C., although it may have been introduced somewhat earlier as well. It is first found in the southern part of China, and then moves north, which strongly suggests this a completely separate development from that of western torsion artillery. The Chinese not only developed a less expensive trigger mechanism, but an important innovation allowed them to mass produced this weapon. The Chinese had developed cast iron, as they had discovered the use of coal, which could heat a furnace hot enough to melt iron. This made the production of crossbows much cheaper in the East than was possible in the West. Thus, the crossbow in China is used much more as an infantry weapons, and not simply in sieges. The Chinese also invented a more effective siege artillery piece, called the "trebuchet," which used a weight, rather than torsion, to hurl a rock and was much more powerful.

Of course, cast iron would eventually transform technology worldwide. Steel is a product of carbon in iron. While it was not yet introduced deliberately, natural carbon deposits were exploited in the 4th century in Spain and in China, and there was the development of quench hardened steel.

There had also been many developments in the civilian world during the Age of War that were important in improving the ability to wage war. The increasing needs of government, which included larger and more expensive armies, led to greater sophistication in taxation, which in turn led to larger government. The provincial system, which we have already discussed as developed by the Assyrians and taken over by the Persians, was also used by the Hellenistic, Roman, and Parthian kingdoms that succeeded the Persians. This type of administrative unit, the province, was adopted by the Indians as well, perhaps in imitation of the Persians, who bordered them to the west. And we see the equivalent of provinces, although they are often called different types of names, but the equivalent of provinces, that is, administrative districts, was also being adopted in China, although this was certainly an independent development.

In the west coinage spread, often through conquest, and the need to pay armies, reaching west to Gaul and Spain on the Atlantic and east to India. The Chinese economy became monetized, but it had a separate history. The invention of coinage and the spread in its use was probably also connected to the needs of warfare. Chinese coins were mainly of bronze, and although gold and silver were occasionally used, as was iron, nothing like the silver standard or gold standard developed in China in this early period. Rather the Chinese dynasties established standard weights for bronze coins. Once established, the use of Chinese coinage expanded enormously, from Central Asia, throughout East and southeast Asia.

With the spread of coinage, and subsequent monetization, economic systems improved, and more writing and literacy led to better contract and credit systems, even banks which, although still primitive by modern standards, gave kingdoms more flexibility in supplying armies. Trade had become an increasingly important part of economies throughout the core, and trade networks grew both in size and sophistication. Shipping also improved both along rivers, especially in China, and on the open seas, such as the Mediterranean, Indian Ocean, and along the Pacific coast of Asia. Trade brought piracy, especially in sea trade, so all the imperial states developed war fleets, both to protect trade and to project their power. In the west these navies normally operated on seas, such as the Mediterranean. But in China, the east-west trajectory of rivers made them more important as military boundaries, and the Chinese built sophisticated river ships to guard them.

Previously virtually all trade had been in luxury items or in metals, but now food began to be transported over long distances. This improved military logistics considerably, and often the private companies or public institutions gathered, stored, and shipped grain and other staples, were requisitioned or contracted during wartime. Indeed, for the first time we see private contracting being used on a large scale to provide food, weapons, and other equipment, especially by the Romans. Larger armies could now operate over longer distances. The Hellenistic kings, for example, led armies up to 100,000 men in campaigns ranging from Italy to India.

Both trade and military conquest had a great deal to do with the spread of writing. The Phoenicians, developing their trade routes to supply silver for the Assyrian army, lent their alphabetic writing system to the Greeks. In turn Greek colonization led to the adoption of the Greek version of the Phoenician alphabet by the Etruscans, Romans, Celts, and others. The conquest of the Aramaean tribes, both into Mesopotamia and Syria-Palestine, led to their script, Aramaic, also adapted from Phoenician, becoming widely used. Since empires covered many different linguistic regions, a common language and writing system was necessary. The Persians used Aramaic, which was used from Egypt to Afghanistan. Aramaic, in turn, is adapted to write languages in such as Sanskrit, and in Central Asia, to write Sogdian, a little known but highly influential Iranian language.

In China, an official dialect of Chinese developed, written in the script invented in the Shang dynasty. In all these cases, the spread of a common language and script, and the need to teach it, led to the rise of various types of literature, including religious texts, poems, stories, and novels, and the rise of historical literature, which included, in all cases, descriptions of war. Writing also allowed for better administration of military forces but also facilitated the exchange of information for tactical and strategic purposes, as well as others, for example intelligence about foreign peoples.

It is during this Age of War that we see the writing of the first specialized military manuals. Few such Greek manuals of the period survive, one of Aeneas Tacticus, for example, and another by Xenophon. But it is apparent that there were many more. In India an early version of the Arthashastra may have been written. This text was attributed to Chandragupta's minister Kautilya, whom we will discuss in a later lecture. And although it is usually seen as a kind of Machiavellian handbook on political science, much of it deals with how to fight wars.

The Age of War is also the period of classic Chinese warfare, reflected in Sun-tsu's writing. Another military theorist, Sun Bin edited Sun-tsu's *Art of War* and wrote his own military treatise, and several others. What is striking about much of this military writing is how much it concentrated on the use of tricks, called "stratagems" in Greek, to defeat the enemy, not by force but by cleverness. It is not entirely clear if this is just an accident of survival, as these texts were more interesting to copyists, or if they reflect something about the military culture of the period.

We have seen how the Age of War led to the rise of fiercely competing states. A fundamental problem with the regimes of this period is that the empires were never able to consolidate, or co-opt, the power of their nobles, who were a constant factor in the ongoing warfare. In the next lecture, we shall see how, all through the core, monarchs arose who were finally able to establish stable centralized empires: those of imperial Rome, Mauryan India, and Han China.

Timeline

B.C.

c. 4000......................................First evidence of horse
                                              domestication.

c. 1600......................................Rise of the Shang dynasty in China.

c. 1450......................................New type of bronze sword
                                              developed, possibly contributing
                                              to catastrophic invasions in the
                                              Near East.

c. 1000......................................The Dorian invasion, leading
                                              to the establishment of the Greek
                                              city-states.

c. 900..The first evidence of the use of
                                              cavalry, in Assyria; first evidence of
                                              civilization in Mesoamerica.

c. 745..Tiglath-Pileser III reforms the
                                              Assyrian military and establishes the
                                              Neo-Assyrian Empire.

c. 594..Solon institutes constitutional
                                              reforms in Athens, giving a degree
                                              of power to the hoplites.

c. 560..The rise of the Persian Empire under
                                              Cyrus the Great.

480 ....The unified city-states of Greece
                                              defeat invading Persian forces.

c. 400..The Chou dynasty collapses
                                              and the Warring States period
                                              begins in China.

336–323.....................................Alexander the Great conquers the
                                              Persian Empire.

c. 250..The Parthians take over Persia,
                                              establishing trade control between
                                              the West and China.

220 ....The unification of China under the Ch'in dynasty.

202 ....Rome defeats Carthage, ending the Punic War.

A.D.

66–73..."Jewish War" with the Roman Empire.

c. 100..Maize introduced to North America from Mesoamerica, prompting the development of agricultural civilizations.

c. 395..Christianity becomes the official religion of the Roman Empire.

570 ....Birth of the prophet Muhammad.

751 ....After defeating the Spanish Muslims, Charles Martel becomes king of the Franks and establishes the Carolingian dynasty; Muslim forces defeat Tang forces at the Battle of the Talas River.

1085 ....Christian kingdoms from northern Spain capture Toledo from the Spanish Muslims.

1204 ....Fourth Crusade.

1288 ....Oldest surviving example of a metal handgun, from China.

1403 ....Florence changes its definition of usury, allowing Christians to practice banking and opening up the credit market.

1453 ....Ottoman capture of Constantinople.

1494 ....Treaty of Tordesillas divides the non-European world into Spanish and Portuguese hemispheres.

1543	Portuguese traders introduce the harquebus to the Japanese.
1571	The Battle of Lepanto, signaling an end to Ottoman control over the Mediterranean.
1595	Justus Lipsius publishes *On the Roman Military in Five Books*.
1637–1638	Shimabara Rebellion in Japan.
1644	The Manchu conquer the Ming in China.
1756	The outbreak of the Seven Years' War between Britain, France, and Spain.
1792	The U.S. passes the Militia Acts, subjecting every "able-bodied white male" to military service.
1793	France institutes the *levée en masse*, or mass conscription.
1832	Carl von Clausewitz's posthumous influential military study, *On War*.
1864	The First Geneva Convention, organized by Henri Dunant.
1867	The Meiji Restoration in Japan leads to the establishment of a modern army and navy.
1885	Ferdinand Mannlicher introduces the first semiautomatic weapon; Hiram Maxim introduces the first modern machine gun.
1893	William Britain introduces the first cast-lead toy soldier.
1911	The first bombs are dropped in war, in Libya.

1914	Archduke Ferdinand assassinated; World War I begins.
1919	Treaty of Versailles ends World War I.
1928	Kellogg-Briand Treaty outlaws war "as an instrument of national policy."
1939	German-Soviet nonaggression pact signed; World War II begins.
1945	The founding of the United Nations.
1946	The Nuremberg War Crimes Trials.
1954	First atomic submarine launched.
1983	The first suicide truck bombing occurs in Lebanon.
1991	The fall of the Soviet Union.
1993	John Keegan's *A History of Warfare*, in which he argues that warfare is an expression of culture.

Glossary

Ahura Mazda: Zoroastrian Persian god.

alii: The ruling class of Hawaii; the descendents of conquerors from Tahiti, they ruled over the commoners. *See also* **Kanakas**.

Amazons: A mythical tribe of women warriors, who lived on the steppes. The idea probably derives from the real use of women in fighting by steppe peoples.

Amr al-Mumin (**Commander of the Faithful**): Military and political title of Muhammad and his successors.

anarchism: A revolutionary movement arising in the 19th century that rejected government. Loosely organized groups of anarchists launched one of the first terrorist campaigns, exploding bombs and assassinating political leaders in various countries.

apocalypse: The idea, drawn from Zoroastrianism and borrowed into both Judaism and Christianity, that the world will come to an end in a final battle between good and evil.

Arianism: An ancient division of Christianity; followed by many of the Germans who took over the western Roman Empire.

aristocrat (or **noble**): A man who holds a leading position in a society on the basis of high birth. Aristocracy and nobility can be created in war but then become hereditary, either in law or practice.

Arya: A term that can mean "chariot noble" and is seen in the linguistic term "Aryan" as well as in the toponyms "Iran" and "Ireland."

askari: From an Arabic word for "soldier," it refers to Africans enlisted into colonial, Western-style regiments. *See also* **sepoy**.

assault rifle: A type of rifle, first introduced by the Germans in 1944, that could be switched from semiautomatic to automatic fire.

Assur: Assyrian god of war and primary (henotheistic) deity.

asymmetrical war: A 21st-century term, referring to the two sides in a conflict using different types of warfare—typically terrorism on one side and conventional operations on the other.

automatic: A firing system in which the recoil or gas from a shot both reloads the next bullet and fires it. The firer need only keep a finger on the trigger to fire a constant stream of bullets.

Bactrian camel: Two-humped camel used on the steppes, as a pack animal but not as a mount in warfare.

banners: A type of military organization introduced into China by the Manchu Ch'ing dynasty.

Bantu: A branch of the Niger-Congo language family; speakers of these languages migrated south into central and southern Africa, using iron tools and weapons.

bomber: An airplane designed primarily to drop explosives on a target located on land or sea.

boomerang: A curved wooden throwing stick, used as a weapon in Australia.

breech-loader: A firearm that can be loaded from the rear and not from the muzzle.

Brown Bess: A model of flintlock musket; used by the British army from the late 17th century through the 18th century.

caliph: The religious title of the successors to Muhammad.

cannon: A large gun, usually a long, thick barrel mounted on a carriage.

cartridge: Originally referred to a paper package containing both gunpowder and ball that made loading easier. Later, it refers to a metal casing that includes not only powder and bullet, but primer as well.

cataphract: A heavily armored horseman, whose horse was also armored.

Catholic Church (or more correctly, **Roman Catholic Church**): A division of Christianity once confined to Europe, now the largest in the world.

cavalry: Soldiers or warriors who fight from horseback.

chain-mail: Armor made out of iron or steel rings.

chassepot: The first practical bolt-action rifle, introduced in 1866.

citadel: A fortress or stronghold built on a high point over a city or settlement.

cleanliness of blood (*limpieza de sangre*): A belief arising in 16th-century Spain that only those of Christian descent (as opposed to converted Muslims) could be nobles. It is thought to be a major factor in the rise of modern racism.

Comancheria: A large territory in the American West during the 18th and 19th centuries, within which the Comanche controlled fur hunting and trading. It stretched from the northern portion of Spanish control in New Mexico to French Louisiana, along the Mississippi.

commerce raiding: *See **guerre de course**.*

commissioned officer: A category of officer in the regimental system who has received a commission of rank originally issued by the king or central government. Commissions could originally be bought and sold but later were issued to individuals by the government.

communism: A revolutionary movement of the 19th and 20th centuries based on the theories of Karl Marx and believing in an inevitable clash between economic classes.

composite bow: A bow made up of both wood and bone, held together with sinew, which is more powerful than an equivalently sized simple bow made only of wood.

Confucianism: A Chinese ideology that stresses virtue and piety toward ancestors.

constabulary units: Colonial military and paramilitary organizations, generally made up of indigenous troops and Western officers, used as police and in counterinsurgency.

core: A common cultural and technological region, which ultimately covered a broad area of Europe, North Africa, and Asia, running from the Atlantic to the Pacific.

corned gunpowder: An improved form of gunpowder, in which the ingredients are soaked in vinegar or urine, then dried, forming small spheres. This treatment made the powder not only more powerful but also more stable, and easier to accurately measure.

corsairs: Pirate ships, especially those of the Muslim states of North Africa, that engaged primarily in seizing crews and passengers for sale as slaves.

crossbow: A mechanical bow that increases firing power by means of spring-loading.

Crusade: Originally referred to a series of wars initiated by, or approved by, the pope, with the intent of recapturing Jerusalem and later of spreading Christianity or suppressing heresy. More broadly, it is used for any war or movement with a Christian evangelical motivation.

Cultural Revolution: Movement initiated by Mao Tse-tung to suppress opposition to his rule; millions were displaced, and hundreds of thousands died.

culverin: An early type of cannon.

cuneiform: First form of writing developed in Mesopotamia.

daric: A type of gold coin introduced by the Persians.

dharma yuddha: Literally "dharma war" or "right path war," a term used to refer to wars intended to spread, or defend, either Buddhism or Hinduism.

dialectic: Idea, introduced by Friedrich Hegel, that an idea or event (thesis) interacts with its opposite (antithesis) to produce a synthesis, which in turn becomes a new thesis.

drill: The practice of military arts, especially of the manual of arms originally used to load and fire guns, and of the steps necessary in military marching.

dromedary: One-humped camel, used both as a pack animal and as a mount in warfare.

dynamiters: A 19th-century term for terrorists.

emergent property: Idea that elements come out of an interaction of some sort.

En: Sumerian priest-king who first ruled Mesopotamian city-states.

encomienda: A land grant widely used by the Spanish in the New World. While it gave the colonist control over the labor of the Indians on the land, unlike a fief, it involved nonmilitary service.

enlisted man: A category of soldier in the regimental system who enters service by being listed on the regiment's rolls, as opposed to being commissioned.

factor: A trader in the employ of a mercantile company, usually in charge of a fixed trading post, called a factory.

fascism: A 20th-century ideology characterized by nationalism, militarism, and often racism.

federates: A late Roman institution, begun in the 4th century A.D., of using tribal forces, who fought under their own kings and had their own territory, as part of the Roman army.

feudalism: A term originally used to refer to the political and military system used in Europe during the Middle Ages, in which knights and nobles received fiefs in exchange for military service. It is more generally used to refer to any system in which land tenure is given in exchange for military service.

fighter: An airplane designed primarily to shoot down enemy airplanes.

fletch: Feathers placed at the end of a dart or arrow to stabilize it in flight and improve accuracy.

flintlock: A type of spring-operated firing mechanism for muskets, in which the trigger pull releases a hammer holding a flint, which strikes a metal plate, causing a spark that ignites the gunpowder.

flower war: A type of ritual warfare conducted by the Aztecs and other Mesoamericans whose primary purpose was to obtain captives for human sacrifice.

frigate: A fifth-rate warship of the sailing age. *See also* **rate**.

fubing: The Chinese conscription system introduced by the Han and revived by the Tang.

galleon: Type of ship developed in Europe; lacked oars and was entirely wind driven. Multiple masts carried a full rigging, and portholes on the sides allowed cannons to be fired from below the deck.

ge: Chinese dagger-ax, often on a pole, sometimes translated as "halberd."

general staff: A division of a Western-style army exclusively devoted to operational planning.

genocide: A legal term coined by the Polish jurist Raphael Lemkin to refer to the attempted destruction of an entire people or its culture.

Greek fire: An incendiary weapon that took at least two forms—one a solid that exploded on impact and the second a liquid that was lit and projected toward the enemy. Invented in the 7th century, its exact formula remains a matter of debate, although it certainly included naphtha (natural petroleum) and sulfur.

grog: Rum mixed with water, an unpopular 18th-century change to the British Royal Navy liquor ration.

guerre de course: Literally "war on trade," also called "commerce raiding"; a type of warfare in which enemy merchant vessels were targets.

guerrilla war: A type of fighting involving hit-and-run tactics, often used by insurgents and revolutionaries.

gunpowder: An explosive formula of charcoal, sulfur, and potassium nitrate, usually in the form of saltpeter.

harquebus: French corruption of the Dutch *hackbut* ("crooked butt"), it is also known as the matchlock gun. The butt of the gun is bent, allowing the shoulder to take the recoil and for aiming down the barrel.

henotheism: The belief that while there are many gods, one god should be worshipped above all the rest. The Assyrian treatment of Assur is an example.

hieroglyphics: First form of writing developed in Egypt.

high explosive: An explosive formula using compounds such as nitroglycerin to produce very large explosions. An early version was dynamite, patented by Alfred Nobel in 1867. It was used in artillery shells, bombs, and mines.

Holocaust: The Nazi genocide against the Jewish people of Europe. Some 6 million Jews were murdered by deliberate starvation, overwork, and exposure, as well as by shooting and gassing.

hoplite: A type of Greek soldier, named after the large round shield (*hoplon*) he carried. Hoplites were heavily armored spearmen who fought in a solid formation called a phalanx. Citizens of city-states who had enough wealth to buy hoplite equipment were required to do so, and to serve in the army.

Horus: Egyptian falcon-god who sometimes functions as a war god.

human intelligence (HUMINT): The obtaining of information about the enemy through agents, often spies.

hussar: Saber-armed light cavalry used by most European armies in the 19th century. This type of cavalry was borrowed from the Hungarian, the name from the Latin *cursarius* (the same root as corsair).

Hyksos: A group of chariot warriors, probably Canaanites, who conquered Egypt in the 17th century B.C.

Indo-European: Language family that includes European languages such as Germanic, Romance, and Slavic, as well as Iranian and Indian languages.

intelligence: The collection and analysis of information, generally military and often secret, about the enemy.

ironclad: Originally a wooden ship with iron armor plating; later a ship made entirely of iron.

Janissary: An elite Ottoman soldier, first raised in the 14th century and recruited from Christian children who were raised as Muslims. Originally put through an intensive training program and among the first units to use firearms and military music. By the 18th century, the system had begun to deteriorate. The word comes from the Turkish *yeni çeri* ("new soldier").

Jesuits (or **Society of Jesus**): A monastic order organized along paramilitary lines but using knowledge as a weapon to spread Catholicism and oppose Protestantism.

jihad: Literally "struggle," its military meaning referred either to the spread of Islam by military force or to the ejection of non-Muslims (principally Christians) from land that had already been subject to Islam.

Kanakas: Hawaiians of the commoner class, frequently used as sailors in Western fleets. *See also* **alii**.

khaki: A dust color used in military uniforms, first by the English and then by many Western forces. The word comes from Hindi.

khan (or **khagan**): A Turkish term for the head of a tribal confederation on the steppes.

kilombo: A military compound used by the Imbagala, a group of marauders active in 16th-century Angola. The term passes into Portuguese as *quilombo*. *See also* **Maroon states**.

knobkerry: A wooden club with a ball-shaped head; like a mace.

Kshatriya: A warrior class found in both early Iran and India.

Kumarbi myth: Story in which younger gods overthrew older ones; an early example of divine warfare.

lascar: A sailor from India or Southeast Asia on a Western-style ship. The term comes either from the Persian *lashkar* (military camp) or from the Arabic *al-askar* (the soldier). *See also* **askari**; **Kanakas**.

lateen sail: A triangular sail that allows a ship to tack, or sail against the wind.

legalism: A Chinese ideology that stressed obedience to the state.

letter of marque: A document issued by a government authorizing private vessels to attack and seize enemy merchant ships. *See also* **privateer**.

levy: Commoners, often peasants, conscripted into military service.

limes (pl. ***limites***): Roman border fortification.

linear B: A type of writing used in Mycenaean Greece.

longbow: A simple bow whose firing power is increased by increasing the length of the bow.

lugal: Sumerian war-king, literally "big man."

ma'at: Egyptian notion of universal harmony, which could be disrupted by, or renewed by, war.

mace: A type of club with a stone or metal head.

machine gun: A weapon designed to fire a large stream of bullets in a short period. Early ones were crank operated (such as the Gatling gun, patented in 1865), but the true machine gun, introduced in 1885, was an automatic weapon. *See also* **automatic**.

Mahayana: One of the two main divisions of Buddhism.

Mamluks (also **Mamelukes**): Muslim slave soldiers; also the slave dynasty that ruled Egypt from the 13th to the 16th century and dominated it until the 19th.

man of war: *See* **ship of the line**.

mandate of heaven: The idea, introduced by the Chou, that Tien, the god of heaven, transferred the imperial dynasty from a corrupt family to one that was deserving.

Manichaeism: An offshoot from Zoroastrianism, with Christian influence, that became a popular religion among the steppe peoples, especially the Turks, before they converted to Islam.

margin: A cultural and technological region outside of the core, including central and southern Africa, the Americas, and Oceania.

Marian reform: A number of innovations, attributed to Gaius Marius, that principally allowed proletarians (those without enough wealth to buy arms) to serve in the army.

Maroon states: A political unit set up, principally in South and Central America, by escaped slaves (Maroons) and others. Called *quilombos* in Portuguese.

Maryannu: A class of chariot nobility found in the Near East; possible cognate of the Indo-European "Arya."

Mauser: The first bolt-action rifle to use an all-metal cartridge, introduced in 1871. It greatly increased the rate of fire.

mercantile companies: Private firms granted government monopolies over all trade in a particular region. Examples were the Dutch and English East Indian companies, the Hudson Bay Company, and the Royal African Company. They were an important element in European imperialism.

mercenaries: Contracted or privately paid soldiers, usually foreign, who sell their services to a government.

Messiah: A figure, borrowed from Zoroastrianism into both Judaism and Christianity, who is to lead the forces of God against those of the evil one and establish a Kingdom of Heaven on earth.

militarism: A term that can mean either a warlike tendency on the part of a state or a predominance of the military within the state.

military academy: A school, first developed in 18th-century Europe, designed to train commissioned officers.

military revolution: A term originally used to refer to the changes in 16th-century European warfare; now used more generally to refer to any period of dramatic innovation, especially in weaponry.

militia: A military force made up of civilians, it can be either volunteer or compulsory.

mine: In the military sense, originally a tunnel, either collapsed with a fire or later filled with gunpowder, used mainly in siege warfare. It later came to refer to explosives triggered by electricity or by pressure, used in both naval and land versions.

Minié ball: A type of bullet, invented by Claude-Étienne Minié in 1847, that allowed the use of muzzle-loading rifles. Grooves in the bullet's rear caused it to expand and hug the rifling, making it spin and giving it much better range and accuracy.

Mithra: Persian god popular with soldiers.

modern war: A category developed by the anthropologist Harry H. Turney-High. He defined it as the use of tactics and of command and control. The term is used more loosely to refer to warfare in the 19th and 20th centuries.

Mohism: A Chinese ideology that stressed pacifism and love for others.

Monophysitism: One of the divisions of Christianity, mainly practiced in the Near East and East Africa.

mortar: Originally "trench mortar"; a firing tube into which a rocket-propelled shell is dropped, used since the early 20th century as an infantry support weapon.

muscular Christianity: A loose movement within American and British Protestantism that advocated an aggressive approach to the spread of Protestant Christianity, identified with "civilization."

musket: Originally a smaller version of the matchlock; with the introduction of the flintlock, it became the term for all nonrifled long firearms.

Nabi: "Prophet"; the religious title of Muhammad.

national socialism (also **Nazism**): The German fascist movement, characterized by its military aggressiveness and fanatical anti-Semitism.

Naue II sword (or **tongue-hilt sword**): A type of sword made with a solid blade and tongue, first made in bronze and then in iron.

needle gun: The first practical breech-loading rifle, introduced in 1848.

Nergal: Sumerian god of war.

Nestorians (Church of the East): A division of Christianity that spread across Central Asia to China in the Middle Ages.

Nisaean horses: Large breed of horses raised first in the Ferghana Valley in the steppes, called by the Chinese "blood-sweating horses."

nobles of the sword (*noblesse d'epée*): French aristocrats who served as officers in the professional French army.

noncommissioned officer: A category of officer in the regimental system that receives its rank from the commander of the regiment.

oracle bone script: The first form of writing developed in China.

Orthodoxy: A division of Christianity that was once the imperial religion of the Byzantine Empire and is now in several national groupings, the largest of which is Russian Orthodoxy.

pacifism: The belief that war is not a justifiable means of solving political or social problems.

Pali canon: Early Buddhist writings.

pan-Arabism: A political movement that arose in the 19th century that advocated uniting all Arab speakers, regardless of religion, into a single nation.

pan-Islamism: A political movement that arose in the 19th century that advocated uniting all Muslim states into a single political unit, usually conceived of as a new caliphate.

pastoralism: An economic system reliant on the herding of animals and trade with, and raiding of, settled cultures.

pentekonter: A 50-oared ship used by early Greek pirates.

percussion cap: A small metal cap filled with mercury fulminate that replaced flint in the firing mechanism of muskets beginning in the 1830s.

philology: The science of reconstructing ancient texts, an important element in the Renaissance and the 16th-century military revolution.

pike: A long spear, over 10 feet in length, usually held with both hands.

poison gas: The use of various toxic substances in gaseous form as a weapon. They range from asphyxiating agents to blistering agents to nerve agents.

polis (pl. **poleis**): A Greek city-state.

primer: Originally the gunpowder placed on a flintlock's pan, which ignited the main charge in the barrel. Later it came to refer to the charge placed at the back of a metal cartridge that, upon being hit by the firing pin, ignites the main charge.

primitive war: A category developed by the anthropologist Harry H. Turney-High. He defined it as a lack of tactics and of command and control. The term is used more loosely to refer to the warfare of hunter-gatherers or of prehistoric cultures.

privateer: A private vessel authorized to attack an enemy merchant vessel and seize its cargo; a form of legalized pirate. *See also* **letter of marque**.

Protestantism: A division of Christianity that arose out of Catholicism in the Reformation of the 16th century. In its Calvinist form, it had a great deal of influence on armies and war.

Quakerism: A division of Protestantism characterized by a lack of church hierarchy and by pacifism.

rate: A category of Western-style warship from the 17th to the 19th century, based on the number of guns it carried.

regiment: A type of military unit, developed in 16th-century Spain and France, that became the basis for Western-style military organization.

rifling: Spiraling etched inside the barrel of a gun, which causes the bullet or shell to spin, increasing accuracy. *See also* **Minié ball**; **breech-loader**.

roll call: An institution of regimental culture in which the unit is assembled and the presence or absence of each soldier is orally reported to the commander.

sangha: Sanskrit for "community," it can refer to a military unit, a military guild, or a community of monks. A *gana-sangha*, often translated "republic," seems to be a steppe confederation.

schar: The armed retainers of a German king or noble, they included both freemen and slaves.

scurvy: A vitamin deficiency common among sailors on long voyages. Causes the loss of teeth, and in extreme cases, death. Cured in the 18th century by the introduction of food containing vitamin C, such as sauerkraut and limes.

Sea Peoples: A group of tribes, fighting on foot and armed with swords, that invaded the Near East in the 13th century.

sekbans: Units of settler soldiers, armed with matchlocks, who joined with peasants during a series of 16th-century revolts against Ottoman rule.

Sekhmet: Egyptian goddess who brought both war and disease.

self-strengthening movement (*tsu ch'iang*): A 19th-century movement to modernize the Ch'ing dynasty, and especially its military, that ultimately failed.

semiautomatic: A firing system in which the recoil or the gas from a shot reloads the next bullet. The firer need only pull the trigger to fire the next shot.

sepoy: From the Persian word for "soldier," it came to mean an Indian serving in a colonial, European-style regiment, especially in the service of the East India Company or British army. *See also* **askari**.

settler soldier: A system in which a family is awarded a farm in exchange for providing one adult male to the army. If the soldier cannot be provided, the land is forfeited back to the government.

sextant: A device for determining a ship's location based on the position of stars, vital in long distance navigation.

shah: An Iranian term originally meaning the head of a tribal confederation; later used to refer to a king or emperor in Persian-speaking states.

shan-yu (or *chan-yu*): A term meaning "ruler," used by Chinese sources in reference to steppe people.

shekel: First a weight, the basis of the Assyrian silver taxation system; later a coin of that weight.

Shi'a: One of the two major divisions of Islam.

shih: Chinese term for a chariot noble or warrior; later came to mean "gentleman" in the Confucian sense.

ship of the line: The largest of the sailed warships of the 17th to 19th centuries, from first rate to fourth rate. *See also* **rate**.

Sicarii: A Messianic group that assassinated Jewish supporters of Roman rule; the first religious terrorists.

signals intelligence (SIGINT): The obtaining of information about the enemy by intercepting communications, often involving code breaking.

Sikhism: A religion that developed in the Punjab in reaction to the upheaval of the Mughal invasion. The Sikhs created an independent state and were (and are) renowned warriors.

single whip: A tax reform instituted by the Ming dynasty, effectively placing China on the silver standard. Due to China's huge economy, this drove the international search for, and trade in, silver for the next several centuries.

sloop: A small Western-style warship carrying fewer than a dozen guns.

smart bomb: A bomb that is dropped from an aircraft and then guided to its target by radio or video.

smokeless powder: An explosive formula made up of single-base powders, such as nitrocellulose, and double-base powders, such as nitroglycerin. Introduced in the 1880s, it eliminated the thick smoke that had permeated battlefields since the 16th century.

social Darwinism: An ideology of the 19th and 20th centuries derived loosely by applying Darwin's theory of evolution to human societies. Its generally racist followers included both militaristic branches, which believed war strengthened the race, and pacifists, who believed war weakened the race.

***Sol Invictus* (Unconquerable Sun)**: A monotheistic deity whose worship some emperors tried to make the state religion of Rome; a precursor to imperial Christianity.

spear-thrower: A notched stick that, by effectively lengthening the throwing arm, allows a spear to be thrown farther and with more power. Also known by the Aztec term *atlatl*.

special forces: Elite units that use guerrilla-style tactics and are common in counterinsurgency operations.

square rigging: Square or rectangular sails that propel a sailing ship forward. *See also* **lateen sail**.

steam turbine: A more effective method of propelling ships, invented in 1884. It extracts thermal energy from steam to drive pistons instead of having the steam directly drive the pistons, as in previous steamship designs. This revolutionized the design of both military and civilian ships.

stirrups: Rings suspended from a saddle that aid a horseman, especially when fighting from horseback.

Stoicism: A variety of Greek philosophy popular among military officers in both Greek and Roman times. It was revived in the Renaissance.

submarine: A ship designed to travel underwater. Early designs go back to the 18th century, but they were first used operationally in the American Civil War. The first fully operational propulsion submarine was launched by the Peruvian navy in 1879.

Sudanic Kingship: A term used to refer to the centralized monarchies of West Africa (formerly known as the Western Sudan), characterized by a semidivine kingship and standing military forces.

Sunni: One of the two major divisions of Islam.

Taoism: A Chinese ideology that stresses withdrawal from the world.

tensility: The ability of a metal to be both strong and flexible.

terrorism: The use of deliberate attacks on civilians, with the intention of undermining civil and military authority.

Theosophy: A 19th-century spiritual organization, important in the pacifist and anticolonial movements, and a great influence on Mahatma Gandhi.

Theravada: One of the two main divisions of Buddhism.

tinku: A kind of ritual warfare carried out by the Incas, Quechua Indians, and other indigenous peoples of South America.

torpedo: Originally a term for a naval mine, it later was used to described the "fish torpedo"—a self-propelled underwater missile carrying an explosive.

torsion artillery: Machines that propel a stone or bolt by means of torsion, usually by means of twisting a rope with a crank and then releasing it.

trebuchet: A large siege machine that hurled a stone by means of a weighted fulcrum.

trireme: An oar-driven warship with a ram, probably invented by the Phoenicians and later borrowed by the Greeks and Romans.

tufek: A Persian term, originally used for tubes used to blow Greek fire, and after the 15th century used to refer to firearms, especially the harquebus or matchlock.

tumulus: A burial mound often used by steppe peoples to inter nobles, also called a kurgan.

uhlan: A lancer; a type of light cavalry used by most European armies in the 19th century. This type of cavalry was borrowed from the Poles, but the term is Turkish (*oghlan*, meaning "lads" or "boys").

universal service: A form of conscription introduced in the 19th century in which every adult male is liable for a term of serving in the military, usually partly in active service and partly in a reserve.

Vedic religion: The religious ideology and practices of the Aryans who invaded India, mixed with elements of the indigenous Indus Valley religion.

veterans: Both in the Roman army and in modern, Western-style armies, former soldiers who obtain certain financial payments and/or privileges due to their military service.

Wahhabism: A puritanical sect of Sunni Islam, which arose in Arabia in the 18th century.

war poet: Specifically, a group of English war veterans who wrote generally antiwar poems during and after the First World War. More generally, any poet who writes about war.

wokou: Japanese pirates active from the 13th to the 16th century. These were sometimes Chinese masquerading as Japanese.

Yahweh Tzaba'ot: Usually translated "Lord of hosts," it literally means "Yahweh of the army" or "Yahweh of war."

Zionism: A Jewish nationalist movement that arose in the 19th century and culminated in the establishment of the state of Israel.

Zouave: Originally French, this is a type of elite unit, with a distinctive uniform adapted from an Algerian tribe of this name. They wore baggy pantaloons and a tight vest, and this had an impact on fashion, especially women's fashion.

Biographical Notes

Abbas I (1571–1629): Shah, or ruler, of the Safavid Persian Empire, he imported Western weapons and tactics, defeating both the Ottoman Turks and the Portuguese.

Abu Bakr (c. 573–634): Arab Muslim political and military figure who became the first successor (caliph) to Muhammad. He suppressed a series of anti-Islamic revolts in Arabia in the ridda wars.

Ackerman, Robert (b. 20th century): American archaeologist who discovered the oldest known evidence of the bow and arrow in the Americas.

Aeneas Tacticus (fl. 4th century B.C.): Greek writer of military handbooks; only one, *How to Survive under Siege*, survives. He may be the Arcadian general of the same name who fought at the Battle of Mantinea (362 B.C.).

Aha (fl. c. 3100 B.C.): Traditionally regarded as the second pharaoh of the First Dynasty of Egypt, who first invaded Nubia, or Kush, to the south.

Akbar (1542–1605): Mughal emperor who vastly expanded the dynasty's rule in India.

Alcibiades (451/0–404/3 B.C.): Athenian aristocrat, general, and politician; a student of Socrates.

Aleksey I (1629–1676): Russian czar under whose reign the Russian empire expanded enormously in size.

Alexander III (a.k.a. **Alexander the Great**; 356–323 B.C.): King of Macedonia who conquered the Persian Empire and invaded India.

Ali, Muhammad (1769–1849): Albanian Egyptian military and political figure who attempted to create a modernized state in Egypt. His bid to conquer the Ottoman Empire failed, but he founded a dynasty that ruled Egypt until 1952.

Ammianus Marcellinus (c. 330–395): Roman military officer and historian.

Andreski, Stanislav (a.k.a. **Stanisław Andrzejewski**; 1919–2007): Polish British sociologist and author of *Military Organization and Society* (2nd ed., 1968).

Apuleius (a.k.a. **Lucius Apuleius Platonicus**; c. 125–c. 180): North African Roman writer; author of *The Golden Ass*, a humorous novel in which soldiers are featured in several scenes.

Archer, Christon (b. 1940): Canadian military historian; coauthor of *A World History of Warfare* (2002).

Archilochus (d. c. 652 B.C.): Greek lyric poet who described his military adventures in a light-hearted manner.

Aristotle (384–322 B.C.): Greek philosopher; student of Plato and tutor of Alexander the Great.

Arkush, Elizabeth (b. 20th century): American anthropologist who researches precontact warfare in South America.

Ashoka (304–232 B.C.): King of the Indian Mauryan dynasty who after a series of conquests converted to Buddhism and embraced pacifism.

Atahualpa (c. 1500–1533): Ruler of the Incan Empire; defeated and killed by the Spanish.

Ataturk, Kemal (1881–1938): Turkish military and political figure who established the Turkish Republic and became its dictator as president.

Augustine (354–430): Roman convert to Christianity who became a major theologian. He developed the Catholic idea of the "just war."

Augustus Caesar (a.k.a. **Gaius Julius Caesar Octavianus**; 63 B.C.–A.D. 14): The first Roman emperor, he established the professional imperial Roman army.

Aurangzeb (1618–1707): Mughal emperor who ended the dynasty's toleration of Hinduism, leading to its increasing weakness.

Babur (a.k.a. **Zahir ud-Din Muhammad**; 1483–1530): Founder of the Mughal dynasty. He wrote the *Baburnama*, an autobiography that includes an account of his conquest of India.

Baibars (1223–1277): Mamluk sultan of Egypt who defeated both a Mongol invasion and the Crusaders.

Bakunin, Mikhail (1814–1876): Russian revolutionary and leading anarchist thinker and leader.

Bassford, Christopher (b. 1953): American military historian and Professor of Strategy at the National War College in Washington DC.

Belloc, Hilaire (1870–1953): French British writer.

Bernadotte, Jean-Baptiste (1763–1884): French soldier who rose from the rank of private to become a marshal of France and then king of Sweden.

Besant, Annie Wood (1847–1933): Irish English spiritual and political figure who became a leader figure in the Theosophical movement and in the Indian independence struggle.

Bessemer, Henry (1813–1898): English inventor and businessman who developed a much-improved method for manufacturing steel.

Black, Jeremy (b. 1955): British military historian and coauthor of *War in World History: Society, Technology and War from Ancient Times to the Present* (2008).

Bligh, William (1754–1817): British naval officer most famous for the mutiny on the HMS *Bounty* and his subsequent 3,600-mile voyage in a lifeboat.

Bluetooth, Harald (c. 935–c. 985): King of Denmark who converted to Christianity.

Bolzano, Bernard (1781–1848): German logical philosopher and pacifist who argued that war was counterproductive and thus should be abolished.

Boris I (c. 825–907): First ruler of Bulgaria to convert to Christianity, in 864. When a group of pagan nobles revolted against Christian rule, he slaughtered them.

Browning, John (1855–1926): American inventor; one of the most important figures in the development of semiautomatic and automatic weapons.

Buddha (a.k.a. **Siddhartha Gautama**; fl. c. 6th or 5th century B.C.): Indian prince and spiritual leader; founder of Buddhism.

Burns, Ken (b. 1953): American documentarian who produced popular series on the Civil War and World War II.

Capa, Robert (1913–1954): American war correspondent and photojournalist who took one of the most famous photographs of 20th-century war, of a Spanish Republican soldier being shot dead.

Capra, Frank (1897–1991): American film director and documentarian who made the series *Why We Fight* for the United States Signal Corps.

Cardigan, Earl of (James Thomas Brudenell; 1797–1868): English noble and military officer who commanded the Light Brigade during their famous charge.

Cassiodorus (c. 490–c. 585): Roman historian who served as a politician under King Theodoric in Italy.

Chandragupta (c. 340–293 B.C.): Indian military figure and founder of the Mauryan dynasty.

Charlemagne (a.k.a. **Carolus Magnus**; 747–814): King of the Franks and first Holy Roman emperor. He conquered a large part of western Europe and began the Christianization of Germany by conquering the Saxons.

Chirino, José (d. 1796): African Indian leader of a slave revolt in Venezuela.

Chivington, John (1821–1892): American minister and militia officer; an abolitionist and Indian fighter.

Christie, Walter (1865–1944): American inventor and arms manufacturer whose suspension system for tanks revolutionized armored warfare.

Chu Te (1886–1976): Chinese revolutionary and military figure who developed the rural guerrilla tactics usually attributed to Mao Tse-tung.

Churchill, Winston (1874–1965): English officer, war correspondent, politician, and author who was prime minister of Great Britain during World War II and authored a number of books on wars he participated in.

Cobden, Richard (1804–1865): British businessman and politician; a promoter of both free trade and pacifism.

Columbus, Christopher (1451–1506): Italian explorer who sailed to the Americas on behalf of the Spanish monarchy. His voyages opened the New World to European conquest.

Confucius (K'ung Fu-tsu; 551–479 B.C.): Chinese political advisor and social philosopher whose ideas had a dramatic impact on East Asian ideology.

Constantine I (272/3–337): Roman emperor and convert to Christianity who legalized the religion and supported it with imperial power.

Cortez, Hernan (1485–1547): Spanish commander who conquered the Aztec Empire.

Crane, Stephen (1871–1900): American journalist and novelist; author of *The Red Badge of Courage* (1894).

Creasy, Edward (1812–1878): British Whig historian and author of *Fifteen Decisive Battles of the World* (1851).

Cromwell, Oliver (1599–1658): English politician and military leader, he formed the New Model Army and, after the overthrow of the monarch, became dictator of England.

Custer, George Armstrong (1839–1876): American cavalry officer who was killed at the Battle of the Little Big Horn, popularly called Custer's Last Stand.

Cyrus (a.k.a. **Kurush**; c. 575–530 B.C.): Founder of the Achaemenid Persian Empire.

Da Gama, Cristovao (c. 1516–1542): Son of Vasco da Gama, he led an expedition to aid the emperor of Ethiopia against Muslim invaders, in which he was killed.

Da Gama, Vasco (c. 1460–1524): Portuguese explorer who was the first to sail from Europe to India via the southern tip of Africa and the first to command European warships in the Indian Ocean.

Da Vinci, Leonardo (1452–1519): Italian scholar, engineer, and artist who designed fortifications and engines of war.

Darius I (a.k.a. **Darayavaus**; c. 549–486 B.C.): Usurper who took the throne of the Persian Empire in a revolt, though his propaganda shows him as the empire's savior. He established the satrap system and many other elements of Persian imperial rule.

Darwin, Charles (1809–1882): English scientist and author of *The Origins of Species*, he developed modern evolutionary theory.

David (fl. c. 1000 B.C.): King of Israel; used mercenaries in his conquests and to put down revolts.

Dawidowicz, Lucy (1915–1990): American historian and author of *The War against the Jews* (1975).

De Montalvo, Garci (d. 1541): Spanish writer whose works, such as *Amadis of Gaul*, inspired the Spanish conquistadors.

Dhu Nawas (a.k.a. **Yusuf Asar Athar**; fl. c. 520): Arab Jewish king of Himyar in modern Yemen. His persecution of Christians led to an Ethiopian invasion of the peninsula.

Diamond, Jared (b. 1937): American evolutionary biologist and world historian; author of *Germs, Guns and Steel* (1998).

Diderot, Denis (1713–1784): Prominent French writer of the Enlightenment and publisher of the *Encyclopedia or Systematic Dictionary of the Sciences, Arts, and Crafts* (1751–1772).

Dix, Otto (1891–1969): German artist and veteran of World War I. His postwar paintings were a powerful indictment of war and militarism.

Douglass, Frederick (1818–1895): African American abolitionist, politician, and author.

Drews, Robert (b. 1930): American classics professor and author of *The End of the Bronze Age: Changes in Warfare and the Catastrophe Ca. 1200 B.C.* (1993).

Dunant, Henri (1828–1910): Swiss businessman and founder of the International Red Cross; key organizer of the Geneva Convention.

El Cid (a.k.a. **Rodrigo Diaz de Vivar**; c. 1040–1099): Spanish military figure who fought on both sides of the Christian-Muslim wars in Spain.

Engels, Friedrich (1820–1895): German writer who, along with Karl Marx, developed modern communist theory. Known for his idea of dialectical materialism.

Fawkes, Guy (1570–1606): English Catholic military figure and spy whose "gunpowder plot" to blow up the Protestant English Parliament in 1605 was one of the first modern terrorist conspiracies.

Festinger, Leon (1919–1989): American psychologist who developed the idea of cognitive dissonance.

Flagg, James (1877–1960): American painter and illustrator who created the poster "I Want YOU for the U.S. Army."

Flynn, Dennis (b. 1945): American professor of economics who has written on the importance of China in the early modern global silver trade.

Forsyth, Alexander J. (1769–1843): Scottish inventor of the first workable percussion cap, one of the inventions leading to the modern rifle.

Franco, Francisco (1892–1975): Spanish military and political dictator who overthrew the Spanish Republic and established a fascist dictatorship with himself as caudillo (leader).

Freud, Sigmund (1856–1939): Austrian psychologist who explained behavior by positing an unconscious mind. His theories have been discredited.

Fulton, Robert (1765–1815): American inventor who built the first practical steamboat.

Gandhi, Mahatma (or **Mohandas**; 1869–1948): Indian political figure key in winning Indian independence, and one of the greatest pacifists of all time. He is best known for his principle of ahimsa (nonviolence).

Ganga Zumba (fl. 1670): Angolan Brazilian ruler of the Quilombo dos Palmares, one of the largest of the states formed by runaway slaves.

Gannibal, Abram Petrovich (1696–1781): Ethiopian Russian general and military engineer.

Garibaldi, Giuseppe (1807–1882): Italian revolutionary, military leader, and politician who was key in the unification of Italy.

Gat, Azar (b. 1959): Israeli military historian and author of *War in Human Civilization* (2006).

Gelawdewos (a.k.a. **Claudius**; 1521/2–1559): Emperor of Ethiopia who, with the help of Portuguese harquebusiers, defeated a Muslim invasion.

Genghis Khan (a.k.a. **Temujin**; 1162–1227): Mongol khan who founded the largest contiguous empire the world has ever known.

Giap, Vo Nguyen (b. c. 1911): Vietnamese revolutionary and military figure who successfully combined guerrilla and conventional warfare to defeat both France and the United States.

Giráldez, Arturo (b. 20th century): Spanish American professor of modern languages who has written on the importance of China in the early modern global silver trade.

Gobineau, Arthur de (1816–1882): French writer and author of *An Essay on the Inequality of the Human Races* (1853), one of the earliest works of modern racial theory.

Gordon, Charles (1833–1885): English military officer who was given command of the Chinese Ever Victorious Army during the Taiping Rebellion and also was an officer in the Egyptian army in the Sudan.

Grant, Ulysses S. (1822–1885): American military and political figure; commanded U.S. forces in the Civil War and became president of the United States.

Graves, Robert (1895–1985): English officer, war poet, and novelist; author of *Goodbye to All That*, a popular antiwar novel.

Greenburg, Joseph (1915–2001): American linguist who proposed that most American Indian languages belong to a single language family.

Gribeauval, Jean-Baptiste de (1715–1789): French artillery officer who made important improvements to cannons.

Grignard, Victor (1871–1935): French chemist and Nobel Prize winner who did poison gas research for the French army.

Grotius, Hugo (1583–1645): Dutch legal scholar; author of *On the Law of War and Peace* (1625).

Guevara, Ernesto "Che" (1928–1967): Argentine revolutionary who popularized rural guerrilla war in Latin America, despite his lack of success.

Gustavus Adolphus (1594–1632): Swedish king and military figure whose reorganization of the Swedish army influenced Western warfare.

Haber, Fritz (1868–1934): German chemist and Nobel Prize winner who did poison gas research for the German army.

Hadrian (a.k.a. **Publius Aelius Hadrianus**; 76–138): Roman general and emperor. He is best known for improving Rome's border defenses and for building Hadrian's Wall in Britain.

Hammurabi (a.k.a. **Hammurapi**; fl. c. 1770 B.C.): Amorite king of Babylon and founder of the Old Babylonian Empire.

Han Wu-ti (140–87 B.C.): Sixth emperor of the Chinese Han dynasty; one of the most important conquerors and military reformers of the period.

Ha-Nagid, Samuel (a.k.a. **Samuel ibn Naghrela**; 993–1056): Spanish Jewish political and military figure who was commander in chief for the Muslim ruler of Granada, a post his son Joseph also held.

Hanson, Victor Davis (b. 1953): American military historian and author of *The Western Way of War: Infantry Battle in Classical Greece* (1989) and *Carnage and Culture: Landmark Battles in the Rise of Western Power* (2001).

Hartley, Aidan (b. 1965): American journalist and war correspondent who has written on warfare in contemporary Africa.

Hegel, Georg W. F. (1770–1831): German philosopher known for his idea of the historical dialectic.

Henry the Navigator (1394–1460): Portuguese prince who masterminded Portugal's explorations down the coast of West Africa.

Herodotus (c. 485–c. 425 B.C.): Greek historian and author of the *History*, an account of the Persian Wars.

Hesiod (fl. c. 700 B.C.): Greek poet and author of *Works and Days*, a description of life in the early Greek city-state, in which he criticized his brother Perses.

Hobbes, Thomas (1588–1679): English philosopher; wrote in *Leviathan* (1651) that because of war, life in the state of nature was "solitary, poor, nasty, brutish and short."

Homer (fl. c. 750 B.C.): Purported author of the Greek epics the *Iliad* and the *Odyssey*.

Honda, Tadakatsu (1548–1610): Japanese general who was made a lord (daimyo) due to his military abilities.

Hoover, J. Edgar (1895–1972): American police official who served as director of the Federal Bureau of Investigation. Under his direction, the FBI took over all counterintelligence and some intelligence functions during World War II.

Howe, Julia Ward (1819–1910): American abolitionist and author who wrote the lyrics to *The Battle Hymn of the Republic*.

Hulagu Khan (1217–1275): Mongol conqueror of the Near East and founder of the Il-Khanid dynasty.

Hung Hsiu-ch'uan (1814–1864): Hakka Chinese religious and political figure who led the Taiping Rebellion.

Hypatia of Alexandria (d. 415): Pagan philosopher and mathematician; murdered by Christian monks.

Ibn Abī Tālib, 'Alī (c. 599–661): Arab Muslim military and political figure who became the fourth caliph. He was defeated and replaced by Mu'awiyah, the first Umayyad caliph.

Ibn al-'As, 'Amr (c. 583–664): Arab Muslim military commander who conquered Egypt for Islam.

Ibn 'Alī, Hussein (626–680): Arab Muslim political and military figure, he led a Shi'ite revolt against the Umayyad and was defeated and killed.

Ibn al-Walīd, Khālid (592–642): Arab Muslim military figure who won many battles during the rise of Islam.

Ismail I (1487–1525): Shi'ite Muslim from northwestern Iran who became the first shah, or ruler, of the Safavid Persian Empire.

Ivan IV (a.k.a. Ivan the Terrible; 1530–1584): Russian political and military figure who became the first czar of the Russian empire.

Jagger, Charles Sergeant (1885–1934): British sculptor who served as an officer in World War I. He is best known as a creator of war memorials.

Jahan (1592–1666): Mughal shah who won wars against the Portuguese and Rajputs and built the Taj Mahal.

Jaspers, Karl (1883–1969): German philosopher who coined the term "axial age."

Jesus of Nazareth (c. 6–35): Jewish religious figure; founder of Christianity.

Jogaila (a.k.a. **Vladislav II Jagiello**; c. 1362–1434): First Christian ruler of Lithuania; laid the foundation for the kingdom of Poland-Lithuania, which dominated Eastern Europe for centuries.

John I (1167–1216): King of England; forced by his barons to sign the Magna Carta.

John Hyrcanus I (c. 175–104 B.C.): High priest and ruler of Judah who conquered neighboring Samaria and Idumaea and allied Judah to the Romans.

Joselowicz, Berek (1764–1809): Jewish Polish cavalry commander, he raised an all-Jewish hussar regiment during the 1794 revolt and served in Napoleon's Polish forces.

Josephus (**Flavius Josephus**; 37/8–c. 100): Jewish Roman military commander and author of *The Jewish War* (c. 75).

Julian II (c. 1443–1513): Italian pope who fought in armor and founded the Swiss Guards.

Julius Caesar (100–44 B.C.): Roman general and politician who took control of the Roman republic and laid the groundwork for the Roman Empire.

Jung, Carl (1875–1961): German psychologist. His theories have been discredited.

Kader, Abdel (1808–1883): Algerian military and political figure who fought the French occupation of Algeria.

Kalakaua, David (1836–1891): Hawaiian noble, politician, and military officer who was elected king of Hawaii.

Kamehameha I (c. 1738–1819): Hawaiian military and political figure who unified the islands and founded the Kingdom of Hawaii.

K'ang-hsi (1654–1722): Chinese emperor of the Ch'ing dynasty, he defeated the Portuguese, took Taiwan, and expanded Chinese control to the northwest.

Kautilya (fl. 300 B.C.): Indian author of the political-military treatise *Arthashastra*, he is traditionally identified with Chanaka, an adviser to King Chandragupta (c. 340–293 B.C.), who was founder of the Mauryan Empire.

Keegen, John (b. 1934): British military historian and author of *The Face of Battle* (1976) and *A History of War* (1993).

Keeley, Lawrence (b. 20th century): Professor of anthropology at the University of Illinois at Chicago and author of *War before Civilization* (1996).

Kidd, William (c. 1645–1701): Scottish privateer who, despite having a letter of marque from the king of England, was hanged as a pirate.

Kiefer, Anselm (b. 1945): German artist who has produced antiwar sculptures dealing with the allied bombing of Germany during World War II.

Kipling, Rudyard (1865–1936): English author and poet whose works illustrated 19th-century English imperialism.

Kosciusko, Thaddeus (1746–1817): Polish military and political figure who fought in the American Revolution and led an unsuccessful uprising against Russia.

Krupp, Alfred (1812–1887): German businessman who built his family's steel company into one of the leading arms manufacturers in the world.

Kubilai Khan (1215–1294): The last ruler of the unified Mongol Empire and the first emperor of the Chinese Yüan dynasty.

Kuo Hsing-Yeh (a.k.a. **Coxinga**; **Cheng Ch'eng Kung**; 1624–1662): Chinese Ming dynasty military figure who drove the Dutch from Taiwan and established an anti-Ch'ing stronghold there.

Ladd, William (1778–1841): American abolitionist and pacifist who organized the American Peace Society in 1828.

Lafayette, Marquis de (**Gibert du Motier**; 1757–1834): French aristocrat, revolutionary, and political leader, he fought in the American and French revolutions.

Lamar, Hedy (1913–2000): Austrian American film actress and coinventor, with composer George Antheil (1900–1959), of a frequency-hopping spread spectrum device.

Lavoisier, Antoine (1743–1794): French scientist called the Father of Modern Chemistry; his work made possible modern explosives.

Lawrence, T. E. (a.k.a. **Lawrence of Arabia**; 1885–1935): British military officer who helped lead the Arab revolt against the Ottomans in World War I and was an early theoretician of guerrilla warfare.

Le Tellier, Michel (1603–1685): French politician who, as secretary of state for military affairs, introduced military and political reforms that transformed the French army. His son, the Marquis de Louvois (1641–1691), continued and expanded his work.

Lemkin, Raphael (1900–1959): Polish jurist who developed the modern legal basis for war crimes and coined the term "genocide."

Lennon, John (1940–1980): English musician, songwriter, and antiwar activist who wrote "Give Peace a Chance."

Leopold II (1835–1909): King of Belgium; known for his conquest, and cruel exploitation, of the Congo.

Lind, James (1716–1794): English naval surgeon who discovered the cause of scurvy.

Lipsius, Justus (1547–1606): Flemish scholar who edited a number of classical military texts and whose teaching influenced modern military theory.

Louis XIV (1638–1715): French king whose military victories and reforms made France the main power in Europe for more than a century.

Loyola, Ignatius (1491–1556): Spanish soldier and founder of the Society of Jesus (Jesuits), he was a leader in the Counter-Reformation.

Lugalzagesi (fl. c. 2280 B.C.): Sumerian king who first united Mesopotamia into a single empire.

Luther, Martin (1483–1546): German theologian whose writings began the Protestant Reformation.

Lycurgus (fl. c. 750 B.C.): Purported founder of Sparta's constitution and military training system (*agoge*). His role, and even his existence, has been doubted.

Machiavelli, Niccolo (1469–1527): Italian diplomat and scholar, he was the author of *The Prince* and *Discourses on Livy*, influential political and military works.

Mahan, Alfred Thayer (1840–1914): American naval officer and military theorist; author of *Influence of Sea Power upon History* (1890).

Mannlicher, Ferdinand (1848–1904): German inventor of the magazine clip, which made possible the semiautomatic gun.

Mao Tse-tung (1893–1976): Chinese revolutionary leader and writer on guerrilla warfare.

Marco Polo (1254–1324): Venetian merchant who traveled from Italy through the Mongol Empire, visiting China and Southeast Asia.

Marighella, Carlos (1911–1969): Brazilian revolutionary and author of the *Minimanual of the Urban Guerrilla* (1969).

Marius, Gaius (c. 157–86 B.C.): Roman military commander and politician. The Marian reform, which transformed the Roman army, was attributed to him.

Marx, Karl (1818–1883): German revolutionary theorist and founder of the modern communist movement.

Maurice of Nassau (1567–1625): Dutch political and military figure whose organization and training of the Dutch army revolutionized modern warfare.

Maxim, Hiram (1840–1916): American British inventor of the modern machine gun.

Mazurkewicz, Josephine (1784–1896): French military surgeon who served both in the Napoleonic and Crimean wars.

McCarthy, Joseph (1908–1957): United States senator from Wisconsin whose investigations into communists in the government and military became a byword for political persecution.

McCrae, John (1872–1918): Canadian officer and military surgeon who wrote one of the most famous war poems of the 20th century, "In Flanders Fields." He died of pneumonia while commanding a field hospital.

McKinley, William (1843–1901): President of the United States; assassinated by an anarchist.

McNamara, Robert (b. 1916): American statistician, businessman, and politician who developed the theory behind firebombing during World War II and was United States secretary of state during the Vietnam War.

McNeil, William H. (b. 1917): Canadian American historian and author of *The Pursuit of Power*: *Technology, Armed Force, and Society since A.D. 1000* (1982).

Moore, Robin (1925–2008), **and Barry Sadler** (1940–1989): American cowriters of the popular song "The Green Berets," which became an unofficial anthem for many special forces units around the world.

Morillo, Stephen (b. 20th century): British American military historian and coauthor of *War in World History: Society, Technology and War from Ancient Times to the Present* (2008).

Mo-tzu (a.k.a. **Mo Ti**; c. 470–391 B.C.): Chinese philosopher known for his teachings of universal love and pacifism.

Muhammad (c. 570–632): Arabian political, military, and religious figure; founder of Islam.

Murad IV (1612–1640): Ottoman Turkish sultan who stabilized the empire and won a series of victories against the Safavid Persians.

Napoleon I (a.k.a. **Napoleon Bonaparte**; 1769–1821): French military and political figure who created a French empire that dominated Europe for a decade. His campaigns and military theories were very influential in the 19th century.

Narmer (fl. c. 3100 B.C.): Subject of the Narmer Palette, which shows a king subduing enemies. Considered to be the unifier of Egypt and first pharaoh.

Naue, Julius (1833–1907): German archaeologist and art historian who categorized Bronze Age swords. The Naue II, or tongue-hilt, sword is named after him.

Nebuchadnezzar II (a.k.a. **Nabu-kudurri-usur**; c. 630–562 B.C.): King of the Neo-Babylonian Empire who conquered Judah and deported its king and aristocracy to Babylon.

Nehemiah (fl. c. 5th or 4th century B.C.): Jewish Persian official placed in charge of Judah by the Persian king, he rebuilt the walls of Jerusalem.

Nelson, Horatio (1758–1805): British naval officer who revolutionized naval tactics.

Nietzsche, Friedrich (1844–1900): German philosopher known for his ideas of the superman and the will to power.

Nightingale, Florence (1820–1910): English nurse, author, and statistician who founded modern military nursing.

Nixon, Richard (1913–1994): President of the United States during the Vietnam War.

Nordenfeldt, Thorsten (1842–1920): Swedish inventor and businessman; founded an arms company that designed antiaircraft guns and submarines.

Nostradamus (a.k.a. **Michel de Nostredame**; 1503–1566): French astrologer and poet whose prophecies were popularized by the Nazi propaganda ministry.

Ono, Yoko (b. 1933): Japanese American artist and pacifist who produced much conceptual antiwar art, both with her husband John Lennon and after his death.

Ötzi (fl. c. 3300 B.C.): Nickname of a man whose body was found in the Ötztal Alps in 1991. His remains were frozen, which allowed the reconstruction of his violent death.

Owen (1893–1918): English officer and war poet of World War I who wrote "Dulce et Decorum Est," one of the most powerful war poems of the 20th century. He was killed in action.

Palmcrantz, Helge (1842–1880): Swedish inventor and businessman. He designed an automatic gun, originally for antisubmarine use, that was key in antiaircraft gun design.

Pan Ch'ao (32–102): Han Chinese general who conquered the Tarim Basin in Central Asia and campaigned as far west as the Caspian Sea.

Parker, Ely (a.k.a. **Donehogawa**; 1828–1895): Seneca Indian American military officer and politician. He served as adjutant to Ulysses S. Grant and was present at Lee's surrender. He rose to the rank of Brigadier General and headed the Bureau of Indian Affairs.

Parker, Geoffrey (b. 1943): British American military historian and author of *The Military Revolution: Military Innovation and the Rise of the West, 1500–1800* (1988).

Parsons, Charles Algernon (1854–1931): Naval engineer who designed the steam turbine engine.

Parvataka (fl. c. 330 B.C.): King of the Indian kingdom of Paurava who fought Alexander the Great in 326 B.C. at the Battle of the Hydaspes River.

Peel, Robert (1788–1850): English politician who formed the first modern police force in London.

Peisistratus (c. 590–528/7 B.C.): Tyrant who ruled Athens with the support of the hoplite class at the beginning of the Peloponnesian War.

Pericles (c. 495–429 B.C.): Greek politician who dominated the Athenian democracy through the elected post of general (*strategos*).

Peter I (1672–1725): Russian czar who modernized the Russian military and state.

Picasso, Pablo (1881–1973): Spanish French artist whose painting *Guernica* (1937) became an icon of the horrors of modern war.

Pinkerton, Allan (1819–1884): Scottish American detective and head of the U.S. intelligence service during the Civil War. He developed human intelligence techniques such as shadowing and undercover work.

Pizarro, Francisco (c. 1471–1541): Spanish commander who conquered the Incan Empire.

Plato (c. 428/7–348/7 B.C.): Greek philosopher and student of Socrates. An aristocrat, he was an opponent of democracy.

Plutarch (c. 45–c. 120): Greco-Roman historian and biographer.

Pol Pot (a.k.a. **Saloth Sar**; 1925–1998): Cambodian revolutionary leader whose short rule of Cambodia (1975–1979) led to the death of more than a million people.

Polybius (c. 203–120 B.C.): Greek politician who was taken to Rome as a hostage and authored a history of the rise of the Roman Empire.

Reagan, Ronald (1911–2004): President of the United States at the end of the Cold War.

Remarque, Erich Maria (1898–1970): German veteran of World War I and author of the classic antiwar novel *All Quiet on the Western Front* (1928).

Richard the Lion-Heart (1157–1199): King of England and Crusader.

Richter, Gerhard (b. 1932): German artist who painted a number of works dealing with the Allied bombing of Germany in World War II.

Rockwell, Norman (1894–1978): American painter and illustrator.

Rosenthal, Joe (1911–2006): American war correspondent and photojournalist who took "Raising the Flag of Mount Suribachi."

Rousseau, Jean-Jacques (1712–1788): French philosopher known for his idea of the "noble savage."

Saladin (a.k.a. **Yusuf ibn Ayyub**; 1138–1193): Kurdish Muslim military and political figure. He drove the Crusaders out of Palestine and founded the Ayyubid sultanate.

Sargon of Akkad (fl. c. 2250 B.C.): King who founded the Akkadian Empire, between Elam (modern Iran) and the Mediterranean. Pioneered the use of the professional army and composite bow.

Sassoon, Siegfried (1886–1967): English officer and one of the war poets of World War I, he was highly decorated but wrote "A Soldier's Declaration" when he refused to return to the front. Rather than being court-martialed, he was treated as shell-shocked.

Sawma, Rabban (c. 1220–1294): Turkish Christian monk, born in Beijing, who traveled west through the Mongol Empire. He was sent as an ambassador to the pope, visiting Constantinople, Italy, and France.

Shaka Zulu (1787–1828): Zulu military leader and politician.

Shakespeare, William (1564–1616): English poet and playwright.

Shang Yang (d. 338 B.C.): Minister in the state of Ch'in whose military and political reforms, following the legalist tradition, led to Ch'in victories and the unification of China.

Shay, Jonathan (b. 1941): American psychologist and author of *Achilles in Vietnam: Combat Trauma and the Undoing of Character*.

Shih Huang-ti (259–210 B.C.): Military figure who unified China, founded the Ch'in dynasty, and became the first Chinese emperor.

Shirley, Anthony (1565–1635), **and Robert Shirley** (c. 1581–1628): Two English brothers—merchants and adventurers—who trained the Safavid Persian army in modern European warfare.

Shostakovich, Dmitri (1906–1975): Russian composer who composed both patriotic ("Song of the Red Army," 1943) and antiwar ("Supporters of Peace March," 1950) orchestral pieces.

Siemienowicz, Kazimierz (c. 1600–c. 1651): Polish Lithuanian artillery general, whose book *The Complete Art of Artillery* (1650) was used as a basic text for centuries.

Smith, Adam (1723–1790): Scottish scholar whose book *The Wealth of Nations* (1776) laid the foundations of modern economic theory.

Smith, Joseph (1805–1844): American religious figure; founder of the Latter Day Saints (Mormons).

Socrates (c. 470–399 B.C.): Athenian thinker who is considered the founder of Greek philosophy.

Solon (c. 630–c. 560 B.C.): Greek statesman whose constitutional reforms first gave power to the Athenian hoplite class.

Ssu-ma Ch'ien (c. 145–86 B.C.): Chinese official in the Han dynasty; author of *Records of the Grand Historian*, an important source for Chinese history.

Stalin, Joseph (1878–1953): Russian revolutionary and political figure who was dictator of the Soviet Union during World War II.

Stendhal (a.k.a. **Henri-Marie Beyle**; 1783–1842): Author of *The Charterhouse of Parma* (1839), which featured a graphic description of the Battle of Waterloo.

Stephen I (c. 970–1038): First Christian king of Hungary, he was canonized as a saint.

Stirling, David (1915–1990): British officer who organized the Special Air Service, a special forces unit during World War II.

Sun Bin (d. 316 B.C.): Author of a Chinese military classic, which was rediscovered in a tomb in 1972.

Sun Tzu (a.k.a. **Sun Wu**; fl c. 525 B.C.): Author of the Chinese military classic *The Art of War*.

Sun Yat-sen (1866–1925): Chinese revolutionary and politician; helped organize the revolution that overthrew the Ch'ing dynasty.

T'ai Tsung (599–649): Chinese military commander who helped his father overthrow the Sui dynasty and become first emperor of the Tang dynasty. T'ai Tsung became the second Tang emperor and conquered an enormous area of East Asia.

Tamurlane (a.k.a. **Timur i-lang**; 1336–1405): Turko-Mongol military and political figure who tried, unsuccessfully, to restore the unified Mongol Empire.

Tandy, David (b. 20th century): Classics professor and author of *Warriors into Traders: The Power of the Market in Early Greece* (1997).

Tennyson, Lord Alfred (1809–1892): English poet whose *Charge of the Light Brigade* became one of the best-known poems of the 19th century.

Theodoric (454–526): King of the Ostrogoths and ruler of Italy, he was both a German king and a literate and cultured Roman.

Thucydides (c. 460–c. 395 B.C.): Athenian general and historian; author of the *History of the Peloponnesian War*, the model for subsequent Greek and Roman historical works.

Tiglath-Pileser III (r. 745–727 B.C.): Assyrian king and conqueror who established the Assyrian professional army and founded the Neo-Assyrian Empire.

Tolstoy, Leo (1828–1910): Russian writer, author of *War and Peace* (1865), and influential pacifist.

Trotsky, Leon (1879–1940): Russian revolutionary who organized and led the Red Army, which maintained Bolshevik power during the Russian Civil War. He was murdered by a Soviet agent in Mexico City.

Truman, Harry S (1884–1972): President of the United States during the Korean War and the beginning of the Cold War.

Tseng Kuo-fan (1811–1872): Han Chinese official, scholar, and military leader, he helped suppress the Taiping Rebellion.

Turney-High, Harry H. (1899–1982): American anthropologist and author of *Primitive War* (1949).

Umar (a.k.a. **Omar**; c. 581–644): Arab Muslim political and military figure who became the second caliph. Under his rule, the Sassanid Persian Empire and most of the Byzantine Empire were conquered for Islam.

Upton, Emory (1839–1881): American military officer and theorist who took a world trip to report on various military forces.

Urban II (1042–1099): Pope who launched the First Crusade and developed the idea of plenary indulgence to encourage participation in it.

Ut, Huynh Cong (b. 1951): Vietnamese American war correspondent and photojournalist who took a famous picture of a young girl suffering from a napalm bomb attack.

Vallaster, Josef (1910–1943): Austrian farmer who joined the Nazi SS and served in several extermination camps. He was in charge of gassing tens of thousands of Jews at Sobibor, where he was killed in an inmate uprising. His name was placed on a war memorial in his village as "killed in action" but was later removed by the mayor.

Van de Mieroop, Marc (b. 20th century): American specialist in Near Eastern history; author of *The Ancient Mesopotamian City* (1997).

Vauban, Sebastien de (1633–1707): French military engineer who revolutionized siege warfare.

Vernon, William (1684–1757): English naval officer and politician who helped reform the British navy. Mount Vernon in Virginia is named for him.

Verulanus, Johannes Sulpitius (fl. 15th century): Early German printer who published some of the earliest printed military works.

Von Clausewitz, Carl (1780–1831): Prussian officer and military theorist; author of *On War* (1832).

Von Dreyse, Johann (1787–1867): German inventor of the first practical bolt-action rifle, the needle gun.

Von Grimmelshausen, Hans Jakob (1621–1676): German writer and author of *Simplicius Simplicissimus* (1669), a humorous novel set in the Thirty Years' War.

Von Hippel, Theodor (b. 19th century): German officer who helped organize the Brandenburgers, one of the first special forces units of World War II.

Von Humboldt, Alexander (1767–1835): German scientist and explorer; one of the founders of modern biology.

Von Lettow-Vorbeck, Paul (1870–1964): German officer who led a very successful guerrilla-type campaign in East Africa during World War I.

Von Wallenstein, Albrecht (1583–1634): German Catholic general and politician who commanded the armies of the Holy Roman Empire during the Thirty Years' War.

Walker, Mary (1832–1919): American military doctor awarded the Medal of Honor for her service in the Civil War.

Wang Fu (c. 78–163): Han dynasty scholar and author of *Comments of a Recluse* (*Ch'ien-fu lun*), which recommended the disciplining of unruly soldiers.

Ward, Frederick Townsend (1831–1862): American Chinese sailor and mercenary who, as a Chinese citizen and official, trained and led the Ever Victorious Army, the first modern Chinese military unit.

Wei Yüan (1794–1856): Chinese scholar and historian; author of *Illustrated Treatise on the Maritime Kingdoms* (1844), the first explanation of Western-style warfare in Chinese.

Wemp, Daniel (b. c. 1980): Papua New Guinean of the Handa clan; subject of the article "Vengeance is Ours" by Jared Diamond.

Wen (a.k.a. **Yang Jian**; 541–604): Chinese military and political figure who became the first emperor of the Sui dynasty. He converted to Buddhism.

Wilhelm II (1859–1941): King of Prussia and emperor (kaiser) of the German Empire during World War I.

Wilson, Woodrow (1856–1924): President of the United States during World War I.

Wingate, Orde (1903–1944): British officer and a key figure in the development of modern special forces.

Wright, (Philip) Quincy (1890–1970): American political scientist and author of *A Study of War* (1942; revised and abridged edition, 1964).

Wright, Wilbur (1867–1912), **and Orville Wright** (1871–1948): American brothers who developed the first practical heavier-than-air craft, or airplane.

Wu Ling (c. 326–299 B.C.): King of Chao, one of a number of warring Chinese kingdoms. He instituted a military reform, introducing the methods of steppe warfare to his army.

Xenophon (c. 430–c. 355 B.C.): Aristocratic Athenian general, historian, and writer of military works. He was a student of Socrates.

Yang Ti (569–618): Chinese Buddhist, the younger son of emperor Wen, and successful general, who maneuvered his brother out of power and the murdered his father to become emperor.

Yuan Shih-kai (1859–1916): Chinese military and political figure. He commanded the imperial Chinese army; made himself the president of the Chinese republic; and shortly before his death, proclaimed himself emperor of China.

Zaharoff, Basil (1849–1936): Greek British businessman and arms dealer who became a popular archetype for the international arms trade.

Zarathustra (a.k.a. **Zoroaster**; fl. c. 600 B.C.; sometimes dated to c. 1000 B.C. or earlier): Persian prophet and founder of Zoroastrianism.

Bibliography

Ágoston, Gábor. *Guns for the Sultan: Military Power and the Weapons Industry in the Ottoman Empire*. New York: Cambridge University Press, 2008. A recent study, based on Turkish archival records, of the successful adoption of guns by the Ottomans.

Allsen, Thomas. *Mongol Imperialism: The Policies of the Grand Qan Möngke in China, Russia and the Islamic Lands*. Berkeley: University of California Press, 1987. This academic monograph focuses on Genghis Khan's little-known grandson Möngke and in the process brings out much detail on warfare during the height of the Mongol Empire.

Amitai-Preiss, Reuven. *Mongols and Mamluks: The Mamluk-Ilkhanid War, 1260–1281*. New York: Cambridge University Press, 2004. A scholarly analysis of the important, and generally overlooked, struggle that confirmed Islam as the primary religion and culture of the Middle East.

Anderson, J. K. *Military Theory and Practice in the Age of Xenophon*. Berkeley: University of California Press, 1970. This remains the classic introduction to the 4th-century B.C. military revolution and is still well worth reading.

Anderson, Matthew. *War and Society in Europe of the Old Regime: 1618–1789*. New York: St. Martin's Press, 1988. This work is a good introduction to the reforms of the French government and military that laid the basis for the professional forces of the 18th century.

Anderson, Robin. *A Century of Media, A Century of War*. New York: Peter Lang, 2006. A study of censorship and propaganda, rather than of media in warfare, this is a somewhat tendentious but readable introduction.

Andrew, Christopher, and Vasili Mitrokhin. *The Sword and the Shield: The Mitrokhin Archive and the Secret History of the KGB*. New York: Basic Books, 1999. Books by retired spies should always be read with a grain of salt, but this is a fascinating, and disturbing, account of the success of Soviet spying in the West, as well as its ultimate failure due to a closed mind-set among Russia's leaders.

Anthony, David W. *The Horse, the Wheel, and Language: How Bronze-Age Riders from the Eurasian Steppes Shaped the Modern World*. Princeton, NJ: Princeton University Press, 2007. This is by far the best recent discussion of the domestication of the horse and the spread of the chariot. Although his argument for horse riding preceding the chariot is problematic, it is still a must read.

Archer, Christon I., ed. *The Wars of Independence in Spanish America*. Wilmington, DE: Scholarly Resources, 2000. This is not a narrative history but rather a good collection of articles and chapters focusing on different incidents and aspects of the South American wars of independence.

Archer, Christon I., John R. Ferris, Holger H. Herwig, and Timothy H. E. Travers. *World History of Warfare*. Lincoln: University of Nebraska Press, 2002. Still the best in-depth textbook on global warfare. The chapters in this anthology are general solid, with some exceptions, such as the chapter on Islam.

Arnold, Thomas F. *The Renaissance at War*. New York: Smithsonian Books, 2006. Part of an excellent series of surveys of military history, this volume provides a clear and up-to-date introduction to this important subject.

Ayalon, David. *Gunpowder and Firearms in the Mamluk Kingdom: Challenge to a Mediaeval Society*. New York: Routledge, 1979. The second edition of a study first published in the 1950s, this is still the best (and virtually only) study of one of the most important military cultures of the Western core to successfully adapt to the gun.

Bachrach, Bernard. *Armies and Politics in the Early Medieval West*. Brookfield, VT: Variorum, 1993. A collection of articles, not all on military subjects, by one of the leading historians of medieval war. The military studies are worth the price of admission.

Bachrach, David. *Religion and the Conduct of War, c. 300–c. 1215*. Rochester, NY: Boydell, 2003. This academic study focuses on the tension between Christian pacifism and holy warfare, especially in the context of the Crusades.

Barfield, T. J. *The Perilous Frontier: Nomadic Empires and China*. Oxford: Basil Blackwell, 1998. While more focused on diplomacy than war, this work is both an introduction to the steppe powers that led to the fall of the Han and a model for studying steppe relations throughout the core.

Bassford, Christopher, and Edward J. Villacres. "Reclaiming the Clausewitzian Trinity." *Parameters*, Autumn 1995. The best short introduction to Clausewitz's thought; very successful in placing him as modern history's leading military theorist.

Beah, Ishmael. *A Long Way Gone: Memoirs of a Boy Soldier*. New York: Farrar, Straus and Giroux, 2007. While every detail may not be correct, this autobiography of a child soldier in Sierra Leone is a moving and chilling view into the nature of warfare in modern Africa.

Beckett, Ian. *Modern Insurgencies and Counter-Insurgencies*. London: Routledge, 2001. This is a good survey of both the wars themselves and the development of the theories of guerrilla warfare and how to combat it.

Bigler, David L. *Forgotten Kingdom: The Mormon Theocracy in the American West, 1847–1896*. Spokane, WA: Arthur H. Clark, 1998. While this is not a military history, Bigler writes about the Mormon-Indian wars, the fights with the United States, and the role of the Nauvoo Legion in both independent Deseret and the Utah territory.

Black, Jeremy. *The Age of Total War: 1860–1945*. Westport, CT: Praeger, 2006. This book is an excellent introduction to the development and course of modern warfare into the first half of the 20th century.

———. *European Warfare, 1494–1660*. New York: Routledge, 2002. This book is one of the best, if not the best, introductions to the period, balancing both land and naval warfare.

———. *War and the New Disorder in the 21st Century*. New York: Continuum, 2004. One of the best military historians working today looks at the world's wars since the year 2000.

Black, Jeremy, and Philip Woodfine, eds. *The British Navy and the Use of Naval Power in the Eighteenth Century*. Atlantic Highlands, NJ: Humanities Press International, 1989. This volume includes the papers given at a conference held in 1987 on various subjects of British sea power, including naval administration and strategy.

Boggs, Carl, and Tom Pollard. *The Hollywood War Machine: U.S. Militarism and Popular Culture*. Boulder, CO: Paradigm, 2007. This work is flawed, in my view, by its imperialist American slant, but it contains an excellent critique of the antiwar films of the Vietnam era and is a good survey of the portrayal of war in American film.

Boot, Max. *War Made New: Technology, Warfare and the Course of History*. New York: Gotham Books, 2006. Covers the period from the 16th century to the present, with a good survey of the technological advances in weapons design during the Industrial Revolution.

Brantlinger, Patrick. *Rule of Darkness: British Literature and Imperialism, 1830–1914.* Ithaca, NY: Cornell University Press, 1988. A postmodern approach and a cultural view of imperialism can make this tough reading for a military historian, but it is full of great examples of imperial ideology.

Brauer, Jurgen, and Hubert van Tuyll. *Castles, Battles and Bombs: How Economics Explains Military History.* Chicago: University of Chicago Press, 2008. This remarkable work applies economic theory to warfare.

Brewer, John. *The Sinews of Power: War, Money and the English State, 1688–1783.* Cambridge, MA: Harvard University Press, 1990. A superb study of how Britain created the financial instruments, both in taxation and deficit spending, that led to it becoming a great power.

Brown, D. K. *Warrior to Dreadnought: Warship Development 1860–1905.* Annapolis, MD: Naval Institute Press, 1998. A highly technical but very enlightening study of how the Industrial Revolution created the modern warship.

Brummett, Palmira. *Ottoman Seapower and Levantine Diplomacy in the Age of Discovery.* Albany, NY: State University of New York Press, 1994. Focusing on both military and economic factors, this is a superb study of Turkish naval operations in the 16th century, putting the Ottomans back on the world stage, where they belong.

Budiansky, Stephen. *Air Power: The Men, Machines, and Ideas That Revolutionized War, from Kitty Hawk to Gulf War II.* New York: Viking, 2004. While not groundbreaking, this is a clear and reliable survey of a complex subject.

Campbell, Brian. *War and Society in Imperial Rome.* London: Routledge, 2002. This is a short, highly readable, scholarly study putting the Roman military in its social, political, and economic context.

Chambers, James. *The Devil's Horsemen: The Mongol Invasion of Europe.* New York: Atheneum, 1979. The classic work on Mongol military history, it is still one of the best introductions to the subject.

Chase, Kenneth. *Firearms: A Global History to 1700.* Cambridge: Cambridge University Press, 2003. A good introduction to the subject from a world historical perspective, it focuses not only on the Chinese invention, but also on the European improvement, of gunpowder.

Cipolla, Carlo. *Guns, Sails and Empire: Technological Innovations and the Early Phases of European Expansion, 1400–1700*. New York: Minerva Press, 1965. Still a classic, this is a groundbreaking analysis of the role of technology in European naval conquests. It is less useful on the non-European reactions to the new innovations, but still very valuable.

Citino, Robert. *From Blitzkrieg to Desert Storm: The Evolution of Operational Warfare*. Lawrence: University of Kansas Press, 2004. While the book is long and detailed, it is a good follow-up to this course, as it extends beyond our range to look at warfare in the second half of the 20th century.

Clayton, Anthony. *Frontiersmen: Warfare in Africa since 1950*. London: UCL Press, 1999. While its theory about modern African war has been criticized, this is a good survey of warfare on the continent, especially the conflicts surrounding decolonization.

Contamine, Phillippe. *War in the Middle Ages*. Translated by Michael Jones. New York: Basil Blackwell, 1984. While focused on western Europe, and with a difficult academic style, this is classic and full of valuable detail.

Cook, Weston. *The Hundred Years War for Morocco: Gunpowder and the Military Revolution in the Early Modern Muslim World*. Boulder, CO: Westview Press, 1994. This book is a rare exploration of the impact of the 16th-century military revolution in a non-European region—in this case, Muslim North Africa.

Corvisier, Andre. *Armies and Societies in Europe, 1494–1789*. Translated by Abigail T. Siddall. Bloomington: Indiana University Press, 1979. This translation of a French classic of military history is full of detail and analysis.

Cotterell, Arthur. *The Chariot: The Astounding Rise and Fall of the World's First War Machine*. Woodstock, NY: Overlook, 2005. More scholarly than its breathless title indicates, this book suffers somewhat from disorganization and a lack of thoroughness but is still a valuable read, especially for its focus on India and China.

Crone, Patricia. "The Early Islamic World." In *War and Society in the Ancient and Medieval Worlds*, edited by K. Raaflaub and N. Rosenstein, 309–332. Cambridge, MA: Harvard University Press, 1999. By far the best short introduction to the Islamic military available; a must-read for anyone interested in the subject.

————. *From Arabian Tribes to Islamic Empire: Army, State and Society in the Near East c. 600–850*. Burlington, VT: Ashgate, 2008. A very expensive book, best checked out of the library, this collection of articles by one of the leading, and most controversial, scholars of Islam working today focuses on the Muslim military during its rise.

Davies, Brian L. "The Development of Russian Military Power, 1453–1815." In *European Warfare, 1453–1815*, edited by Jeremy Black. New York: St. Martin's Press, 1999. An in-depth analysis of the growth of the Russian gunpowder empire, this chapter dispels some misconceptions in the process.

Dawidowicz, Lucy. *The War against the Jews, 1933–1945*. New York: Holt, Rinehart and Wilson, 1975. While neither the most recent nor the most comprehensive work on the Holocaust, this is an excellent starting point on Nazi anti-Semitic ideology and its genocidal results, emphasizing its militaristic aspects.

Dawley, Alan. *Changing the World: American Progressives in War and Revolution*. Princeton, NJ: Princeton University Press, 2003. This account of the history of American progressives during World War I and its aftermath is unique for Dawley's fusion of social and international history.

De Pauw, Linda Grant. *Battle Cries and Lullabies: Women in War from Prehistory to the Present*. Norman: University of Oklahoma, 2000. While not reliable for the ancient period, this is a highly readable introduction to women in combat. The sections on the 18th and 19th centuries are quite good.

DeVries, Kelly. *Medieval Military Technology*. Orchard Park, NY: Broadview, 1992. A great introduction to the often confusing details of armor, weapons, and fortifications in the Middle Ages. It is Eurocentric, however, and weak on some areas, such as Greek fire.

DiMarco, Louis A. *War Horse: A History of the Military Horse and Rider*. Yardley, PA: Westholme, 2008. While lacking illustration, this is a fine, up-to-date introduction to the subject of cavalry, ranging from antiquity to the present. DiMarco's book is very readable and full of interesting facts and stories.

Drews, Robert. *Early Riders: The Beginnings of Mounted Warfare in Asia and Europe*. New York: Routledge, 2004. The best book on the subject of the beginnings of cavalry; the author argues strongly for a 9th-century date and its origins in the Near East, not the steppes.

————. *The End of the Bronze Age: Changes in Warfare and the Catastrophe Ca. 1200 B.C.* Princeton, NJ: Princeton University Press, 1993. Not only is this the classic modern study of the collapse of the Bronze Age palace empires, it is also a persuasive argument for the importance of the sword revolution.

Duffy, Christopher. *The Military Experience in the Age of Reason.* New York: Atheneum, 1987. This book is the best introduction to the military culture of the 18th century, with a good contrast between the lives of private soldiers and officers in the regimental society.

Dzengseo. *The Diary of a Manchu Soldier in Seventeenth-Century China.* Translated by Nicola Di Cosmo. New York: Routledge, 2006. The author of this diary, which gives a rare eyewitness look at an early modern non-Western army, was an officer in the Manchurian forces fighting in southwestern China in the 1670s and 1680s.

Elliot, J. H. *Empires of the Atlantic World.* New Haven, CT: Yale University Press, 2006. A good study of the contrasting methods used by the Spanish and British in their colonization of the New World.

Enloe, Cynthia. *Ethnic Soldiers: State Security in Divided Societies.* Athens: University of Georgia Press, 1980. A theoretical, rather than historical, approach and concerned largely with the 20th century, it is nevertheless one of the few works that cogently discuss the role of ethnicity in the 19th-century military.

Farris, William W. *Heavenly Warriors: The Evolution of Japan's Military, 500–1300.* Cambridge, MA: Harvard University Press, 1992. While not focused specifically on bushido, this is a good introduction to the origins of the samurai and their way of warfare.

Farwell, Byron. *Mr. Kipling's Army: All the Queen's Men.* New York: W. W. Norton, 1981. Short and highly readable, this is one of the best introductions to the culture of a 19th-century army and the regimental system.

Ferguson, Nial. *The Cash Nexus: Money and Power in the Modern World, 1700–2000.* New York: Basic Books, 2000. This book is a superb analysis of the role of warfare in the development of modern financial institutions.

Ferguson, R. Brian. "A Paradigm for the Study of War and Society." In *War and Society in the Ancient and Medieval Worlds*, edited by K. Raaflaub and N. Rosenstein. Cambridge, MA: Harvard University Press, 1999. This essay is written in the context of ancient and medieval warfare. It is very valuable, however, because of the global reach of the volume and especially because of the way the author, an anthropologist, works the evidence of premodern warfare from around the world into a useful theoretical framework.

Ferill, Arthur. *The Origins of War*. London: Westview Press, 1985. Somewhat dated but still valuable, an argument for the Neolithic origins of war. Short and readable, it is a good place to start for the basic evidence and arguments.

Forsyth, James. *A History of the Peoples of Siberia*. Cambridge: Cambridge University Press, 1994. While primarily focused on the Russian invasion of the region, this work takes a rare look at warfare among the north Asian peoples and is a very good study of the military aspects of the fur trade.

French, Shannon E. *The Code of the Warrior: Exploring Warrior Values Past and Present*. Lanham, MD: Rowman & Littlefield, 2003. The author both analyzes and advocates for warrior codes, such as chivalry and bushido; furthermore, she compares such systems through history and around the world.

Fukui, K., and D. Turton. *Warfare among East African Herders*. Osaka, Japan: National Museum of Ethnology, 1979. While an anthropological study, rather than a military one, this collection of articles focuses on a little-discussed topic.

Fussell, Paul. *The Great War and Modern Memory*. New York: Oxford University Press, 1975. Quite possibly the best book ever written on culture and war, this is a must-read for military historians, especially of the 20th century.

Gabriel, Richard. *The Culture of War: Invention and Early Development*. New York: Greenwood Press, 1990. This is an integrated study of war from its origins through the Bronze Age. While it does not cover East Asia, it is wide-ranging in the Western core.

Garlan, Yvon. *War in the Ancient World: A Social History*. Translated by Janet Lloyd. New York: W. W. Norton, 1975. An older (and Eurocentric) study, this is nevertheless a classic work and valuable for the relation of war with ancient social structure.

Gat, Azar. *War in Human Civilization*. Oxford: Oxford University Press, 2008. Not a military history, but a well-argued thesis on the interaction of war and culture, it is a must-read for military historians.

Gilmartin, John. "The Cutting Edge: An Analysis of the Spanish Invasion and Overthrow of the Incan Empire, 1532–1539." In *Transatlantic Encounters*, edited by K. Andrien and R. Adorno. Berkeley: University of California Press, 1992. This chapter remains the best short discussion in English of the role of military technology in the conquest of Peru.

———. *Gunpowder and Galleys*. Cambridge: Cambridge University Press, 1974. While focused mainly on the 16th century, this is one of the few books that discuss the impact of the gun on naval warfare before the development of the galleon.

Gnirs, Andrea M. "Ancient Egypt." In *War and Society in the Ancient and Medieval Worlds*, edited by K. Raaflaub and N. Rosenstein, 71–104. Cambridge, MA: Harvard University Press, 1999. This chapter is a study of the organization of the Egyptian army in the New Kingdom and very useful for understanding (non-Greek) armies of the period. There is a particularly good discussion of the chariot forces.

Gommans, Jos. *Mughal Warfare: Indian Frontiers and Highroads to Empire, 1500-1700*. New York: Routledge, 2002. One of the few books on premodern South Asian warfare published outside India, this excellent (but expensive) book will repay a trip to the local university library.

Gommans, Jos, and Dirk Kolff, eds. *Warfare and Weaponry in South Asia, 1000–1800*. New York: Oxford University Press, 2001. The military history of premodern India is poorly served, and it is especially difficult to find works published outside of India. This is beginning to change, as evidenced by this scholarly anthology.

Graff, David A. *Medieval Chinese Warfare, 300–900*. New York: Routledge, 2002. A fine survey on a subject rarely written about (at least in English), although there is more focus on logistics and administration than weapons and tactics.

Gunaratna, Rohan. *Inside Al Qaeda: Global Network of Terror*. New York: Berkley Books, 2003. A fascinating analysis of the structure of the al-Qaeda terrorist organization, the model asymmetric military force of the last 20 years.

Habeck, Mary R. *Storm of Steel: The Development of Armor Doctrine in Germany and the Soviet Union, 1919-1939*. Ithaca, NY: Cornell University Press, 2003. Based on archival research, including previously secret Soviet documents, this is an excellent analysis of the theoretical and experimental work that led to the blitzkrieg.

Hale, John. *War and Society in Renaissance Europe*. Baltimore, MD: Johns Hopkins University Press, 1986. This is an excellent study of the interaction of the military and the Renaissance, with a good balance of the influence in both directions.

Hanson, Victor Davis. *The Western Way of War: Infantry Battle in Classical Greece*. London: John Curtis/Hodder & Stoughton, 1989. While his thesis may be problematic, this is the very best book on the mechanics of Greek hoplite warfare.

Hassig, Ross. *Aztec Warfare: Imperial Expansion and Political Control*. Norman: University of Oklahoma Press, 1988. A comprehensive and compelling presentation of the history of the dramatic Aztec conquest of central Mexico.

———. *War and Society in Ancient Mesoamerica*. Berkeley: University of California Press, 1992. This study, by the leading expert in the field, takes a long-term and paradigmatic approach and does not confine itself to Aztec warfare in the contact period.

Head, Duncan. *The Achaemenid Persian Army*. Stockport, UK: Montvert, 1992. While not an academic study, this is one of the few comprehensive looks at the Persian army in this critical period.

Headrick, Daniel. *The Tools of Empire: Technology and European Imperialism in the Nineteenth Century*. New York: Oxford University Press, 1981. The book argues that technology did not just provide the means for European expansion, but the motivation as well.

Helgeland, John. "Christians and the Roman Army A.D. 173–337." *Church History* 43, no. 2 (June 1974): 149–163. While not a military history, one of the few studies that seriously considers the importance of Christians in the imperial Roman army before its full Christianization in the 4th century.

Hildinger, Erik. *Warriors of the Steppe: A Military History of Central Asia, 500 B.C. to A.D. 1700*. New York: Sarpedon, 1997. This book is a good introduction to the basics of steppe warfare; it emphasizes continuity, thus sometimes missing some important changes.

Housely, Norman. *Religious Warfare in Europe, 1400–1536*. Oxford: Oxford University Press, 2002. This book not only links 16th-century European religious war to its antecedents in the

Crusading movement, but despite its title, it is also global in its approach.

Howard, Michael. *War and the Liberal Conscience*. New York: Columbia University Press, 2008. This is the second edition of a classic history of liberal pacifist and antiwar movements and ideology.

Hui, Victoria Tin-bor. *War and State Formation in Ancient China and Early Modern Europe*. New York: Cambridge University Press, 2005. This work challenges the notion that the nation-state is solely a European phenomenon. The author's view is shared by Azar Gat and extended in his *War in Human Civilization*.

Hyland, Ann. *The Horse in the Ancient World*. Westport, CT: Praeger, 2003. A solid popular survey of the horse in antiquity, this work is full of practical insights and draws on non-European sources.

Imber, Colin. *The Ottoman Empire, 1300–1650: The Structure of Power*. New York: Palgrave Macmillan, 2002. A straightforward political history, it covers the Ottoman religious warfare not only in Europe but globally as well.

Johnson, Curtis. *Redeeming America: Evangelicals and the Road to Civil War*. Chicago: I. R. Dee, 1994. This book focuses on theological movements in antebellum America and is a good introduction to militant ideas within American Protestantism.

Kang, Sa-Moon. *Divine War in the Old Testament and the Ancient Near East*. New York: W. de Gruyter, 1989. While technical, this is an excellent study of the origins of religious warfare, with much valuable detail.

Karsh, Efraim. *Islamic Imperialism*. New Haven, CT: Yale University Press, 2006. This study argues that jihad has always been an integral part of Islam. Not all will agree with its conclusions, but it is a valuable survey of the subject.

Keegan, John. *A History of Warfare*. New York: Vintage, 1994. Less of a historical survey than an argument for the primacy of culture in warfare. While still a necessary read, its approach is appearing more and more dated.

———. *Intelligence in War*. New York: Vintage, 2004. Focusing on the effectiveness of intelligence gathering in war, this is one of the best introductions to the subject.

Keeley, Lawrence. *War before Civilization: The Myth of the Peaceful Savage*. New York: Oxford University Press, 1996. A scholarly but readable work, this is the best recent anthropological study of primitive war. This book has changed our understanding of early and marginal warfare.

Keen, Maurice. *Chivalry*. New Haven, CT: Yale University Press, 1984. A scholarly and readable introduction to chivalry that treats it as an aristocratic military code.

Kennedy, Hugh. *The Armies of the Caliphs: Military and Society in the Early Islamic State*. London: Routledge, 2001. While it might be tough going for one not familiar with the period, this is an excellent study of the development of the professional armies of the caliphate.

Knightley, Phillip. *The First Casualty: The War Correspondent as Hero and Myth-Maker from the Crimea to Iraq*. 3rd ed. Baltimore, MD: Johns Hopkins University Press, 2004. A thorough history of war journalism, this makes an excellent introduction to the interaction of war and the media.

Kuklick, Bruce. *Blind Oracles: Intellectuals and War from Kennan to Kissinger*. Princeton, NJ: Princeton University Press, 2006. A powerful critique of the mistakes of the academic analysts and think tanks that dominated—and to some extent still dominate—American strategic thinking.

Kurlansky, Mark. *Non-Violence: The History of a Dangerous Idea*. New York: Modern Library, 2008. While somewhat preachy and patchy in spots, this book is full of interesting detail on the history of pacifism and nonviolence.

Lee, A. D. *War in Late Antiquity*. Malden, MA: Basil Blackwell, 2007. While focusing almost exclusively on the late Roman army, this work puts the military and warfare in social, political, and economic context.

Li, Nan. *Chinese Civil-Military Relations: The Transformation of the People's Liberation Army*. New York: Routledge, 2006. An analysis of the changing role of the Chinese military in the politics—and economy—of communist China.

Lloyd, Alan B. "Philip II and Alexander the Great: The Moulding of Macedon's Army." In *Battle in Antiquity*, edited by Alan B. Lloyd, 169–198. London: Duckworth, 1996. This is a short and readable discussion of the importance of military reform in Alexander the Great's success.

Loewe, Michael. "The Campaigns of Han Wu-Ti." In *Chinese Ways in Warfare*, edited by Frank A. Kierman Jr. Cambridge, MA: Harvard University Press, 1974. This chapter is an excellent study of Han warfare, as well as of the military leadership of one of China's greatest conquerors.

Lutz, James Michael, and Brenda J. Lutz. *Terrorism: Origins and Evolution*. New York: Palgrave Macmillan, 2005. One of the few works on the subject that views terrorism in a broad historical and global perspective.

Lynn, John A. *The Bayonets of the Republic: Motivation and Tactics in the Army of Revolutionary France, 1791–94*. Urbana: University of Illinois Press, 1984. In this valuable study, Lynn delves into the question of discipline and combat effectiveness in an army that was in some respects raised from scratch.

Lyons, Malcolm C., and D. E. P. Jackson. *Saladin: The Politics of the Holy War*. New York: Cambridge University Press, 1982. Not for beginners, but the use of Arabic sources gives this in-depth biography a firmly Muslim perspective.

Madden, Thomas F. *The New Concise History of the Crusades*. Lanham, MD: Rowman & Littlefield, 2005. This is an excellent introduction to this period of medieval religious warfare; it takes both sides into consideration and puts events into a contemporary perspective.

Malone, Patrick. *The Skulking Way of War: Technology and Tactics among the New England Indians*. Baltimore, MD: Johns Hopkins University Press, 2000. Although this text is mainly concerned with the impact of firearms, the first chapter discusses precontact warfare in eastern North America.

Mawdsley, Evan. *The Russian Civil War*. Boston: Allen & Unwin, 1987. A short introduction to a very complicated and brutal struggle, this text focuses on the question of how and why the communists won.

McNeill, William. *The Pursuit of Power: Technology, Armed Force, and Society since A.D. 1000*. Chicago: University of Chicago Press, 1982. A classic work by one of the first great world historians; despite its flaws, is an important argument for the importance of market economies in the growth of military power.

Mielczarek, Mariusz. *Cataphracti and Clibinarii: Studies on the Heavy Armoured Cavalry of the Ancient World*. Translated by Maria

Abramowicz. Lodz, Poland: Oficyna Naukowa MS, 1993. The author, a Polish professor of archaeology, is one of the world's experts in the cavalry of ancient Central Asia. Although published in Poland, the book is available on the Internet.

Miller, Nathan. *Broadsides: The Age of the Fighting Sail, 1775–1815.* New York: Wiley, 2001. A highly readable introduction into how the wooden world functioned, especially useful for its focus on the professionalism of both crew and officers.

Morillo, Stephen. "Guns and Government: A Comparative Study of Europe and Japan." *Journal of World History* 6 (1995): 75–106. This article is an excellent study on the similarities and differences in the use of the gun at either end of the core.

Morillo, Stephen, Jeremy Black, and Paul Lococo. *War in World History.* New York: McGraw-Hill, 2008. A very good introduction to the subject, but it suffers somewhat from being too short for a global survey of military history.

Murphey, Rhoads. *Ottoman Warfare, 1500–1700.* New Brunswick, NJ: Rutgers University Press, 1999. While focusing mainly on the 17th century, this work argues that the Ottomans successfully adopted the European-style gun and integrated it into their military system.

Nalty, Bernard. *Strength for the Fight: A History of Black Americans in the Military.* New York: Free Press, 1989. Though focused on the modern period, this remains the best academic introduction to the issue of race in the American armed forces.

Neier, Aryeh. *War Crimes: Brutality, Genocide, Terror, and the Struggle for Justice.* New York: Times Books, 1998. This work, by a Holocaust survivor and former head of Amnesty International, is both a historical survey and an analysis of war crime tribunals.

Niditch, Susan. *War in the Hebrew Bible: A Study in the Ethics of Violence.* New York: Oxford University Press, 1993. Not a study in ethics but an analysis of the various attitudes toward war in the biblical text. Densely argued but well worth reading.

O'Connell, Robert L. *Of Arms and Men: A History of War, Weapons, Aggression.* New York: Oxford University Press, 1989. An excellent study discussing the impact of weapons on warfare. As it was written during the Cold War, the latter section is somewhat dated but still well worth reading.

Otterbein, Keith. *How War Began.* College Station: Texas A&M University Press, 2004. While arguing for the existence of Paleolithic war, this book challenges the idea that war is natural to humans. This is the most important recent book on war's origins.

Overy, Richard. *Why the Allies Won*. New York: Norton, 1995. A well-argued thesis that the economic flexibility of the Western powers, and the inefficiency of the fascist ones, played a key role in Allied victory in World War II.

Palmer, Michael A. *Command at Sea: Naval Command and Control since the Sixteenth Century*. Cambridge, MA: Harvard University Press, 2005. A superb study of the problems of control and command at sea and how European navies solved them.

Parker, Geoffrey. *Europe in Crisis, 1598–1648*. Malden, MA: Blackwell, 2001. An updated version of a survey textbook on this period of intense European religious wars, by the author of *The Military Revolution*.

———. *The Military Revolution: Military Innovation and the Rise of the West 1500–1800*. 2nd ed. Cambridge: University of Cambridge Press, 1996. A classic work—one that changed the writing of military history. It is a must-read.

Peers, Douglas M. *Between Mars and Mammon: Colonial Armies and the Garrison State in India, 1819–1835*. New York: Tauris Academic Studies, 1995. Most books on colonial militaries focus on warfare, but this book is a study of the garrison army of India and its relationship to civilian authority.

———, ed. *Warfare and Empires: Contact and Conflict Between European and Non-European Military and Maritime Forces and Cultures*. Brookfield, VT: Ashgate/Variorum, 1997. This is an interesting collection of articles on various aspects of the spread of military culture around the world. Especially good on India.

Perdue, Peter C. *China Marches West: The Qing Conquest of Central Eurasia*. Cambridge, MA: Belknap Press, 2005. This is a recent and comprehensive study of Ch'ing military expansion and conflicts with neighboring states, with ample attention to questions of administration and logistics.

Perlmutter, David D. *Visions of War: Picturing Warfare from the Stone Age to the Cyber Age*. New York: St. Martin's Press, 1999. A readable and thought-provoking study of the representation of war in images, it is the best work on the subject.

Perrin, Noel. *Giving Up the Gun: Japan's Reversion to the Sword, 1543–1879*. Boston: D. R. Godine, 1979. While some of Perrin's points have been challenged by more recent scholarship, this groundbreaking work on the de-gunpowdering of Japan is still well worth reading.

Porter, Bruce D. *War and the Rise of the State: The Military Foundations of Modern Politics*. New York: Free Press, 2002. Written by a political scientist, this work makes a powerful case that not only do states make war, but war makes states.

Postgate, J. N. *Taxation and Conscription in the Assyrian Empire*. Rome: Biblical Institute Press, 1974. While dense and highly technical, and dealing only tangentially with the army, this is an invaluable study of the administration that made the Assyrian Empire so influential.

Prucha, Francis Paul. *The Sword of the Republic: The United States Army on the Frontier, 1783–1846*. New York: Macmillan, 1968. This remains an important study of the importance of the army in opening the American frontier—not by war, but by building infrastructure.

Ralston, David. *Importing the European Army: The Introduction of European Military Techniques and Institutions in the Extra European World, 1600–1914*. Chicago: University of Chicago Press, 1990. While primarily focused on 19th-century interactions, it does discuss the 18th century in some detail.

Ramold, Steven J. *Slaves, Sailors, Citizens: African Americans in the Union Navy*. DeKalb: Northern Illinois University Press, 2002. This study focuses only on the Civil War, but it is a good introduction to the integrated nature of crews throughout the wooden world.

Reed, Nelson. *The Caste War of the Yucatan*. Stanford, CA: Stanford University Press, 2001. A scholarly but readable account of the little-known Mayan independence movement and its Christian connections.

Reiter, Dan, and Allan C. Stam. *Democracies at War*. Princeton, NJ: Princeton University Press, 2002. Basically a book of political theory, this is still a good read for historians looking at the way that 20th-century democratic ideology impacted war making.

Roth, Jonathan P. "War." In *The Cambridge History of Greek and Roman Warfare. Vol. 1: Greece, the Hellenistic World and the Rise of Rome*, edited by Philip Sabin, Hans van Wees, and Michael Whitby, 368–398. Cambridge: Cambridge University Press, 2007.

This chapter discusses military methodology in the Hellenistic and Roman republican periods, focusing on logistics and command.

Russell-Wood, A. J. R. *The Portuguese Empire, 1415–1808*. Baltimore, MD: Johns Hopkins University Press, 1998. While not a military history, this work gives a good introduction to the details of European world expansion.

Saideman, Stephen M., and R. William Ayres. *For Kin or Country: Xenophobia, Nationalism and War*. New York: Columbia University Press, 2008. This new work emphasizes the importance of nationalism in the wars of the 20th century.

Sajer, Guy. *The Forgotten Soldier*. Translated by Lily Emmet. New York: Harper & Row, 1971. There have been attempts, wrong in my view, to question the authenticity of this autobiographical account by a soldier on the Eastern Front in World War II, but German soldiers have confirmed its powerful narrative.

Sandars, Nancy. *The Sea Peoples: Warriors of the Ancient Mediterranean, 1250–1150 B.C.* London: Thames and Hudson, 1985. This is a thorough and readable introduction to the late Bronze Age and the complex problem of the Sea Peoples.

Sandler, Stanley. *The Emergence of the Modern Capital Ship*. Newark: University of Delaware Press, 1979. This book focuses mainly on the development (in late 19th-century Britain) of the mastless, turreted warship and is a good introduction into this vital period of naval innovation.

Scheina, Robert L. *Latin America's Wars, Volume I: The Age of the Caudillo, 1791–1899*. Washington, DC: Brassey's, 2003. Remarkably, this is the first book in English published on the subject. It is an excellent study of the region's 19th-century wars and warfare.

Schwartz, Seth. *Imperialism and Jewish Society, 200 B.C.E. to 640 C.E.* Princeton, NJ: Princeton University Press, 2001. This is an innovative and thought-provoking work—one of the few that addresses the complex interaction between Judaism and the Roman Empire.

Seaton, Philip A. *Japan's Contested War Memories: The "Memory Rifts" in Historical Consciousness of World War II*. New York: Routledge, 2009. This book makes the point that the Japanese rewriting of history is by no means a feature of their culture but is common in modern societies.

Showalter, Dennis E. *Railroads and Rifles: Soldiers, Technology, and the Unification of Germany*. Hamden, CT: Archon Books, 1975. A classic monograph that discusses the effects of technological change on society as a whole but maintains its focus on the military and warfare.

Sidebottom, Harry. *Ancient Warfare: A Very Short Introduction*. Oxford: Oxford University Press, 2004. Part of a great series of such books, this is excellent introduction to ancient warfare, as well as a well-argued critic of the idea of the so-called Western way of war.

———. "Philosopher's Attitudes to Warfare under the Principate." In *War and Society in the Roman World*, edited by John Rich and Graham Shipley. London: Routledge, 1993. A well-argued and readable introduction to the various ideological views of warfare among Roman intellectuals. This is very important work for understanding both pre-Christian and Christian attitudes.

Smail, R. C. *Crusading Warfare, 1097–1193*. New York: Cambridge University Press, 1995. Despite its name, this book is as much on Muslim as on European warfare and a good introduction to both, but be prepared for untranslated Latin quotations!

Smaldone, Joseph P. *Warfare in the Sokoto Caliphate: Historical and Sociological Perspectives*. New York: Cambridge University Press, 1977. This sociological study of a highly militarized culture has ramifications outside the history of African warfare, itself a neglected topic.

Spence, Jonathon D. *God's Chinese Son: The Taiping Heavenly Kingdom of Hong Xiuquan*. New York: W. W. Norton, 1997. This is the best introduction to one of the most important military events of the 19th century and its ideological roots.

Starkey, Armstrong. *European–Native American Warfare, 1675–1815*. Norman: University of Oklahoma, 1998. This book stresses both the relative success of Indians early on and the importance of European adoption of Native American tactics in order to defeat them.

Stoecker, Sally. *Forging Stalin's Army: Marshal Tukhachevsky and the Politics of Military Innovation*. Boulder, CO: Westview Press, 1999. This is an excellent study of the debate over ideology and professionalism in military theory in the first decades of the Soviet Union.

Suri, Jeremi. *Power and Protest: Global Revolution and the Rise of Detente*. Cambridge, MA: Harvard University Press, 2003. This work argues that the worldwide cultural upheavals of the 1960s had a profound impact on the strategic thinking of the period.

Sweeney, Michael S. *Secrets of Victory: The Office of Censorship and the American Press and Radio in World War II*. Chapel Hill: University of North Carolina Press, 2000. While confined to the United States and World War II, this book illuminates many of the practical and ideological issues of censorship throughout the 20th century.

Taber, Robert. *The War of the Flea*. London: Granada, 1965. The classic study of 20th-century guerrilla warfare, it remains the first stop for anyone interested in understanding the subject.

Taylor, Philip M. *Munitions of the Mind: A History of Propaganda from the Ancient World to the Present Era*. Manchester, UK: Manchester University Press, 2003. Although it focuses almost entirely on the West, this is a comprehensive and well-written introduction to the subject of propaganda, especially in the modern period.

Tilly, Charles. *Coercion, Capital, and European States, A.D. 990–1990*. Cambridge, MA: Basil Blackwell, 1990. A broad-ranging study that goes up to the 20th century; but very valuable in its discussion of the economy and medieval warfare.

Upton, Emory. *Armies of Asia and Europe: Embracing Official Reports of the Armies of Japan, China, India, Persia, Italy, Russia, Austria, Germany, France, and England*. New York: Greenwood Press, 1968. First published 1878. This is a reprinted edition of a remarkable primary source, not only for comparing the makeup of European and non-European armies, but for illuminating the mind-set of the 19th-century military professional.

Vagts, Alfred. *A History of Militarism: Civilian and Military*. New York: Free Press, 1959. This is an older work but still a classic well worth reading. It covers the development and importance of militarism in 19th- and 20th-century Europe.

Van Creveld, Martin. *The Culture of War*. New York: Presidio Press, 2008. While this book covers the culture of war from the ancient world to the present, it is especially valuable in understanding how military culture reacted to industrialism.

———. *Technology and War from 2000 B.C. to the Present.* New York: Collier Macmillan, 1989. An excellent work from one of the leading military historians. Not simply an introduction, it argues several very thought-provoking ideas on the interaction of technology and war.

Van Wees, Hans. *Greek Warfare: Myths and Realities.* London: Routledge, 2004. An excellent and up-to-date discussion of many of the problems of Greek warfare, although less useful on the navy than the army.

———. *Status Warriors: War, Violence and Society in Homer and History.* Amsterdam: J. C. Gieben, 1992. While its conclusions are often challenged, this is an excellent introduction to the problem of warfare in Homer. It is both scholarly and readable.

Vayda, Andrew Peter. *Maori Warfare.* Wellington, New Zealand: Polynesian Society, 1960. An old and difficult to find monograph, this is one of the few in-depth discussions of precontact Polynesian warfare.

Vergruggen, J. F. *The Art of Warfare in Western Europe during the Middle Ages: From the Eighth Century to 1340.* Translated by Sumner Willard and S. C. M. Southern. New York: North-Holland, 1977. Originally published in the 1950s and then updated in the 1970s, this is a dense read but worthwhile for its brilliant analysis of medieval Western warfare.

Victoria, Brian Daizen. *Zen at War.* New York: Weatherhill, 1979. While primarily focused on Japanese Buddhism during World War II, this is one of the few books on the subject of Buddhist holy war.

Vincent, Steven. *In the Red Zone: A Journey into the Soul of Iraq.* Dallas, TX: Spence, 2004. An insightful look at the early years of the Iraq conflict by a journalist who traveled widely throughout the country and who ultimately died there at the hands of terrorists.

Voldeman, Daniele, and Luc Capdevila. *War Dead: Western Societies and the Casualties of War.* New York: Columbia University Press, 2007. This is a study not only of cemeteries and war memorials but of how casualties are treated by the military and the society of different countries, revealing much about their cultures.

Wallinga, H. T. *Ships and Sea-Power before the Great Persian War: The Ancestry of the Ancient Trireme.* Leiden, Netherlands: E. J. Brill,

1993. This work is an important and iconoclastic study of the origins of the trireme and shipping in the first half of the 1st millennium B.C.

Ward, Harry. *The War for Independence and the Transformation of American Society*. London: Routledge, 1999. A fascinating look at how the war changed not only the American military but the broader society as well.

Weatherford, Jack. *Genghis Khan and the Making of the Modern World*. New York: Crown, 2004. This highly readable work by an anthropologist is less about Genghis Khan himself than about the impact of the Mongols on world history.

Weber, David J. *The Spanish Frontier in North America*. New Haven, CT: Yale University Press, 1994. This book, now available in a shorter version for students, emphasizes the reciprocal relationship between the Spanish and native peoples, not least in military matters.

Webster, David. "Ancient Maya Warfare." In *War and Society in the Ancient and Medieval Worlds*, edited by K. Raaflaub and N. Rosenstein, 333–360. Cambridge, MA: Harvard University Press, 1999. An excellent discussion of the changing attitude toward Mayan warfare brought about by the decipherment of their script.

Wesseling, H. L. *The European Colonial Empires: 1815–1919*. Translated by Diane Webb. New York: Longman, 2004. This is a scholarly text that successfully combines a narrative description with an overall analysis of 19th-century European imperialism.

Westad, Odd. *The Global Cold War*. Cambridge: Cambridge University Press, 2005. By focusing on the Cold War in the third world, this work brings out how the ideologies of the two superpowers were not always translated into the nationalistic and other realities on the ground.

Whitby, Michael. "Reconstructing Ancient Warfare." In *The Cambridge History of Greek and Roman Warfare. Vol. 1: Greece, the Hellenistic World and the Rise of Rome*, edited by Philip Sabin, Hans van Wees, and Michael Whitby, 54–84. Cambridge: Cambridge University Press, 2007. Detailed but highly readable, this is an excellent introduction to the use of primary sources in understanding ancient warfare.

Winter, Jay. *Remembering War: The Great War between Memory and History in the Twentieth Century*. New Haven, CT: Yale University Press, 2006. While burdened somewhat by academic jargon, this is a good survey of the various ways in which the First World War was memorialized and remembered.

Yates, Robin D. S. "Early China." In *War and Society in the Ancient and Medieval Worlds,* edited by K. Raaflaub and N. Rosenstein, 7–45. Cambridge, MA: Harvard University Press, 1999. A start for Eurocentric military historians, this is a short but well-written introduction to warfare in China in the early period.

Zarrow, Peter. *China in War and Revolution, 1895–1949.* New York: Routledge, 2005. A good introduction to the wrenching changes, driven primarily by warfare, that China went through in the first half of the 20th century.

Zorlu, Tuncay. *Innovation and Empire in Turkey: Sultan Selim III and the Modernisation of the Ottoman Navy.* New York: Tauris Academic Studies, 2008. A good example of the excellent work of a new generation of Turkish scholars on military history now appearing in English.

Zürcher, Erik. *The Buddhist Conquest of China.* Leiden, Netherlands: E. J. Brill, 2006. A reprint of a work originally published in 1959, but still the best work on the subject available in English. Like all books published by Brill (including my own) this is too expensive for most people to buy—so check it out of the library.

Notes